# Enhancing Teaching Practice

# in HIGHER EDUCATION

# Praise for the book

'Everything you wanted to know about ways of improving teaching and learning, but might have been too reluctant to enquire into. Each chapter addresses a key aspect, is taut and accessible to busy practitioners, and its main points easily understood. Large literatures are opened invitingly to the reader and are assimilated with ease. Helen Pokorny and Digby Warren have demonstrated just how helpful good editing can be. I recommend this book wholeheartedly.'
**Ron Barnett, Emeritus Professor of Higher Education, Institute of Education, University College London**

'This is a timely collection of chapters covering the key topics new and existing lecturers and learning support staff need to understand to find their way through the rapidly changing HE landscape. This scholarly volume provides an informative, practical and readable guide to the professionalisation of teaching and learning in higher education. I highly recommend it.'
**Professor Mick Healey, Higher Education consultant and researcher**

'This book offers an excellent overview of the areas of activity, knowledge and values that are important for all teachers in higher education. Each of the chapters articulate forms of learning that are interactive, engaging and inclusive of the diversity of learners encountered in higher education today. The authors have blended theoretical underpinnings, highly practical approaches and the use of insightful questions throughout the text, to create a highly thoughtful and useful guide for staff.'
**Dr Catherine Bovill, University of Glasgow**

'This book is a valuable resource for anyone concerned with academic professional development in the changing landscape of higher education. Chapters provide considered and reflective explorations into what it means to both teach and learn at university, rather than simply offering a 'how to do it' approach. In so doing, the volume challenges HE educators to take a fresh approach to their own professional values.'
**Mary Lea, The Open University**

'I am delighted to offer an endorsement for this volume which I think makes a significant and powerful contribution to the literature in the field. This timely book contains a wealth of practical advice while being soundly research-informed and evidence-based. At a time when globally higher education institutions are seeking ways to recognise and reward teaching excellence, this book is invaluable. The range of contributors to this book is impressive and they are clearly guided by a strong editorial influence, which ensures its coherence.'
**Sally Brown, Emerita Professor, Leeds Beckett University**

Enhancing Teaching Practice

in HIGHER EDUCATION

Edited by **HELEN POKORNY | DIGBY WARREN**

Los Angeles | London | New Delhi
Singapore | Washington DC | Melbourne

Los Angeles | London | New Delhi
Singapore | Washington DC | Melbourne

SAGE Publications Ltd
1 Oliver's Yard
55 City Road
London EC1Y 1SP

SAGE Publications Inc.
2455 Teller Road
Thousand Oaks, California 91320

SAGE Publications India Pvt Ltd
B 1/I 1 Mohan Cooperative Industrial Area
Mathura Road
New Delhi 110 044

SAGE Publications Asia-Pacific Pte Ltd
3 Church Street
#10-04 Samsung Hub
Singapore 049483

Editor: James Clark
Editorial assistant: Robert Patterson
Production editor: Tom Bedford
Copyeditor: Solveig Gardner Servian
Proofreader: Bryan Campbell
Indexer: Silvia Benvenuto
Marketing manager: Dilhara Attygalle
Cover design: Naomi Robinson
Typeset by: C&M Digitals (P) Ltd, Chennai, India
Printed and bound by CPI Group (UK) Ltd,
Croydon, CR0 4YY

**Library of Congress Control Number: 2015948613**

**British Library Cataloguing in Publication data**

A catalogue record for this book is available from
the British Library

MIX
Paper from
responsible sources
FSC® C013604
www.fsc.org

ISBN 978-1-4462-0284-5
ISBN 978-1-4462-0285-2 (pbk)

At SAGE we take sustainability seriously. Most of our products are printed in the UK using FSC papers and boards.
When we print overseas we ensure sustainable papers are used as measured by the PREPS grading system.
We undertake an annual audit to monitor our sustainability.

This book is dedicated to Helen Peters and to inspirational, caring and committed teachers and colleagues everywhere.

# Contents

# List of Figures and Tables

## Figures

## Tables

# About the Editors

**Helen Pokorny** is Principal Lecturer in Learning and Teaching in Higher Education at the University of Westminster. She started teaching in Higher Education in 1988 and has taught at all levels of undergraduate and postgraduate study in Business and Professional Development. She became an Education Developer in 2010 and has worked with colleagues on a range of research and professional development activities and projects including first year transition and curriculum development, developing students' sense of belonging, students' perceptions of effective feedback, and raising the attainment of Black and Minority Ethnic (BME) students. She has maintained throughout her career an abiding commitment to the recognition of prior learning, both teaching and researching in this area, and is a founding Director of the *Prior Learning International Research Centre* (PLIRC) based in Canada. She is a Senior Fellow of the Higher Education Academy and is the Academic Lead for the University of Westminster's Professional Recognition and Enhancement Scheme for Teaching.

**Digby Warren** is Associate Professor of Higher Education and a University Teaching Fellow at London Metropolitan University. Digby has been working in the field of higher education development for over 20 years. His chief area of expertise is curriculum development and associated teaching, learning and assessment processes, about which he has produced over 30 conference papers, published articles and book chapters – with a focus on student diversity issues and transformational approaches. Currently Head of the *Centre for the Enhancement of Learning and Teaching* (CELT), as a consultant member (2004–2008) of the *Oxford Centre for Staff and Learning Development* (OCSLD) he delivered workshops at a number of UK universities, and was also co-editor of conference proceedings for the London series of International Conferences on the Scholarship of Learning & Teaching (2005–2010). His role includes teaching on CELT's MA in Learning & Teaching in HE as Course Leader, organising professional development activities and coordinating the University's CPD scheme for academic practice. On the international front, he played a lead role in the highly rated EU-funded Tempus Project on 'Quality Assurance through Professional Development' (2011–2014), using curriculum development as a driver for innovation.

# About the Contributors

**Dr Pauline Armsby** coordinates pedagogic research at the University of Westminster in the Department of Leadership and Professional Development, and teaches on the MA Higher Education and Doctorate in Professional Studies (Education). Over the last 20 years, Pauline has developed and managed a range of different Work Based Learning (WBL) programmes from undergraduate to doctorate level, for distance provision internationally, for Higher Education practitioners, and with collaborative partners. She has also worked with a range of organisations to accredit their activity, and to maintain Higher Education quality and standards. Her research and publications are on Work Based Learning as a field of study, practitioner doctorates, and the accreditation of prior experiential learning. Previously, Pauline worked in Adult, Further and Higher Education facilitating personal and professional development courses. Pauline's undergraduate degree, master's and doctoral qualifications are in psychology and occupational psychology, and she has a Postgraduate Certificate in Post Compulsory Education.

**Jennifer Bright** has been working at the University of Westminster since October 2000, initially as a teacher of academic writing and currently as Senior Lecturer in Teaching and Learning, developing and teaching on continuing professional development programmes for academic staff and graduate teaching assistants. She also has a liaison role on a teacher education programme at Westminster International University in Tashkent. She first encountered mindfulness in 1991 when she was introduced to Thich Nhat Hanh's *The Miracle of Mindfulness*. Since then, she has maintained a commitment to using a mindful approach as she finds it invaluable in both personal and professional life. She is a founding member of the Contemplative Pedagogy Network.

**Tom Burns** and **Sandra Sinfield** are co-authors of *Teaching, Learning and Study Skills: A Guide for Tutors* (Sage, 2004) and *Essential Study Skills: The Complete Guide to Success at University* (4th edition to be published by Sage in 2016).

In a previous life, Tom Burns, who has always been interested in theatre and the arts and their role in teaching and learning, led the Hainault Action Group in setting up adventure playgrounds and devising community events and festivals for the local community. Whilst still a student, Tom set up and ran the first International Dario Fo Festival – with symposium, theatre workshops for students and local people and full dramatic performances by the Fo-Rame theatre troupe of *The Tiger's Tale* and *The Boss's Funeral*.

Sandra Sinfield has worked as a laboratory technician, a freelance copywriter, an Executive Editor (*Medicine Digest*, circulation 80,000 doctors) and in the voluntary sector with the Tower Hamlets Research and Resource Centre and with the Islington Green School Community Play *Whose Life is it Anyway?* written by Alan Clarke and produced at Sadler's Wells.

Together Tom and Sandra have taken a production of John Godber's *Bouncers* on a tour of Crete music venues, written and made a feature film (*Eight Days from Yesterday*) and produced teaching and learning courses and materials in a range of settings. Their *Take Control* video won the IVCA gold award for education, and has been embedded in an online study resource (*Six Steps to Success* – http://learning.londonmet.ac.uk/epacks/soccer/).

Tom Burns and Sandra Sinfield are both Senior Lecturers in Educational and Learning Development and University Teaching Fellows, based in the *Centre for the Enhancement of Learning and Teaching* (CELT) at London Metropolitan University. In addition, both are actively involved in the *Association for Learning Development in Higher Education* (www.aldinhe.ac.uk). Most recently they have developed the student-facing *Study Hub* (www.londonmet. ac.uk/studyhub) and the staff-facing *Take5* website and blog (http://learning. londonmet.ac.uk/epacks/take5/) – the latter of which is designed to seed, share and support staff engagement with engaging and innovative learning, teaching and assessment practices. They continue to develop learning, teaching and assessment innovations with a special focus on engaging praxes that ignites student curiosity and develops power and voice.

**Sibyl Coldham** is Director of Professional Learning Development at the University of Westminster. She coordinates learning and teaching development across the University. Sibyl has worked in educational development for over 30 years and has considerable experience in practice-orientated learning, developing reflection as a tool for learning, and in learning and assessment design for professional competence. She trained as a secondary teacher before joining the London School of Acupuncture and Traditional Chinese Medicine, where her role was Staff and Curriculum Development. She helped to develop practice-based clinical assessment and introduced reflection, inter-professional working and action learning as the basis for student and staff professional development and ethical working. From 2005–2010 Sibyl was the Director of the *Centre for Excellence in Professional Learning from the Workplace* (CEPLW). The focus of the CEPLW was to develop practice-orientated approaches and work integrated learning in course design and assessment, and more widely across the University.

**Dr Steven Cranfield** is Senior Lecturer in Pedagogic Research in Higher Education in the Department of Leadership and Professional Development, University of Westminster Business School, and course leader of the MA in Higher Education. He obtained his PhD in Education at the Institute of Education, London, studying under Professor Ronald Barnett. A Senior Fellow of the Higher Education Academy, Steven teaches and researches on leadership and management and on academic and professional practice. At Westminster he jointly coordinates the Higher Education and Theory (HEAT) network as well as the Translaborate network which explores the confluence of ideas of translation and collaboration. He is co-author (with Valerie Iles) of *Developing Change Management Skills* (SDO, 2004) and co-translator (with Claudio Tedesco) from the Spanish of the poetry of Francisco Brines, *Of Purest Blue* (Get A Grip, 2010). A founder member of the Leavis Society, he is the author of a forthcoming book *F. R. Leavis: The Creative University*, to be published by Springer.

**Dr Rebecca Eliahoo** is Principal Lecturer (Lifelong Learning) at the University of Westminster. She is a Senior Fellow of the Higher Education Academy and her professional interests lie in the field of teacher education, staff development and mentoring. She completed an investigation into mentors' experiences supporting trainees during initial teacher training for her Masters dissertation and a study of the professional development needs of English teacher educators in the Further Education sector for her PhD thesis. In 2003, she won a Walter Hines Page scholarship to study language and widening participation in the recruitment of teachers in Texas, USA, and in both 2005 and 2012 she was awarded University of Westminster Teaching Fellowships for excellence in teaching and learning. Before qualifying as a lecturer, Rebecca was deputy editor, features editor and reporter on a number of publications specialising in industrial design and marketing and wrote regularly for national newspapers.

**Charl Fregona** is a Senior Fellow of the Higher Education Academy, and a national SEDA (Staff and Educational Development Association) Fellow. She is Principal Lecturer in E-learning Development, University Teaching Fellow and Head of the e-learning unit within the *Centre for the Enhancement of Learning and Teaching* (CELT) at London Metropolitan University. She has practised in both school and higher education settings and spent some time in her early career as national training manager for an educational software design company. Charl has been involved in continuing professional development in higher education for the past 16 years, and is currently teaching course modules in *Web-based Learning, Facilitating Online Learning and Collaboration* and *Applying Learning Technologies* within the MA in Learning and Teaching in Higher Education. Her research interests are in the social justice implications of higher education policy with regard to disruptive technologies.

**Dave Griffiths** is a former Senior Lecturer in Educational and Learning Development at London Metropolitan University and is now a part-time Lecturer in Leadership and Professional Development at Hertfordshire University. He is a Senior Fellow of the Higher Education Academy and a Master Practitioner of NLP. Dave has over 40 years' experience of delivering staff development, the last 16 of which were spent within London Metropolitan University as a team member of the *Centre for the Enhancement of Learning and Teaching* (CELT), assisting the professional development of staff in Learning and Teaching roles. Now in semi-retirement, he is concentrating on professional skills development of staff in leadership posts in the public, private and voluntary sectors. His research interests include: human development across the lifespan, transition management, action learning in research, the role of academic supervision in facilitating learning and processes of leadership – inside and outside organisational contexts.

**Dr Kathy Harrington** is Principal Lecturer in Educational and Learning Development in the *Centre for the Enhancement of Learning and Teaching* (CELT) at London Metropolitan University, where she teaches on the Learning and Teaching in Higher Education Master's programme and oversees the experiential route for professional recognition of teaching and fellowship of the Higher Education Academy. Previously she was Academic Lead – Students as Partners at the Higher Education Academy (2012–2014) and Director of the *Write Now* Centre for Excellence in Teaching and Learning (2005–2010), a cross-institutional initiative developing writing and assessment practice within disciplines (www.writenow.ac.uk/). Kathy has trained in working with groups and organisations at the Tavistock Centre, London, and has a particular interest in the psycho-social dynamics of learning and teaching. She is co-author (with Mick Healey and Abbi Flint) of *Engagement Through Partnership: Students as partners in learning and teaching in higher education* (Higher Education Academy, 2014), and co-editor (with Theresa Lillis, Mary Lea and Sally Mitchell) of *Working with Academic Literacies: Case studies towards transformative practice* (Parlour Press, 2016).

**Julian Ingle** is a *Thinking Writing* Advisor at Queen Mary University of London. After working as a translator in Barcelona, Julian studied philosophy at the Universities of Middlesex and Essex. Before joining the *Thinking Writing* team at Queen Mary, University of London in 2009, he worked at London Metropolitan University, City University and University College London, where he wrote and taught courses in philosophy, history of ideas and history for adults in continuing education; academic writing and English for academic purposes at post-graduate, undergraduate and foundation level; Spanish language at undergraduate level; and worked on English as Foreign Language teacher training courses at post-graduate and undergraduate level. His work in learning development involved facilitating action learning sets and developing critical and reflective thinking. Much of Julian's recent work in *Thinking Writing* has been with staff and students in medicine, computer science and engineering.

**Susannah McKee** is a Senior Lecturer at London Metropolitan University in the Centre for Access, International Programmes and Academic Support. She has worked in Higher Education for ten years in areas including language and international programmes, an Extended Degree in Social Sciences and Humanities, teacher education and academic support. She has an MA in Learning and Teaching in Higher Education and is a Fellow of the Higher Education Academy. Her research interests include student transitions into Higher Education and widening participation.

**Dr Agata Sadza** is Senior Lecturer in Applied Translation at London Metropolitan University. An experienced teacher and trainer, she is specifically interested in instructional design, especially the application of learning technologies in adult education and the use of web-based technologies to enhance learning, teaching, assessment and feedback provision, within both the Higher Education setting and the professional world. She is a strong supporter of innovative learning and teaching methods, which she often incorporates in her own teaching practice. She holds a PG Diploma in Learning and Teaching in Higher Education and two SEDA certificates (Embedding Technology in Learning and Supporting Learning with Technology). She is Fellow of the Higher Education Academy and is an Associate Member of the Association for Learning Technology. Agata is also a published English–Polish translator and has cooperated with several academic and literary publishing houses.

**Matt Scandrett** is a Senior Lecturer at London Metropolitan University, teaching on the Extended Degree in Social Sciences and Humanities and BSc Criminology. He has 15 years' teaching experience in Higher Education in both the UK and abroad and is a Fellow of the Higher Education Academy. Matt has an MA in Learning and Teaching in Higher Education and is currently undertaking a PhD in Criminology.

# Acknowledgements

Grateful thanks go to our Senior Commissioning Editor James Clark and his team for their sterling support, expertise and encouragement throughout the rich collaborative process among all our authors that has produced this book.

We would also like to thank Sarah, Laura and Mike Pokorny for their patient good humour and all contributors' family and friends whose plans have been disrupted yet who have remained so supportive through the demands of writing this book.

# Introduction: Teaching in the Changing Landscape of Higher Education

Helen Pokorny and Digby Warren

> Education is a vital, demanding, and precious undertaking, and much depends on how well it is done. If it is true to the human being, education must reflect our nature in all its subtlety and complexity. Every human faculty must be taken seriously, including the intellect, emotions, and our capacity for relational, contemplative and bodily knowing … Educate our students as whole people, and they will bring all of who they are to the demands of being human in private and public life. The present and future well-being of humankind asks nothing less of us. (Palmer and Zajonc, 2010: 152–3).

## The changing landscape of higher education

Globally the higher education (HE) sector is experiencing significant challenges and reforms. In the UK a number of policy initiatives have restructured HE from a fully funded system to a market-driven model within a very short period of time. The government White Paper, Students at the Heart of the System (BIS, 2011), set an agenda focused on student choice in a 'market context'. Aligned to this shift has been the introduction of a regime of performance indicators on top of an already extensive quality assurance system (QAA, 2012). University statistical data and student survey data are used to tabulate university positions into 'league tables'. Students as fee-payers are encouraged to use this data to make decisions about where and what to study. Alongside this commodification of HE is a call in the White Paper (section 2.7: 27) to 'restore teaching to its proper position, at the centre of every [HE institution's] mission' that is being taken forward through the development of a 'Teaching Excellence Framework' which aims to recognise universities offering the highest teaching quality. This will be an outcomes-focused, ranking scheme using a clear set of metrics (Johnson, 2015), albeit that a lack of sophisticated conceptualisations of 'teaching excellence' compounds the issue of developing 'comparative mechanisms' that would allow 'effective cross-institutional benchmarking as an enabling process in response to the need for some institutions to improve their engagement with teaching enhancement' (Gunn and Fisk, 2014: 47). The policies that underpin these changes in HE reflect a neoliberal agenda with competition at its heart and a substantive switch from public to private funding of education through the student loan system. Consequently there is also a renewed policy interest in graduate earnings premiums and graduate employment. This places further emphasis on universities working in partnership with employers and taking responsibility for developing students' employability skills. It reflects global trends as HE

> has been increasingly captured by political mandates focusing on market awareness, competitiveness, entrepreneurialism, the reconfiguration of higher education institutions [HEIs] as organizations and their governance models.... HEIs roles and missions are expected to include up-skilling the population and lifelong learning, social inclusion, widening participation, citizenship skills and competences (Magalhães and Veiga, 2013: 64)

with the accent on 'competences' rather than 'knowledge' eroding the 'modern ideal of education' which 'assumes that the exposure of students to knowledge potentially provides emancipatory and transformational features for the individuals involved, providing to society better citizens and specialized workers' (Magalhães and Veiga, 2013: 59).

Within this shifting national context is an ambition to diversify student recruitment and to increase overseas student income. This is a policy objective which has been in tension with UK government initiatives to control immigration. Widening of participation in HE remains an ambition, with the UK committed to doubling the proportion of young people from disadvantaged backgrounds entering HE by 2020 from 2009 levels (Johnson, 2015). In the UK the cap on student numbers has been removed and consequently academics find themselves in a situation in which there is a tremendous strain on resources, while staff:student ratios continue to increase. They are being asked to do more with less, with many competing pressures on their time, including research, and where continuous change is the norm.

One of the emerging agendas is around flexible pedagogies and digital education (Ryan and Tilbury, 2013). Pressures in funding add to pressures to provide flexibility in learning opportunities, support and assessment (Barnett, 2014). Digital learning is now a feature of all provision from face-to-face to distance learning and all modes of delivery in between. It encompasses the use of technology in the classroom, mobile learning, Virtual Learning Environments (VLE), Massive Online Open Courses (MOOCs) and open learning (giving students choice over what, when, at what pace, where, and how they learn). However, students' adoption of social media does not always translate into proficiency with educational uses of technology. Thus academics are often required to support students in the use of technology in order to realise the design benefits of a technology enhanced curriculum.

There has also been a reconfiguring of academic work and an increase in the numbers of UK academics on teaching-only contracts and teaching-focused roles. Locke (2014) suggests that these contractual changes may make academic work less attractive as a career and argues for a reconsideration of academic roles and teaching careers that encourage new forms of professionalism to emerge from within the profession itself, with a focus on teaching as a key element of career progression. Similarly Light et al. (2009: 13–14) call for a reclaiming of professionalism as 'ongoing transformation centred in the learning situation' as opposed to a form of professionalism driven by external accountability pressures for 'standardised professional organisation, practice and evaluation procedures'. As evidenced by Gibbs (2010), improved student evaluations of teaching have been found to correspond to improvements in measures of teaching quality (p.26) and the adoption of 'well-understood pedagogical practices that engender student engagement' (p.5) – which can be promoted through investment in professional development of academic staff (p.14).

The importance of professionalism in teaching in HE is gaining acknowledgement internationally. For example, the European Science Foundation (2012) sees it as central to the integration and regionalisation of European HE and to supporting student mobility within the Bologna process. In Australia, there are national debates and moves towards 'academic professionalisation' (ACPET, 2013), led by the Office of Learning and Teaching that has funded a project to develop a national framework 'to raise the professionalism of higher education teaching' (OLT, 2012).

In the UK, the Professional Standards Framework for Teaching and Supporting Learning (UKPSF, 2011) provides a nationally recognised framework for bestowing professional recognition within HE teaching and learning support through a comprehensive set of professional standards and guidelines for HE providers and leaders.

The UKPSF outlines the 'dimensions' of professional practice within HE teaching and learning support as:

- areas of activity undertaken by teachers and support staff;
- core knowledge needed to carry out these activities at the appropriate level;
- professional values that individuals performing these activities should exemplify (UKPSF, 2011).

Although developments at the macro level influence how we think about the purpose of, and shape, HE work in local contexts, Smith (2010: 727) reassures that 'whilst the language and rhetoric of contemporary higher education may feel inhospitable, the gaps in which to exercise autonomy still remain'. Fanghanel (2012: 2) similarly argues that lecturers 'operate in a space that needs to accommodate the demands of market-oriented practices, and yet contain the aspirations academics have for themselves and for their students, and their passion for knowledge ...'. She sees within the academy 'a rich, critical and empowering potential that can be harnessed to develop approaches to educating students and practising research that address the complexities of today's world' (p.14). The changes imposed on us may lead to interesting questions about who we are as educators, what we value and what we know, as well as what we can no longer take for granted and need to think about afresh. As Tennant et al. argue,

> academics can find space for their own agency in the midst of system wide and institutional policies and practices that serve to frame, as well as delimit and constrain, what counts as good academic work in teaching and research ... [and] that academics can develop a sense of agency through a reflexive engagement with the circumstances in which they find themselves (2010:1).

## The purpose of this book

Thus the purpose of this book is to support colleagues involved in HE teaching and support of learning to engage with current challenges, enhance their educational practice and scholarship and to reflect on their choice of identity as an HE educator – one that fits with their own professional values and articulation of their professional practice. There are a number of cross-cutting themes, one of which is developing resilience and care for our students and their learning, our colleagues and ourselves. 'Care is a resilient value that, despite the pressures, remains fundamental to many in academic life' (Smith, 2010: 722). It also resonates with the notion of authenticity in teaching, which 'involves our caring about the subject balanced and enriched by our caring about what is in the important interest of students' (Kreber, 2007: 3). Other related themes that permeate the chapters are diversity, relationships, dialogue and enquiry. Students enter HE with a wide range of personal biographies, experiences and cultural capital, and developing relational, dialogic approaches to teaching and assessment practice provides the potential for developing shared perspectives and joint understanding of learning goals and processes. It also opens up creative spaces for changing practices and shifting some of the familiar ways of working. The authors aim both to stimulate new ideas and also to provide support for established ways of working. In foregrounding relationships, the authors also remind us that teaching is an affective process and pay attention to the role of emotions – our own and students – as part of the educational experience (Moore and Kuol, 2007).

The book also addresses as cross-cutting themes the 'dimensions' of the UKPSF. The chapters consider, from different perspectives, the UKPSF 'Areas of Activity' which are broadly:

- learning design and planning;
- teaching/supporting learning;
- assessment and feedback;
- planning effective learning environments;
- continuing professional development.

The book provides an overview of key concepts, models and practices that underpin these areas and relate to UKPSF 'core knowledge' requirements including:

- how students learn;
- methods for teaching and assessing;
- learning technologies;
- evaluation of teaching;
- quality assurance and quality enhancement.

The UKPSF professional values around respect, equality and promoting participation in learning permeate the scholarship, research and professional practice from which ideas are drawn.

For lecturers seeking professional recognition, through either accredited courses or experience-based applications, the UKPSF dimensions need to be demonstrated through the successful incorporation of scholarship and/or the findings of pedagogic research. Hence the book aims to:

- empower educators to empower students;
- provide an overview of key concepts models and practices to inspire and support teaching;
- challenge assumptions and outline different approaches to practice;
- support professional development, scholarship and the articulation of ones' own pedagogy and professional values, identity and practice.

Based on extensive secondary research and the authors' own direct experience in HE teaching and/or provision of professional development, the book chapters provide exemplars of practice embedded in the scholarly literature, offering busy academics accessible ideas and a wide range of references from the field. The book uses short case studies and vignettes to illustrate these ideas and practices, and includes relevant guiding principles. Each chapter also has a short list of further reading/web resources (all URLs verified prior to publication) and a set of questions for readers to reflect on their own professional practice and development.

## An introduction to the chapters

**Chapter 2: Course and Learning Design and Evaluation** – Digby Warren explores different concepts and paradigms of 'curriculum' and various models and methods for course and learning design and curriculum evaluation, with varied examples and references to sources where good case studies from a range of disciplines can be found. The chapter is premised on the holistic notion of 'curriculum' as a contextualised practice that encompasses knowledge domain, educational values and principles, teaching, learning, assessment and evaluation.

**Chapter 3: Teaching by Leading and Managing Learning Environments** – Steven Cranfield considers how different environments or settings within which students are asked or required to learn, such as large groups, small groups and laboratory and practice settings, have an impact on how they approach their learning and hence on the design and delivery of teaching. He provides an overview of underpinning principles and concepts before exploring their application in practice.

**Chapter 4: Assessment for Learning** – Helen Pokorny draws on key concepts around the development of a shared frame of reference within assessment communities, to explore approaches to assessment and feedback design and assessment standards. Plagiarism is considered from a socio-cultural perspective and conceptualised as a topic to be addressed through the learning process as much as through the quality assurance process.

Specific attention is given to developing effective groupwork assessment and the assessment of prior experiential learning, as these are significant areas of assessment practice which have their own particular pedagogical issues and practices.

**Chapter 5: Blended Learning** – Charl Fregona, with Agata Sadza adding a resonant case study, explores the options and issues presented by developments in elearning. This chapter considers students' experiences of digital technologies and expectations of elearning and the need for learners to develop critical research skills and 'digital scholarship'. Different approaches to and models for blended learning design are outlined, along with pedagogical strategies for promoting and supporting student participation in blended and online learning.

**Chapter 6: Student Engagement** – Kathy Harrington, Sandra Sinfield and Tom Burns draw on material from the substantial and diverse field of student engagement to chart a path of particular relevance to any university teacher who takes an interest in thinking about and finding fresh ways to enable students' engagement with learning, both within and alongside the curriculum. They focus directly on the interface between teaching and learning, and on the relationship between teachers and students as a vehicle for engagement in all its diversity, providing principles and practices to foster engaged teaching and learning, and examples of engagement within and alongside the curriculum.

**Chapter 7: Embracing Student Diversity** – Susannah McKee and Matt Scandrett examine practical ways in which we might actively embrace diversity for positive change in student experience for all members of the university community through inclusive teaching, whilst recognising that students vary in any number of ways and should be seen first and foremost as individuals. They consider ways of encouraging a sense of belonging and developing an inclusive curriculum and classroom, and of thinking through issues around the student lifecycle and assessment.

**Chapter 8: Engaging with Academic Writing and Discourse** – Julian Ingle examines some of the challenges of teaching academic writing in HE, as well as the difficulties students encounter when learning how to write in their disciplines or subject areas. Taking a multilayered view of university-level writing and the ways it can be understood, the argument of this chapter is that teaching and learning about writing are most effective when situated within the discipline. He considers students' attitudes to writing and provides accounts of practice that illustrate how some of the challenges can be addressed. He also considers how and why we might expand and use the resources and range of texts available to students and staff.

**Chapter 9: Effective Supervision** – Dave Griffiths and Digby Warren consider the complexities of academic supervision that operate at a variety of academic levels, arguing that at the core of the process is an interpersonal relationship that has the potential to enable and validate learning or, conversely, to hinder and subdue it. Their chapter outlines what this complexity means for the practice and process of academic supervision, explores some new perspectives on the different elements that constitute the process, and suggests some practical responses to the many challenges generated by the complexity of supervision today.

**Chapter 10: Work-related and Professional Learning** – Sibyl Coldham and Pauline Armsby outline a range of approaches to developing work-relevant skills, attributes and practices, looking at the openings they offer in terms of developing students' confidence in, and experience of, work processes during their university study. They explore key learning design and assessment strategies used in the various approaches, drawing on literature from workplace learning and practice, as well as HE and employability. To illustrate different approaches they draw on examples from a range of disciplines, their own experience and offer links to substantial case study repositories as further reading.

**Chapter 11: Professional Development** – Jennifer Bright, Rebecca Eliahoo and Helen Pokorny consider that professional growth and development occurs through increased experience of teaching and ongoing evaluation and examination of one's practice in this role. It is therefore wider than participating in workshops and courses and is concerned with examining the cycle of teaching and assessing from different standpoints both individually and collaboratively. In this chapter they consider a range of approaches to professional development including mentoring practice, approaches to peer review of teaching, the Scholarship of Teaching and Learning (SoTL) and the role of 'mindfulness' in professional development and HE teaching.

All of the authors are HE educators of long standing and all find their inspiration from working with colleagues and students to address the challenges of teaching today. It is from this process of collegiality and sharing of ideas that this book is born.

# References

Australian Council for Private Education and Training (ACPET) (2013) 'Higher Education: "Professionalising" the academic workforce', report on a round table discussion. Available at www.acpet.edu.au/article/6415/higher-education-professionalising-the-academic-workforce/ (accessed 28 July 2015).

Barnett, R. (2014) *Conditions of Flexibility: Securing a more responsive higher education system*. York: Higher Education Academy. Available at www.heacademy. ac.uk/sites/default/files/resources/FP_conditions_of_flexibility.pdf (accessed 9 September 2012).

BIS (Department for Business Innovation and Skills) (2011) *Students at the Heart of the System*. Available at www.gov.uk/government/uploads/system/uploads/ attachment_data/file/31384/11-944-higher-education-students-at-heart-of-system.pdf (accessed 21.9.15).

European Science Foundation (2012) 'The Professionalisation of Academics as Teachers in HE. Standing Committee for Social Sciences: Science Position Paper'. Strasbourg: France.

Fanghanel, J. (2012) *Being an Academic*. Abingdon: Routledge.

Gibbs, G. (2010) *Dimensions of Quality*. York: Higher Education Academy. Available at www.heacademy.ac.uk/resource/dimensions-quality

Gunn, V. and Fisk, A. (2014) *Considering Teaching Excellence in Higher Education 2007–2013*. York: Higher Education Academy. Available at https:// www.heacademy.ac.uk/resource/considering-teaching-excellence-higher-education-2007-2013

Johnson, J. (2015) 'Teaching at the Heart of the System', speech by UK Minister of State for Universities and Science to Universities UK, London. Available at www.gov.uk/ government/speeches/teaching-at-the-heart-of-the-system (accessed 28.7.15).

Kreber, C. (2007) 'What's it really all about? The Scholarship of Teaching and Learning as an Authentic Practice', *International Journal for the Scholarship of Learning and Teaching*, 1 (1): 1–4.

Light, G., Cox, R. and Calkins, S. (2009). *Teaching and Learning in Higher Education: The reflective professional*. Thousand Oaks, CA: Sage.

Locke, W. (2014) *Shifting Academic Careers: Implications for enhancing professionalism in teaching and supporting learning*. York: Higher Education Academy. Available at https://www.heacademy.ac.uk/resource/shifting-academic-careers-implications-enhancing-professionalism-teaching-and-supported

Magalhães, A. M. and Veiga, A. (2013) 'What about education in higher education?', in L. R. Smith (ed.), *Higher Education: Recent trends, emerging issues and future outlook*. New York: Nova Science, pp.57–72.

Moore, S. and Kuol, N. (2007) 'Matters of the heart: Exploring the emotional dimensions of educational experience in recollected accounts of excellent teaching', *International Journal for Academic Development*, 12 (2): 87–98.

Office of Learning and Teaching (OLT), Australian Government (2012) 'Academic Workforce 2020: Reconceptualising the professional practice of teaching in higher education'. Available at www.olt.gov.au/project-academic-work-force-2020–framing-national-agenda-professionalising-university-teaching-2012 (accessed 28.7.15).

Palmer, P. and Zajonc, A. (2010) *The Heart of Higher Education: A Call to Renewal – Transforming the Academy through Collegial Conversations*. San Francisco, CA: Josey-Bass.

Quality Assurance Agency (QAA) (2012) *The UK Quality Code for Higher Education*. Available at www.qaa.ac.uk/assuring-standards-and-quality/the-quality-code (accessed 9.9.15).

Ryan, A. and Tilbury, D. (2013) *Flexible Pedagogies: New pedagogical ideas.* York: Higher Education Academy. Available at www.heacademy.ac.uk/sites/default/files/resources/npi_report.pdf (accessed 9.9.15).

Smith, J. (2010) 'Academic identities for the twenty-first century', *Teaching in Higher Education*, 15 (6): 721–7.

Tennant, M., McMullen, C. and Kaczynski, D. (2010) *Teaching, Learning and Research in Higher Education: A critical approach.* Abingdon: Routledge.

UKPSF (2011) *UK Professional Standards Framework for Teaching and Supporting Learning in Higher Education.* York: The Higher Education Academy. Available at www.heacademy.ac.uk/sites/default/files/downloads/UKPSF_2011_English.pdf (accessed 9/9/15).

# 2

# Course and Learning Design and Evaluation

Digby Warren

---

**Chapter overview**

This chapter explores:

- concepts and paradigms of 'curriculum'
- criteria for effective course design
- models for curriculum and learning design
- models and methods of curriculum evaluation

---

## Introduction: concepts of curriculum

As Jenkins (2009: 162–3) observes:

> The formal curriculum is where the worlds of individual faculty [lecturers] and students interact and where the departmental and institutional contexts play key roles in determining what is learnt and how. However, even at the beginning of their careers faculty have the power (in part) to shape the courses they teach.

This chapter concentrates on curriculum development, from the learning design of whole programmes and their constituent units (modules) to short courses and specific sessions. It is premised on a holistic notion of 'curriculum' as a contextualised practice that encompasses knowledge domain, educational values and principles, teaching, learning, assessment and evaluation.

In everyday parlance, 'curriculum' is often a synonym for 'syllabus' or the content of a study programme, but its etymology suggests a much richer concept. It derives from the Latin verb *currere*, meaning to run or race; the noun *curriculum* could refer to a race, a race course or a racing chariot (Goodson, 1997). Analogously, we could think of 'curriculum' as the journey of learning (race) to master required tasks, knowledge and skill (race course) aided by all available resources (racing chariot) – from the student's own aptitudes and motivations to the learning materials, interactions with peers and the steer provided by teachers as subject experts and facilitators of learning. As Sirotnik (1991: 243) puts it: 'Curriculum includes not only the content of subject matters, but how knowledge is organized, how teachers teach, how learners learn and how the whole is evaluated.' Curriculum design, for programmes, modules or individual sessions, is thus concerned with *what* is to be learnt (content); *why* (rationale and philosophy), *how* (process) and *when* (structure) it is to be learnt; and *how* the learning will be *demonstrated* (assessment) and the effectiveness of the teaching and the learning design will be appraised (evaluation) – all of which is shaped by the design principles and wider contexts (disciplinary, institutional, regulatory, political, societal) of the curriculum (see Jackson et al., 2002, for visual representations of the interconnected variables of curriculum).

Critical theorists hold the view of curriculum as a social construct and agency of social and cultural reproduction through which particular knowledges, beliefs, norms and values – usually those that serve the dominant groups and reinforce social hierarchies along class, gender and racial lines – are validated and transmitted from generation to generation (Apple, 1996; Bourdieu and Passeron, 1990; Giroux, 1981, 1983; Goodson, 1997). The curriculum is therefore not 'neutral' but the result of a selection that is produced out of the prevailing political, economic and cultural forces (Apple, 1996: 22).

Linked to this view is the idea of the 'hidden curriculum', meaning the implicit attitudes, norms and values carried in curriculum content, classroom relationships, learning environments and institutional rules and rituals, as part of the socialisation function of education (see Margolis et al., 2001; Kentli, 2009; and Cotton et al., 2013 for elaborations of this concept). For example, Geography courses purvey notions of 'sustainability' that are 'heavily mediated by lecturers' wider beliefs and attitudes' (Cotton et al., 2013: 197) and contradictions may exist between the messages of the formal curriculum and actual organisational practices (in recycling, energy efficiency etc.), which can also be enlightening for students to investigate, using their campus as a 'case study' (Winter and Cotton, 2012). Young black women at a mainly white American college had to confront 'competing definitions about race and gender on a campus that privileged particular constructions' and the 'gaze' of white students and staff who 'often read them through a stereotypical lens' (Eposito, 2011: 155–6). Cheng and Yang (2015) found that both teachers and students, through formal medical classes and informal extracurricular activities, perpetuated 'a heterosexual masculine culture and sexism' that 'eroded' the self-esteem and learning opportunities of female and gay students (also see Hill et al., 2014, on negotiating the hidden curriculum in surgery). Yet the curriculum can also be a site of contestation or resistance, and a space for social transformation – where it is used to foster critical consciousness and democratic citizenship and to enable subordinated groups to reclaim their lives and histories (Apple, 1993; Freire, 1973; Giroux, 1983, 2011).

## Curriculum paradigms

Viewing curriculum in relation to ideological and pedagogical orientations, different paradigms of or approaches to curriculum have been identified. Ross (2000) elaborates on three major curricular models evident in the history of curriculum development in Britain (see pp.128–31):

- *academic* – subject-based, content-driven curricula in which the teacher decides on and transmits approved knowledge, and assessment is prescribed and norm-referenced;
- *vocational* – skills-led, objectives-driven curricula in which the teacher guides students as to what to study, and assessment is summative and criterion-referenced;
- *developmental* – learning-centred, process-driven curricula in which the teacher partners with the students, and assessment encompasses formative and coursework elements.

In the past two decades in higher education (HE), however, there has been a shift towards integrating a developmental approach within discipline-based and professional courses, as curriculum development becomes more consciously shaped by pedagogy and the outcomes-focused impetus of HE and quality assurance policies (see Chapter 1: Teaching in the Changing Landscape of Higher Education), as well as new trends towards working with students as partners in learning and teaching development (see Chapter 6: Student Engagement).

The typology expounded by Grundy (1987) and Cornbleth (1990) classifies curriculum as:

- *'product'* – curriculum is construed as a programme plan (or 'blue print' as Pratt, 1980: 4, defines it) and a product to be delivered to students, as an 'object'; the focus is on content and directing student activity toward meeting pre-set objectives;
- *'process'* – curriculum is understood as the interaction of teachers, students and knowledge, as an 'action'; the focus is on the processes that enable learning and meaning-making, allowing room for experimentation;
- *'praxis'* – curriculum becomes a vehicle for promoting human emancipation, via the exercise of 'critical pedagogy'; while sharing the focus on process, it is geared towards raising students' awareness of dehumanising, inequitable and undemocratic social practices and institutions and developing more egalitarian visions of society. It is this commitment to engendering critical reflection and action to change the world, grounded in the values of 'human well being and the search for truth, and respect for others', that constitutes 'praxis' (Smith, 2011).

Critical pedagogy is distinct from 'critical thinking' (Burbules and Berk, 1999) in that, while it also employs rational analysis to uncover assumptions and discern faulty arguments, it is a consciously 'political and moral project' that aspires to promote equality and democracy via individual and social responsibility as engaged citizens in a globalized society (Giroux, 2011). It entails 'weaving a radical content with liberating teaching practices' (Boyce, 1996: 11), selecting topics, materials and analytical frameworks through which critical consciousness can be developed collaboratively through open dialogue and problem-posing; 'participative assessment' whereby students are involved in appraising their own and their peers' learning (Reynolds and Trehan, 2000); and critical reflection by teachers in reviewing and developing their effectiveness at creating emancipatory learning environments.

From an ontological angle, Barnett (2009) considers the curriculum as 'an educational vehicle to promote a student's development', as the process of 'coming to know' can be 'edifying' through its propensity to foster 'epistemic virtues', i.e. knowledge-based 'dispositions' – such as a 'will to learn', engage, listen and explore new perspectives – and 'qualities' – such as 'courage, resilience, carefulness, integrity, self-discipline, restraint, respect for others, openness, generosity, authenticity' (p.434). This depends on how actively the 'pedagogical relationship' between teachers and students works to elicit these virtues, via the curriculum content (for instance, offering 'contrasting insights and perspectives') and process – enthusing students to engage with each other and put forward their 'own profferings' (p.438). For Barnett, in our modern 'age of supercomplexity' that is 'replete with manifold interpretations' of reality and the uncertainty and insecurity this brings, a 'genuine higher education' needs to go beyond a 'dogma' of knowledge and skills towards engendering these modes of human being(ness) for engaging in such a world (pp.439–40) (also see Barnett, 2015). His vision here builds on his earlier notion of a 'curriculum for critical being' (Barnett, 1997) through which to develop criticality – the hallmark of HE (see Dunne, 2015) – in three domains: *knowledge* (critical reason), *self* (critical reflection) and the *world* (critical action), so that 'understanding' is united with 'performance' and critical values are extended to the societal sphere. 'Knowledge' refers to the discipline-based competences, 'action' to the competences acquired through 'doing' and 'self' to how the discipline influences identity (e.g., 'reflective practitioner'). Exploring how different subject areas accord differing weightings to and differently integrate each of these domains – professional disciplines tend to have a higher degree of integration across the three domains and stronger weighting on 'action' compared to the knowledge emphasis of sciences and humanities (see Barnett et al., 2001; Barnett and Coate, 2005) – can make this model an elucidative framework to interrogate course design and curriculum practice.

## Criteria for effective course design

Various frameworks offer criteria as to what makes for a well-designed course. Common to them all is the principle that course design should be centred on enabling successful, high-level learning. In his influential model, John Biggs (1996, 1999) propounds 'constructive alignment' whereby teaching methods and assessment tasks should engage students in activities through which they can achieve and demonstrate required learning outcomes. His approach rests on constructivist learning theory which posits that 'learners arrive at meaning by actively selecting, and cumulatively constructing, their own knowledge, through both individual and social activity' (Biggs, 1996: 348). (For a critical discussion of challenges and paradoxes in applying constructivism to contemporary higher education, see Schweitzer and Stephen, 2008.) This activity may occur through a range of teacher-led, peer-based and self-study activities – lectures, seminars, practical sessions, groupwork, learning contracts, informal student collaborations (see Chapter 3: Teaching by Leading and Managing Learning Environments) – and assessment methods aimed at encouraging 'deep learning' (Biggs, 1999).

A 'deep' approach is characterised by the academic ideal of critical, integrative, intrinsically motivated learning, as opposed to a 'surface' approach of uncritical, atomistic rote-memorisation, or a 'strategic' grades-orientated, assessment-driven approach which veers between deep or surface learning as required (Marton et al., 1997; Biggs, 2003; Ramsden, 2003). Students' approaches to learning are not fixed dispositions but situational interactions between their motives, learning styles and abilities and the dynamics of the teaching-learning environment (see Entwistle, 2003).

Criteria for design for deep learning are synthesised in Table 2.1, which combines advice from Ramsden (2003) and Biggs (2003) with the 'seven principles for good practice' derived by Chickering and Gamson (1987) and the eight principles for creating 'a supportive critical community of inquiry' proposed by Garrison and Anderson (2003: 18).

Curriculum coherence, as Hounsell and McCune (2002: 20) suggest, also entails alignment to the students, with responsiveness to 'diverse student needs and capabilities', and alignment of learning support and course organisation and management (e.g., teaching spaces, equipment, facilities, course handbooks, feedback from students) to help implement curricular aims. Similar principles are foregrounded by Bovill et al. (2011) in relation to 'course design to engage and empower students', noting the importance of providing for cumulative development throughout the curriculum of students' academic and literacy skills (see Chapter 8: Engaging with Academic Writing and Discourse), and using ongoing feedback to enable learners to be aware of their progress in relation to required standards (see Chapter 4: Assessment for Learning).

A student-focused approach to course design and delivery therefore needs to be inclusive (see Chapter 7: Embracing Student Diversity), creating learning opportunities that 'engage all students meaningfully by encouraging them to draw on and apply their own and others' knowledge' and taking care 'to anticipate, recognise and provide for individuals' specific physical, cultural, academic and pastoral needs' (Hockings, 2010: 47). In their guidelines for 'inclusive curriculum design', Morgan and Houghton (2011) recommend an approach that 'places the student at the heart of the design process' (p.11) and embeds the following principles (pp.12–13):

- *anticipatory* – proactively considers the entitlements of all students in all activity across the whole student life cycle;
- *flexible* – is adaptable to the changing student profile and circumstances;
- *accountable* – encourages staff and student responsibility in meeting equality objectives;

**Table 2.1** Criteria for effective course design

| Criteria for effective design | Biggs (2003)* and Ramsden (2003)# | Chickering and Gamson (1987) | Garrison and Anderson (2003) |
|---|---|---|---|
| Sets clear, high expectations | Clearly stated expectations# | (6) communicates high expectations | (1) negotiable expectations, clearly expressed, encourage deep approaches to learning |
| Embraces student diversity | | (7) respects diverse talents and ways of learning | |
| Encourages student–teacher contact | Teaching and assessing in a way that encourages a positive working environment so students can make mistakes and learn from them* | (1) encourages contact between students and teachers | |
| Enables well-structured knowledge | Teaching that brings out the structure of the topic or subject explicitly* | | (2) coherent knowledge structures (schema) facilitate purposeful and integrative learning |
| Clarifies relevance and meaning of content and tasks | Stimulating teaching which demonstrates lecturer's commitment to the subject and its meaning and relevance to students# | | |
| Promotes critical thinking | Teaching to *elicit* a positive response from students, by questioning and presenting problems, rather than to *expound* information* | | (5) critical discourse confirms understanding and diagnoses misconceptions<br>(6) critical thinking must be modelled and rewarded |
| Encourages student responsibility | | | (3) control creates commitment and encourages personal responsibility to monitor and manage meaningful approaches to learning – also see (1) above |

*(Continued)*

**Table 2.1** (Continued)

| Criteria for effective design | Biggs (2003)* and Ramsden (2003)# | Chickering and Gamson (1987) | Garrison and Anderson (2003) |
|---|---|---|---|
| Offers student choice in content and process | Opportunities to exercise responsible choice in method and content of study# | | (4) choice in content and process is a catalyst for spontaneous and creative learning experiences and outcomes while recognising and valuing intuition and insight |
| Fosters active learning | Teaching and assessment methods foster active engagement# | (3) encourages active learning | |
| Develops collaborative learning | | (2) develops reciprocity and cooperation among students | |
| Ensures time on task | Sufficient time to engage with tasks (*versus* emphasising coverage at expense of depth)* | (5) emphasizes time on task | |
| Assessment is aligned to learning objectives | Principle of constructive alignment* | | (7) assessment must be congruent with expected learning outcomes<br><br>(8) learning is confirmed through assessment |
| Provides prompt and instructive feedback | Feedback on progress encourages deep learning# | (4) gives prompt feedback | |

- *collaborative* – involves partnerships among stakeholders (students, staff, professional bodies, employers etc.) to develop course content and relevance;
- *transparent* – clarifies the rationale for design decisions, promoting awareness of the benefits for all;
- *equitable* – ensures procedures are the same for all students and decisions are fair and transparent.

To that end, they offer a set of generic questions on various aspects of course design (see pp.15–16) to ensure that 'all students' entitlement to access and participate in a course are anticipated, acknowledged and taken into account' (p.14), illustrated with practical examples from two dozen different disciplines (see section three of their publication). The University Design for Learning (UDL) framework also defines cogent principles (derived from learning sciences research) for creating inclusive curricula. It recommends that all courses should offer students:

- *multiple means of representation* to acquire knowledge (course content presented in variety of formats – text, audio, image, video, hyperlinks);
- *multiple means of expression* to demonstrate what they know (varied tools and forms of assessment, supported by exemplars and formative feedback);
- *multiple means of engagement* to motivate them to learn (choice of content and modes of learning) (Hall and Stahl, 2006).

Dell et al. (2015) illustrate how UDL principles can be applied to online courses following practical steps in the guide developed by the University of Arkansas (http://ualr.edu/pace/tenstepsud/ – accessed 31.07.15), and Tobin (2014) proposes a set of creative strategies based on UDL found helpful for increasing 'online student retention'.

# Models for curriculum and learning design

Curriculum development entails how 'a curriculum is planned, implemented and evaluated, as well as what people, processes and procedures are involved' (Ornstein and Hunkins, 2009: 15). Curriculum models can assist designers to undertake course development in a more systematic and considered way. Although curriculum models can be useful as heuristic devices, they are not a 'recipe' and should be informed by teachers' professional judgements as to what are apt approaches to fostering student learning (Knight, 2001; Ornstein and Hunkins, 2009). As Toohey (1999: 25) says, the central question for course design is '*What is most important for these students to know and what might be the best ways for them to learn it?*' (italics in original). To this, Light et al. (2009: 80) add further questions that highlight the centrality of 'assessment' and 'evaluation' to course design:

- How will you know if your students have achieved desired learning?
- How will you know if and how your teaching has contributed to such learning?

Related to the differing conceptions of 'curriculum' (discussed above), curriculum models can be broadly classified as:

- 'product' or rational models, which propose a step-by-step, outcomes-led approach aimed to yield coherent curriculum plans and efficient delivery of education; and
- 'process' models, which focus more on the students' experience and activities for engaging them in meaningful learning (see overview by O'Neill, 2010).

There are many different curriculum models; it is a question of choosing which model(s) are best suited to one's academic discipline.

## Rational models

'Product' or rational models employ means-to-end reasoning in which curriculum content and methods are planned in light of pre-determined learning objectives. Typically, these models – such as systematic 'instructional design' (see Kemp, 1977; Dick et al., 2014 (originally 1978); Romiszowski, 1981) – follow a linear sequence in which:

- the demand for the course is established;
- learner characteristics and needs are considered;
- intended learning outcomes are specified;
- subject content is selected and sequenced;
- teaching and assessment methods are chosen;
- teaching plans and learning materials are devised;
- the course is delivered and evaluated and adjustments are proposed.

The assessment-focused model proposed by Moon (2002, 2007) seeks to ensure a close relationship between level, learning outcomes, assessment and teaching, according to the following sequence:

- use module aims and level descriptors (generic statements of what learners should achieve by the end of a particular level of HE study), translated in subject discipline terms, to write learning outcomes;
- write threshold assessment criteria implied by the learning outcomes;
- develop assessment method(s) to test achievement of these criteria;
- develop a teaching strategy to enable students to attain the threshold criteria;
- implement the module and check the coherence of the cycle, rethinking initial learning outcomes and so on if necessary.

Instead of this 'chronological' kind of model, Cowan et al. (2004: 448) favour a 'logical' but more fluid model, involving 'simultaneous consideration' of assessment, learning and teaching activities in relation to desired learning outcomes, to achieve curriculum alignment (pp.449–50). They propose use of an 'alignment matrix' (p.447) to map activities (shown in vertical columns) to outcomes (listed horizontally), with an additional column for 'evaluation' of how effectively all elements work together.

In reality, curriculum construction is a complex, iterative process in which there is a constant interplay among all the factors that impinge on the curriculum. This is vividly captured in the 'ouija board' model propounded by Jenkins (2002, 2009). He uses the metaphor of an 'ouija board' (a device that uses alphabet letters and a movable pointer for communicating with the spirit world) to convey the idea that the curriculum is influenced by a range of 'forces' which both impact on practice and are shaped by lecturers as they exercise creative choices in curriculum-making. These 'forces' include:

- aims and objectives;
- conceptions of the discipline;
- research interests;
- educational theories, research and pedagogy;
- student needs;
- learning methods and technologies;
- assessment-as-learning;
- credit structures;
- quality and external requirements;
- student time (in and out of class);
- costs and resources.

Curriculum making naturally reflects its context. Luckett (2009) found that the knowledge structure of the discipline combined with the departmental culture had an overriding influence on the curriculum structure. Trowler (2009) and Fanghanel (2009) elucidate how 'teaching and learning regimes' operate at the 'meso-level' to impact on lecturers' academic practice. All these above aspects, however, should be considered for achieving thorough, rigorous curriculum development.

While 'rational curriculum planning' fits well with the quality assurance regimes and managerialist culture prevalent in HE, for Knight (2001: 373–4) it has certain limitations: complex learning is not easily reduced to precise statements of what students will learn, and the approach is 'too efficient' – it needs to allow space for 'creativity, innovation and flexibility' in teaching and learning. Similar cautions about narrow outcomes-based approaches are voiced by Hussey and Smith (2003). Noting that teachers in HE are ironically stuck between 'tight adherence to achieving pre-specified outcomes' and optimising 'the development and support of independent, autonomous and lifelong learners' (p.358), they urge that learning outcomes should be framed 'more broadly and flexibly' (p.367) so as to embrace students' emergent learning and enjoyment too. Tam (2014) argues that while the outcomes-based approach sharpens the focus onto student learning, care should be taken to avoid 'rigidity and conceptual reification' when implementing this approach in curriculum design and teaching. Light et al. (2009: 84–5) contrast two uses of learning objectives:

- the *rational* approach, where courses are designed to produce uniform outcomes to satisfy the goal of standardisation; and
- the *reflective* approach, where courses are designed to offer a 'rich environment of learning experiences to which students will respond in different ways' (p.85), and teachers reflect on objectives to guide ongoing changes to the course and professional judgements-in-action.

## Process model

It is the latter type of approach that characterises the 'process model' advanced by Knight (2001, 2002), influenced by complexity theory. Here, curriculum planning

- arises from imagining good learning activities for engaging students with the subject, and then orchestrating these through
- mapping the learning processes across the set of modules that make up the programme, and
- constructing a 'general specification' of the knowledge/skill areas in which students should be able to make claims to achievement. This 'directs attention' but does not tightly prescribe (in the way outcomes-based planning does) what should emerge from the learning process.

Other important and widely relevant features of this model include:

- meeting criteria for good teaching, such as interest, clarity, enthusiasm, use of varied methods and media and collaborative and reflective learning activities (see Knight 2001: 375);
- ensuring that the assessment system builds the students' capacity to evidence their learning, providing them with responsive feedback (see Chapter 4: Assessment for Learning);
- obtaining timely feedback on the impact of teaching on student learning, making adjustments where necessary.

Given the predominance of outcomes approaches, Knight (2001: 379) suggests that a process-based curriculum designed so as to generate the 'right ingredients' can then be checked against quality assurance standards (such as level descriptors or subject benchmarks) to see whether any required outcomes are 'unlikely to emerge' and fine-tuned as necessary.

## Programme design

For curriculum design of an entire degree programme, the framework devised by Hartman and Warren (1994) combines a 'rational' and 'process' approach whereby the end goal is considered in tandem with a strong focus on the students' characteristics and the learning processes and support that would enable them to develop desired graduate attributes. It entails moving iteratively among the following areas:

- *type(s) of graduate* – nature and value of the discipline; recommendations of professional bodies; society needs; institutional ethos; national education policy;
- *types of students* – background knowledge and prior experience; conceptual understanding; (existing) skills and language competence; approaches/attitudes to studying;
- *curriculum aims* (bearing in mind the ideal graduate) – body of knowledge and level of conceptual and theoretical development; general academic, discipline-specific and personal/interpersonal skills;
- *curricular structures* – semesterised or whole-year courses (modules); co-requisites; double majors (joint degrees); additional educational interventions (such as writing-intensive modules);
- *course (module) design* (with reference to curriculum aims and structure, and the student profile) – content; sequencing of conceptual and skills development; selection of texts; pace and workload; learning and teaching

activities and materials; assessment methods and criteria; feedback to students; monitoring student progress; provision of academic support;
- *resources* – teaching staff; time; funding; consultative (such as input from library, educational development or elearning specialists, industry, employers and practitioners); provision for staff professional development (see Chapter 11: Professional Development).

A useful tool for designing in coherent, progressive learning opportunities across a whole programme is a 'skills matrix' in which the various graduate skills are displayed in vertical columns, then the modules are listed horizontally per year or level of study, and in relation to each module it is identified which particular skills are introduced (I), practiced (P) and/or assessed (A) (see Turner, 2002: 27, for an example). A more sophisticated set of indicators developed by Sumsion and Goodfellow (2004: 333) identifies whether specific skills/attributes are 'assumed, encouraged, modelled, explicitly taught, required [or] evaluated'. This kind of method thus provides a map of how the various modules individually and collectively contribute to the cumulative development of graduate outcomes.

## 'Teaching for understanding' and 'threshold concepts'

When it comes to thinking about what makes for good learning 'encounters' in the subject area (Knight, 2001: 376), a useful model is the Teaching for Understanding (TfU) framework developed by scholars at the Harvard Graduate School of Education (see Perkins, 1993; Wiske, 1998; Wiske et al., 2005). It proposes that courses should create opportunities for students to gain awareness of and demonstrate the four dimensions of understanding (see summary in McCarthy, 2008: 104):

- *purposes* – what drives inquiry in the discipline (or field)?
- *knowledge* – what are key concepts in the discipline?
- *methods* – how is knowledge created and verified in the discipline?
- *forms* – how is knowledge expressed in the discipline?

McCarthy (2008) reveals that where university lecturers adopted this TfU approach it helped to facilitate active learning and 'learning how to learn' among their students.

Allied to TfU is the notion of 'threshold concepts', defined as 'concepts that bind a subject together, being fundamental to ways of thinking and practising in that discipline' (Land et al., 2005: 54). These are construed to be '*transformative* (occasioning a significant shift in the perception of a subject), *irreversible* (unlikely to be forgotten, or unlearned only through considerable effort), and *integrative* (exposing the previously hidden interrelatedness of something)' (p.53) as well as '*troublesome*' where perceived as counter-intuitive or conceptually awkward or absurd (Meyer et al., 2015: 277). During the process of mastering a threshold concept, learners enter into a liminal space as they oscillate between old and emerging understandings, which can cause confusion and uncertainty. Teachers need to offer motivating tasks, empathetic listening and facilitation as students negotiate the new conceptual terrain back and forth (Cousin, 2006; Land et al., 2014). Considerable research has been conducted in a range of disciplines towards identifying threshold concepts in particular fields (as the 'jewels in the curriculum'), to help lecturers prioritise content and ponder ways of teaching them (see Quinlan et al., 2013: 586, for surveys of such work, and Tight, 2014, for a review of theorisation here). Regarding curriculum development, it is recommended that courses should be designed and reviewed according to the sequence of content and processes through which students encounter, explore and internalise threshold concepts – via activities such as scaffolding, use of learning materials and conceptual tools, mentoring and peer collaboration – and demonstrate their understanding through appropriate assessment (Land et al., 2005, 2006). A resonant case study of how threshold concepts have informed curriculum making is the account by Rowe and Martin (2014) of 'Dance 724', a postgraduate module in qualitative research methods and academic writing that prepares students with diverse cultural and educational histories for independent research projects; while their focus is on dance studies, the issues discussed may be common amongst performing artists and practitioners from varied fields transitioning into academic study. Their course sought to address six 'key thresholds' formed by problematic assumptions associated with academic writing and with the nature of research, using pedagogic practices such as 'polylogues' (group discussions which prompt diverse interpretations to emerge), writing tasks repeatedly approached from different angles (akin to choreographic processes of reflection and refinement) and peer review.

## Curriculum design and the research–teaching nexus

Related to the TfU approach is the question of curriculum design that fosters connections between research and teaching. The model in Jenkins et al. (2007: 28–9), and updated in Healey et al. (2014: 16–17), distinguishes between four approaches defined in relation to two axes – (i) emphasis on research content *versus* research process, and (ii) students as audience *versus* participants:

- *research-led* – curriculum is structured around learning content that reflects current research in discipline, which may include staff research;
- *research-tutored* – curriculum is focused around students learning about research findings in small-group critical discussions with lecturers and writing essays;
- *research-orientated* – curriculum promotes a research ethos through teaching that highlights processes of knowledge construction in the discipline and develops students' knowledge of and ability to employ research methodologies and techniques;
- *research-based* – curriculum is organised largely around enquiry-based learning activities (see below), with learning treated as a research-like process.

Case studies of course designs and strategies for course teams to engage students in research and inquiry can be found in Jenkins et al. (2007), Healey and Jenkins (2009) and Healey et al. (2014).

For interdisciplinary and multidisciplinary course design, a theme-based approach can provide for a coherent architecture and conceptual integration, for example building an 'integrated' curriculum around an over-arching 'real world issue' such as 'migration'. Park and Son (2010: 84) clarify that:

> Multidisciplinary learning highlights learning of various topics from diverse disciplines; while interdisciplinary learning has a mixture of diverse disciplines to solve a problem. Transdisciplinary learning, taking interdisciplinary learning a step further, facilitates collaborative learning through a shared conceptual framework.

Constructing a cross-disciplinary course requires careful, collaborative planning, as Bucci and Tranthan (2014) illustrate with reference to their module on 'Children and Violence' combining criminal justice and psychology disciplines. The process entailed *generative*, *refining* and *finalising* stages as the lecturers moved from brainstorming ideas about purposes, goals, content, activities, assignments and readings, to narrowing these down to a 'manageable form', then producing the course documentation and materials (pp.124–6). Benefits of interdisciplinary teaching, they suggest, include expanding the knowledge horizons and insights of both the teachers and learners through courses that deal with current subjects, which keeps the students' interest, and clarifying core (threshold) concepts in light of the interacting disciplines.

## Learning-centred designs

Courses can also be constructed around learning-centred designs, using enquiry-based learning (EBL). This umbrella term describes approaches where learning is driven by processes of enquiry designed to stimulate students' curiosity and promote active and collaborative engagement in finding and applying knowledge for the solution of complex problems and scenarios (Kahn and O'Rourke, 2005). EBL can serve well for enabling experiential learning in terms of Kolb's (1984) learning cycle, creating opportunities for reflection on and abstract conceptualisation from concrete experiences, leading to active experimentation with new ideas. Although adapting to EBL can pose challenges (e.g., fit with students' learning styles; attending to group functioning; securing staff commitment and shifting to the role of 'process facilitator'; assessing the learning process as well as outcomes), perceived benefits include increased student interest, collaborative and independent learning and transferable skills (Deignan, 2009), and EBL can be applied across a spectrum of disciplines – see case studies in Barrett et al. (2005) and the University of Birmingham (n.d.) web page. Forms of EBL include problem-based, case-based and project-based learning (also see Chapter 10: Work-related and Professional Learning).

## Problem-based learning

An approach that has expanded to numerous subject areas since its introduction in medical education in the 1960s (see overview in Hung et al., 2008), here the problem initiates and anchors the learning: 'Instead of requiring that students study content knowledge and then practi[s]e context-free problems, PBL embeds students' learning processes in real-life problems' (p.486). Problems can be presented 'in a variety of formats including: scenarios, puzzles, diagrams, dialogues, quotations, cartoons, e-mails, posters, poems, physical objects, and video-clips' (Barrett, 2005: 56). Working in small groups students unpack the problem, identify then gather and synthesise information required to address it, and propose and critically review solutions. While the PBL group tutorial is at the heart of the process, it can be supplemented by lectures, practicals and skills workshops which serve as resources for tackling the problem (Barrett, 2005). In terms of course design, the curriculum content and process is organised around carefully selected and designed problems of appropriate complexity (see Hung et al., 2008: 496–8) – decision-making, diagnosis-solution, and policy-analysis problems are deemed best suited for PBL (Jonassen and Hung, 2008) – and compatible forms of assessment for appraising the self-reflection and practice-based knowledge, skills and attitudes developed holistically through PBL (see MacDonald, 2005). Checklists can offer a precise tool for assessment of PBL sessions (see Elizondo-Montemayor, 2004). As Savin-Badin (2014) discerns, there are a number of variants ('constellations') of PBL, depending on the disciplinary and pedagogical orientation of courses. For a practical guide to PBL see Jonassen (2010) and Brodie (2013) and case studies in Barrett and Moore (2011), the *Interdisciplinary Journal of Problem-Based Learning* and new *Journal of Problem Based Learning in Higher Education*.

## Case-based learning

Here a realistic case relevant to the course (medicine, law, business, social work etc.) provides the springboard for learning, with students analysing it and making decisions as to the best course of action. Using cases can resonate with students because they provide authentic examples of theory in context, while also requiring learners to exercise high-order thinking skills and presenting opportunities for working in teams (Branch et al., 2014 – includes a range of case studies). Benedict (2010) reports that integrating case-based learning, using virtual patient technology, with PBL practica in an advanced therapeutics course in Pharmacy boosted learning outcomes and was intellectually stimulating and enjoyed by most students. As Altay (2014) evinces in relation to design disciplines (architectural, interior and industrial product design), case-based learning can be successfully combined with role play and project-based learning to achieve 'learner-centred instruction' that strengthened students' analytical, evaluative and creative skills as well as increasing empathy with diverse users for whom they were designing.

## Project-based learning

EBL occurs here through projects that present authentic, real-world challenges, are academically rigorous, and require students to generate, evaluate and implement project ideas and create high-quality products and presentations (see Lee et al., 2014). Success is aided by teaching that supports effective goal-setting, develops project-management skills, and provides project consultation and monitoring, and feedback to students (Garrison, 1999). Project-based learning can be integrated within more traditional courses, using projects for applying knowledge and run alongside lectures (see Engineering case study in Gavin, 2011, which addresses the key elements of curriculum design). Indeed, this 'hybrid' approach may well work better with students engaging with this method for the first time, as they may lack the problem-solving and interpersonal skills to participate in fully-fledged project-based learning (Chua, 2014). Features of course design that can enhance such learning include use of: community partnerships to help students to build networks in the field and provide authentic feedback, which motivates students and overcomes resistance to this method, as their work is open to public scrutiny; learning contracts to improve group dynamics; project calendars to build in progress checks and instil accountability to groups; and rubrics (criteria) to guide assessment, especially where it involves creative products (such as films or brochures) less familiar to the students or staff, reinforced by feedback or evaluation from peers and from clients (Lee at al., 2014). (also see Chapter 10: Work-related and Professional Learning).

EBL courses can also offer scope for a 'negotiated curriculum' in which students have a say in what and how they wish to learn and are assessed, often using a 'learning contract' to specify this. In the case reported by McMahon (2010) students in a module on 'training and development' set their own programme organised around action-planning, weekly self- and peer-assessment, and production of a portfolio to evidence learning outcomes; it had a 'transformative' impact on their self-confidence and abilities as students and as trainers in their places of work. In addition, through 'arts-based inquiry', creative methods using art forms (poetry, narrative, images, painting, dance, drama, music etc.) can stimulate engaged, whole-person learning that deepens students' reflection, conceptual understanding, creativity, confidence, empathy and self-awareness (Warren, 2013).

## 'Community of inquiry' model

The 'community of inquiry' (CoI) model (Garrison and Anderson, 2003; Garrison, 2007) has become influential particularly in relation to online learning where the challenge is to create equivalent dynamics to face-to-face environments (see Chapter 5: Blended Learning). The model construes participants as engaged in deep learning through the confluence of social, cognitive and teaching presence:

- *social presence* is the ability of learners to project their personalities and interact with peers to achieve effective and open communication for sharing ideas and building group cohesion;
- *cognitive presence* is their interaction with content, involving the exploration, construction, resolution and confirmation of understanding through collaboration and reflection;
- *teaching presence* establishes and sustains the CoI, enabling these interactions and worthwhile learning outcomes through the teacher's fundamental role in design, facilitation and direct instruction (Garrison et al., 2010).

Although some researchers question the relative influence of group-based social presence on learners' knowledge construction (Annand, 2011), in the main the CoI framework has proved fruitful both for theoretical exploration of the learning transactions and for guiding learning design in practice (see Swan and Ice, 2010, and special issue of *Internet and Higher Education*, volume 13; and Akyol and Garrison, 2013, which includes case studies on topics such as effective teaching practices, online discussions, student assessment and medical education). The model has, for example, informed studies of video-based instruction in HE courses (Borup et al., 2012), students' use of social media (*Facebook*) as a collective 'third space' for academic networking and 'safe' expression of 'counter scripts' (Rambe, 2012) and students' adoption of democratic principles of responsibility, critique, participation and collaboration in the virtual classroom (Gallego-Arrufat and Gutiérrez-Santiuste, 2015).

## 7Cs model of learning design

The '7Cs' model (Conole, 2013: 77–8) is a framework for designing a 'learning intervention' that 'makes effective use of technologies':

- *conceptualise* – what is the vision of the learning intervention? who is it being designed for? what pedagogical approaches are used?
- *capture* – what Open Educational Resources are being used, and what other resources need to be developed?
- *create* – what kinds of learning activities will the learners engage with?
- *communicate* – what types of communication will the learners be using?
- *collaborate* – what types of collaboration will the learners be doing?
- *consider* – what forms of reflection and demonstration of learning (assessment) are included?
- *consolidate* – how effective is the design? do the different elements work together?

(For online guidance on the use of this model, see websites listed at the end of this chapter.)

## Session design

McAlpine's (2004) model for a 'unit of instruction' covers four main phases linked to Gagne's (1985) 'conditions of learning':

- *engagement* – gain attention of students, clarify learning objectives, stimulate recall of prior learning;
- *informing* – advise students about the subject matter or task, present stimulus material;

- *practice* – provide activities for students to rehearse, perform, apply; provide guidance and feedback on performance, enhance knowledge retention and transfer;
- *assessment* – assess student performance and outcomes.

It is intended both as a 'design tool' and a 'chronology' for the teaching–learning process (the first two phases are short and introductory, with the bulk of time focused on 'practice'), which acts as preparation for formal assessment. However, the 'assessment' could also be an informal, interim evaluation of how far students are developing desired understanding and competencies and whether further teaching is needed (see ideas about 'classroom assessment techniques' below).

# Curriculum evaluation

Evaluation has been broadly defined as 'the purposeful gathering, analysis and discussion of evidence from relevant sources about the quality, worth and impact of provision, development or policy' (CSET, 2008). In curriculum terms, it is distinguished from *assessment*, which pertains to processes used to ascertain whether students have achieved learning outcomes; however, *evaluation* can use assessment data as part of the evidence. In Norris's (1998: 207) nutshell definition: 'curriculum evaluation is about describing the meaning, values and impact of a curriculum to inform curriculum decision making'. In this sense, curriculum evaluation is also process through which to develop 'Scholarship of Teaching and Learning' (see Chapter 11: Professional Development).

## Purposes and approaches

Evaluation is integral to all phases of curriculum development, and it can serve a number of purposes:

- *developmental* – to gauge how well the course or session is meeting students' needs and facilitating desired learning, and to identify where it can be improved;
- *appraisal* – to judge teacher competence for probation, accreditation or promotion;
- *accountability* – to furnish evidence of quality and standards;
- *innovation* – to review the effectiveness of a new approach or method.

(adapted from Light et al., 2009: 241).

There are also different approaches to curriculum evaluation, including:

- *empiricist* – high on reliability and validity;
- *illuminative evaluation* (Parlett and Hamilton, 1972) – providing a close-up, qualitative study of the teaching and learning in context that seeks to discover and document what it is like to be a participant in an innovative programme (as an example from HE, see the evaluation by Clemow, 2007, of the learning process in an interprofessional mentorship course for health professionals);
- *bureaucratic* – driven by institutional procedures using set instruments;
- *collective or participative* – often involving students as investigators as well as subjects. Increasingly students are being incorporated as authentic partners in curriculum development in HE, a process which is challenging but rewarding for all parties and can provide a 'rich experience of learning from students through opening up meaningful dialogue' (Bovill, 2014: 22) (also see Chapter 6: Student Engagement).

A distinction is also made between *extrinsic* evaluation, which is concerned with judging the extent to which espoused objectives are achieved – and accepts that these 'can be stated in relatively unequivocal and measurable terms', and *intrinsic* evaluation, which asks questions about the worth of the stated objectives themselves and whether the experiences provided meet the needs of all interested parties (Gilbert, 2004: 303–304).

Evaluation can be *formative*, conducted during the course to enable immediate adjustments responsive to student learning needs and feedback, as well as *summative*, an overall review undertaken at the end. Diamond (2004) highlights how use of structured, mid-term feedback, collected via small-group discussions led by a trained facilitator (the lecturers were not present), prompted informed changes such as clarification of expectations or content, new teaching strategies or refinements to assessment. 'Classroom assessment techniques' – quick, non-graded in-class activities designed to give both lecturers and students useful feedback on the teaching-learning process (see Angelo and Cross, 1993) – offer a repertoire of exercises for instant, continuous evaluation of course-related knowledge and skills, students' attitudes and values, and their reactions to teaching. Examples are the one-minute paper completed near the end of class ('What was the most important thing you learned'? or 'What important question remains unanswered?'), pros-and-cons grids, skills checklists and reading rating sheets (see Chapter 4: Assessment for Learning).

## Planning and conducting an evaluation

Questions to ask when planning an evaluation include:

- What is the purpose and focus of the evaluation?
- What values and criteria underpin the evaluation?
- From whom and in what form will data be collected?
- Who will collect and analyse data?
- What type of analysis, interpretation, and decision rules will be used and by whom?
- Who will see the results of the evaluation?
- Who will use the results of the evaluation?
- How will the results and actions arising be fed back to the students?

Topics commonly covered in curriculum evaluation include attainment of learning outcomes, subject matter, teaching and learning methods, assessment and feedback practices, learning spaces and facilities, academic support and learning resources. Criteria will relate to the goals of the evaluation: for instance, how far the course promotes 'constructive alignment', 'deep learning' or mastery of 'ways of thinking and practising in the discipline' (see Hounsell and McCune, 2002). These goals could also be determined in light of the 'level' of evaluation being pursued, as per the model formulated by Kirkpatrick (2006) in relation to organisational training:

1. *Reaction* – how students feel about the course/learning experience.
2. *Learning* – their acquisition of new knowledge, skills and attitudes.
3. *Behaviour* – changes in their behaviour in learning or practising.
4. *Results* – usually this refers to benefits to the organisation (such as increased staff morale, productivity or client satisfaction); however, in adapting this model for evaluation of outcomes in HE, Praslova (2010: 222) suggests that this level could include 'alumni employment and workplace success, graduate school admission, service to underprivileged groups or work to promote peace and justice, literary or artistic work, personal and family stability, and responsible citizenship'.

Student evaluations of teaching (SET) have tended to focus mainly on 'level 1', although in their 'comprehensive overview of all meta-analyses' related to SETs, Wright and Jenkins-Guarnieri (2012) concluded that SETs are valid measures of teaching effectiveness and useful tools for improving quality of teaching and, hence, student achievement. Yet research findings also indicate low correlations between SET scores and student learning, so that Tran (2015) urges adoption of a 'learning-focused' approach to evaluation which explores what students can do as a result of the teaching, recognising that educational responsibility lies on both sides. Examples of this approach are the National Survey of Student Engagement (NSSE) in America, or its Australasian version (ACER) (http://research.acer.edu.au/ausse/ accessed 31.07.15), in which 'students' approaches to learning and student learning outcomes were measured as indicators of effective teaching' (Tran, 2015: 56). Also, Frick et al. (2010) have developed a similar instrument for evaluating Teaching and Learning Quality (TALQ) that combines items based on 'first principles of instruction' (Merrill, 2002) with questions about students' own academic learning time and progress on the course.

Ideally, as Harris et al. (2010) explain, curriculum (programme) evaluation should be 'longitudinal, developmental and multilevel', exploring the differences between the '*intended, implemented* and *attained* curriculum' to ensure quality learning and teaching experiences adapted to changes in the educational context are provided; and their health sciences case study shows that 'a carefully planned evaluation can contribute to evidence-based, responsive decision-making throughout the lifespan of the curriculum' (p.488). Likewise, the approach employed Spiel et al. (2006) in evaluating a medical curriculum which revealed a 'discrepancy between educational objectives and their realization' that indicated directions for improvement: first the evaluators 'defined central areas of expertise graduates should possess' and then they asked 'defined learner and teacher groups to evaluate these areas, either as self-assessment or as external/expert assessment' (p.446). A similar systematic approach developed by Hall (2014) for nursing education is the 'BEKA' methodology, applicable to other professional disciplines too: '*Benchmarking* compares curriculum against external standards; *evidencing* drills further into the data in relation to objectives and content mapping, resource mapping [texts, readings etc.], and assessment analysis. *Knowing* involves interviews with stake holders [teachers and learners] to uncover deeper understanding. Lastly *applying* establishes what students actually know and are able to apply' (p.345, italics added). From a 'meta-analysis' of all data, action plans are devised to resolve discrepancies.

## Evaluation methods

Evaluation data can be obtained from different sources using a variety of possible methods:

- *course materials*: outlines, handbooks, tasks, readings, online resources;
- *self-generated*: 'previewing' and 'retracing' specific teaching sessions to pinpoint areas of difficulty and success, usually in consultation with a 'critical friend' (Hounsell, 2003: 205), teaching logs/diaries;

- *students*: instant and informal feedback, suggestions boxes, course committees, questionnaires, focus groups, interviews, shadowing, analyses of assessed work and learning journals for evidence of learning outcomes;
- *peers*: feedback from teaching team, library staff and pedagogical specialists, classroom observations, peer review of other aspects of teaching (such as assessment or VLE design);
- *external*: examiners, employers, professional bodies, supervisors of work/study placements.

Good practice requires using more than one source and type of information, to permit 'triangulation' of data. For detailed points on the use, advantages and constraints of different methods see the *Evaluation Cookbook* (Harvey, 1998) and guide on *Collecting and Using Student Feedback* (Brennan and Williams, 2004). It is also important to 'close the loop' with students, so that they can see that their feedback is valued and acted on. Numerous options here include: feedback in lectures (verbal, summary handout), during induction, minutes or reports, newsletters, noticeboards, email, webpage, student-staff committees and meetings with student representatives.

Online evaluations have become ubiquitous, but often suffer from low response rates, a serious matter given data-driven decision-making in HE nowadays. Survey fatigue and 'nonresponse double-bias' – students with high grades tend most to respond and also to give high ratings – are key issues that could be addressed by better coordination and communication (Adams and Umbach, 2012), explaining the value of the course evaluation process and sending reminders to students, besides ensuring a stable and accessible platform (Norris and Conn, 2005). Furthermore, Park (2014) notes that despite becoming electronic, data collection instruments and response levels remain unchanged. However, 'active participation, high engagement and constructive feedback can be achieved ... where the design of the evaluation questionnaire characterises online learning. In other words, the evaluation can be designed to be one of the scheduled learning activities embedded in the LMS site, which extends from an extra or trivial task to an interactive and communicative form' (p. 1002).

# Conclusion

Course design influences students' perceptions about how classes are conducted and their performance on assessment, as Black et al. (2014) demonstrate in their evaluation of three different types of course design in Marketing. They found that both experiential learning and participative (active) learning designs produced more positive student ratings and better outcomes than traditional 'passive' designs. Angelo (2013: 110) reiterates the main motif here, that 'a well-designed, learning-centered curriculum is one that helps all willing and able students achieve and demonstrate the expected standard of learning more effectively, efficiently and successfully than they could on their own'. Curriculum making for 'higher' education is a complex process but one that can be generative and creative for students as well as teachers, especially when working as partners on the learning journey.

## Questions for reflective practice and professional development

1 How does your curriculum practice embody or reflect your educational philosophy and values?
2 What models of curriculum and learning design are suitable for course design for enabling student learning in your discipline or subject area?
3 What processes and variety of evidence do you employ to review the effectiveness of your course in facilitating student engagement and achievement, both while teaching it and at the end of the cycle?
4 In what ways could you involve students as authentic partners in curriculum development?

## Useful websites

'Imaginative Curriculum' Resources Archive
http://78.158.56.101/archive/palatine/resources/imagincurric/index.html

Frameworks and Toolkits – Higher Education Academy
www.heacademy.ac.uk/frameworks-toolkits/frameworks

Programme and Module Design – University College of Dublin
www.ucd.ie/teaching/resources/programmedesigndevelopment/

JISC: Curriculum Change and Transformation
http://jiscdesignstudio.pbworks.com/w/page/57414310/Curriculum%20Change
%20and%20Transformation

Problem Based Learning Resource Centre – University of Ulster
http://samsara.scic.ulst.ac.uk/~kay/pbl/

UDL On Campus: Universal Design for Learning in Higher Education
http://udloncampus.cast.org/home#.VcDMdflViko

7Cs Framework for Learning Design
online toolkit: www2.le.ac.uk/projects/oer/oers/beyond-distance-research-alliance/
7Cs-toolkit blog created by Grainne Conole: http://e4innovation.com/

Threshold Concepts
www.ee.ucl.ac.uk/~mflanaga/thresholds.html

Evaluation Cookbook
www.icbl.hw.ac.uk/ltdi/cookbook/contents.html

Classroom Assessment Techniques (CATs) – Vanderbilt University
http://cft.vanderbilt.edu/guides-sub-pages/cats/

# References

Adams, M. J. D. and Umbach, P. D. (2012) 'Nonresponse and online student evaluations of teaching: understanding the influence of salience, fatigue, and academic environments', *Research in Higher Education*, 53 (5): 576–91.

Akyol, Z. and Garrison, D. R. (2013) *Educational Communities of Inquiry: Theoretical Framework, Research and Practice*. Hershey, PA: IGI Global.

Altay, B. (2014) 'User-centered design through learner-centered instruction', *Teaching in Higher Education*, 19 (2): 138–55.

Angelo, T. (2013) 'Designing subjects for learning: Practical research-based principles and guidelines', in L. Hunt and D. Chalmers (eds), *University Teaching in Focus: A learning-centred approach*. Abingdon: Routledge, pp.93–111.

Angelo, T. A. and Cross, K. P. (1993) *Classroom Assessment Techniques: A handbook for college teachers* (2nd edn). San Francisco, CA: Jossey-Bass.

Annand, D. (2011) 'Social presence within the community of inquiry framework, *The International Review of Research in Open and Distributed Learning*, 12 (5): 40–56. Available at www.irrodl.org/index.php/irrodl/article/view/924/1855 (accessed 9.9.15).

Apple, M. W. (1993) *Official Knowledge: Democratic Education in a Conservative Age*. New York: Routledge and Kegan Paul.

Apple, M. W. (1996) *Cultural Politics and Education*. New York: Teachers College Press (Columbia University).

Barnett, R. (1997) *Higher Education: A critical business*. Buckingham: SRHE/Open University Press.

Barnett, R. (2009) 'Knowing and becoming in the higher education curriculum', *Studies in Higher Education*, 34 (4): 429–40.

Barnett, R. (2015) *Thinking and Rethinking the University: The selected works of Ronald Barnett*. Abingdon: Routledge.

Barnett, R. and Coate, K. (2005) *Engaging the Curriculum in Higher Education*. Maidenhead: Society for Research into Higher Education & Open University Press.

Barnett, R., Parry, G. and Coate, K. (2001) 'Conceptualising curriculum change', *Teaching in Higher Education*, 6 (4): 435–49.

Barrett, T. (2005) 'What is problem-based learning?', in G. O'Neill, S. Moore and B. McMullin (eds), *Emerging Issues in the Practice of University Learning and Teaching*. Dublin: All Ireland Society for Higher Education (AISHE), pp.55–66. Available at www.aishe.org/readings/2005–1/barrett-What_is_Problem_B_L.pdf (accessed 9.9.15).

Barrett, T. and Moore, S. (eds) (2011) *New Approaches to Problem-based Learning: Revitalising your practice in higher education*. Abingdon: Routledge.

Barrett, T., Mac Labhrainn, I. and Fallon, H. (eds) (2005) *Handbook of Enquiry and Problem-based Learning*. Galway: National University of Ireland Galway, pp.1–12. Available at www.aishe.org/readings/2005–2/contents.html

Benedict, N. (2010) 'Virtual patients and problem-based learning in advanced therapeutics', *American Journal of Pharmaceutical Education*, 74 (8): 1–5.

Biggs, J. (1996) 'Enhancing teaching through constructive alignment', *Higher Education*, 32 (3): 347–64.

Biggs, J. (1999) 'What the student does: Teaching for enhanced learning', *Higher Education Research and Development*, 18 (1): 57–75.

Biggs, J. (2003) *Teaching for Quality Learning at University* (2nd edn). Buckingham: Society for Research into Higher Education/Open University Press.

Black, G. S., Daughtrey, C. L. and Lewis, J. S. (2014) 'The importance of course design on classroom performance of marketing students', *Marketing Education Review*, 24 (3): 213–26.

Borup, J., West, R. E. and Graham, C. R. (2012) 'Improving online social presence through asynchronous video', *Internet and Higher Education*, 15 (3): 195–203.

Bourdieu, P. and Passeron, J.-C. (1990) *Reproduction in Education, Society and Culture* (2nd edn). London: Sage.

Bovill, C. (2014) 'An investigation of co-created curricula within higher education in the UK, Ireland and the USA', *Innovations in Education and Teaching International*, 51 (1): 15–25.

Bovill, C., Bulley, C. J. and Morss, K. (2011) 'Engaging and empowering first-year students through curriculum design: Perspectives from the literature', *Teaching in Higher Education*, 16 (2): 197–209.

Boyce, M. E. (1996) 'Teaching critically as an act of praxis and resistance', *Electronic Journal of Radical Organisational Theory*, 2 (2): 1–14. Available at www.mngt.waikato.ac.nz/ejrot/vol2_2/boyce.pdf (accessed 9.9.15).

Branch, J., Bartholomew, P. and Nygaard, C. (eds) (2014) *Case-based Learning in Higher Education: A learning in higher education anthology*. Faringdon: Libri.

Brennan, J. and Williams, R. (2004) *Collecting and Using Student Feedback: A guide to good practice*. York: Learning and Teaching Support Network Available at www.heacademy.ac.uk/sites/default/files/id352_collecting_and_using_student_feedback_a_guide_to_good_practice.pdf (accessed 9.9.15).

Brodie, L. (2013) 'Problem-based learning', in L. Hunt and D. Chalmers (eds), *University Teaching in Focus: A learning-centred approach*. Abingdon: Routledge, pp.145–63.

Bucci, L. and Trantham, S. (2014) 'Children and violence: An undergraduate course model of interdisciplinary co-teaching', *International Journal of Teaching and Learning in Higher Education*, 26 (1): 122–31.

Burbules, N. C. and Berk, R. (1999) 'Critical thinking and critical pedagogy: Relations, differences, and limits', in T. S. Popkewitz and L. Fendler (eds), *Critical Theories in Education: Changing terrains of knowledge and politics*. New York: Routledge, pp.45–65.

Centre for the Study of Education and Training (CSET), University of Lancaster (2008) *Evaluation Capacity Building 'Toolkit'*. Available at www.lancaster.ac.uk/fass/events/capacitybuilding/toolkit/index.htm#structure (accessed 9.9.15).

Cheng, L-F., Yang, H-C. (2015) 'Learning about gender on campus: An analysis of the hidden curriculum for medical students', *Medical Education*, 49 (3): 321–31.

Chickering, A. W. and Gamson, Z. F. (1987) 'Seven principles for good practice in undergraduate education', *American Association of Higher Education Bulletin*, 39 (7): 3–7.

Chua, K. J. (2014) 'Performance differences between first-time students undergoing hybrid and pure project-based learning', *International Journal of Engineering Education*, 30 (5): 1200–1212.

Clemow, R. (2007) 'An illuminative evaluation of skills rehearsal in a mentorship course', *Nurse Education Today*, 27 (1): 80–87.

Conole, G. (2013) 'Innovative approaches to learning design: Harnessing new technologies for learning', in T. Bilham (ed.), *For the Love of Learning: Innovations from outstanding university teachers*. Basingstoke: Palgrave Macmillan, pp.76–83.

Cornbleth, C. (1990) *Curriculum in Context*. Basingstoke: Falmer.

Cotton, D., Winter, J. and Bailey, I. (2013) 'Researching the hidden curriculum: intentional and unintended messages', *Journal of Geography in Higher Education*, 37 (2): 192–203.

Cousin, G. (2006) 'An introduction to threshold concepts', *Planet*, 17: 4–5. Available at http://journals.heacademy.ac.uk/doi/pdf/10.11120/plan.2006.00170004 (accessed 9.9.15).

Cowan, J., George, J. W. and Pinheiro-Torres, A. (2004) 'Alignment of developments in higher education', *Higher Education*, 48 (4): 439–59.

Deignan, T. (2009) 'Enquiry-based learning: Perspectives on practice', *Teaching in Higher Education*, 14 (1): 13–28.

Dell, C. A., Dell, T. F. and Blackwell, T. L. (2015) 'Applying universal design for learning in online courses: Pedagogical and practical considerations, *The Journal of Educators Online*, 13 (2): 166–92.

Diamond, M. R. (2004) 'The usefulness of structured, mid-term feedback as a catalyst for change in higher education classes, *Active Learning in Higher Education*, 5 (3): 217–31.

Dick, W., Carey, L. and Carey, J. O. (2014) *The Systematic Design of Instruction* (8th edn). Cambridge: Pearson.

Dunne, G. (2015) 'Beyond critical thinking to critical being: Criticality in higher education and life', *International Journal of Educational Research*, 71 (1): 86–99.

Elizondo-Montemayor, L. L. (2004) 'Formative and summative assessment of the problem-based learning tutorial session using a criterion-referenced system', *Journal of the International Association of Medical Science Educators*, 14 (1): 8–14. Available at www.iamse.org/member/article/volume14-1/14-1-8-14.pdf

Entwistle, N. (2003) *Concepts and Conceptual Frameworks Underpinning the ETL Project, Occasional Report 3*. ETL Project: Universities of Edinburgh, Coventry and Durham. Available at www.etl.tla.ed.ac.uk/docs/ETLreport3.pdf (accessed 9.9.15).

Eposito, J. (2011) Negotiating the gaze and learning the hidden curriculum: A critical race analysis of the embodiment of female students of color at a predominantly white institution, *Journal for Critical Education Policy Studies*, 9 (2): 143–64.

Fanghanel, J. (2009) 'Exploring teaching and learning regimes in higher education settings', in C. Kreber (ed.), *The University and its Disciplines: Teaching and learning within and beyond disciplinary boundaries*. London: Routledge, pp.196–208.

Freire, P. (1973) *Education for Critical Consciousness*. New York: Seabury Press.

Frick, T. W., Chadha, R., Watson, C. and Zlatkovska, E. (2010) 'Improving course evaluations to improve instruction and complex learning in higher education', *Educational Technology Research and Development*, 58 (2): 115–36.

Gagne, R. (1985) *The Conditions of Learning* (4th edn). New York: Holt, Rinehart & Winston.

Gallego-Arrufat, M-J. and Gutiérrez-Santiuste, E. (2015) 'Perception of democracy in computer-mediated communication: Participation, responsibility, collaboration, and reflection', *Teaching in Higher Education*, 20 (1): 92–106.

Garrison, D. R. (2007) 'Online community of inquiry review: Social, cognitive, and teaching presence issues', *Journal of Asynchronous Learning Networks*, 11 (1): 61–72.

Garrison, D. R. and Anderson, T. (2003) *E-Learning in the 21st Century: A framework for research and practice*. New York: RoutledgeFalmer.

Garrison, D. R., Cleveland-Innes, M. and Fung, T. S. (2010) 'Exploring causal relationships among teaching, cognitive and social presence: Student perceptions of the community of inquiry framework', *Internet and Higher Education*, 13 (1–2): 31–6.

Garrison, S. (1999) 'Dual Perspectives on the Effectiveness of Project-Based Learning in an Online Environment', *Teaching in the College Community (TCC) Online Conference Proceedings*. Available at http://tcc.kcc.hawaii.edu/previous/TCC%201999/papers/garrison1.html (accessed 9.9.15).

Gavin, K. (2011) 'Case study of a project-based learning course in civil engineering design', *European Journal of Engineering Education*, 36 (6): 547–58.

Gilbert, R. (2004) 'A framework for evaluating the doctoral curriculum', *Assessment and Evaluation in Higher Education*, 29 (3): 299–309.

Giroux, H. A. (1981) *Ideology, Culture and the Process of Schooling*. Philadelphia, PA: Temple University Press.

Giroux, H. A. (1983) *Theory and Resistance in Education: A pedagogy for the opposition*. South Hadley, MA: Bergin and Garvey.

Giroux, H. A. (2011) *On Critical Pedagogy*. New York: Continuum.

Goodson, I. (1997) *The Changing Curriculum: Studies in social construction*. New York: Peter Lang.

Grundy, S. (1987) *Curriculum: Product or praxis?* Lewes: Falmer.

Hall, C. E. A. (2014) 'Toward a model of curriculum analysis and evaluation – Beka: A case study from Australia', *Nurse Education Today*, 34 (3): 343–8.

Hall, T. and Stahl, S. (2006) 'Using universal design for learning to expand access to higher education', in M. Adams and S. Brown (eds), *Towards Inclusive Learning in Higher Education: Developing curricula for disabled students*. Abingdon: Routledge.

Harris, L., Driscoll, P., Lewis, M., Matthews, L., Russell, C. and Cumming, S. (2010) 'Implementing curriculum evaluation: Case study of a generic undergraduate degree in health sciences', *Assessment & Evaluation in Higher Education*, 35 (4): 477–90.

Hartman, N. and Warren, D. (1994) 'Perspectives on a framework for curriculum development created for use in the Faculty of Social Science and Humanities at the University of Cape Town', *South African Association for Academic Development Conference Proceedings*, 1: 234–64.

Harvey, J. (ed.) (1998) *Evaluation Cookbook*. Edinburgh: Learning Technology Dissemination Initiative. Available at www.icbl.hw.ac.uk/ltdi/cookbook/cookbook. pdf (accessed 9.9.15).

Healey, M. and Jenkins, A. (2009) *Developing Undergraduate Research and Inquiry*. York: Higher Education Academy. Available at www.heacademy.ac.uk/sites/ default/files/developingundergraduate_final.pdf (accessed 9.9.15).

Healey, M., Jenkins, A. and Lea, J. (2014) *Developing Research-based Curricula in College-based Higher Education*. York: Higher Education Academy. Available at www.heacademy.ac.uk/sites/default/files/resources/developing_research-based_curricula_in_cbhe_14.pdf (accessed 9.9.15).

Hill, E., Bowman, K., Stalmeijer, R. and Hart, J. (2014) 'You've got to know the rules to play the game: How medical students negotiate the hidden curriculum of surgical careers', *Medical Education*, 48 (9): 884–94.

Hockings, C. (2010) *Inclusive Learning and Teaching in Higher Education: A synthesis of research*. York: Higher Education Academy. Available at https://www.heacademy.ac.uk/resources/detail/resources/detail/evidencenet/Inclusive_learning_and_teaching_in_higher_education

Hounsell, D. (2003) 'The evaluation of teaching', in H. Fry, S. Ketteridge and S. Marshall (eds), *A Handbook for Teaching and Learning in Higher Education: Enhancing academic practice*. London: Kogan Page, pp.200–12.

Hounsell, D. and McCune, V. (2002) *Teaching-Learning Environments in Undergraduate Biology: Initial perspectives and findings. Occasional Report 2*. ETL Project: Universities of Edinburgh, Coventry and Durham. Available at www.etl.tla.ed.ac.uk/docs/ETLreport2.pdf (accessed 9.9.15).

Hung, W., Jonassen, D. H. and Liu, R. (2008) 'Problem-based learning', in J. M. Spector, J. G. van Merriënboer, M. D. Merrill and M. Driscoll (eds), *Handbook of Research on Educational Communications and Technology* (3rd edn). Mahwah, NJ: Erlbaum, pp.485–506. Available at www.aect.org/edtech/edition3/ER5849x_C038.fm.pdf (accessed 9.9.15).

Hussey, T. and Smith, P. (2003) 'The uses of learning outcomes', *Teaching in Higher Education*, 8 (3): 357–68.

Jackson, N., Shaw, M. and Wisdom, J. (2002) 'Imaginative curriculum story: An experiment in collaborative learning', paper produced for the 'Imaginative

Curriculum' project of the former Learning and Teaching Support Network (LTSN) established in UK higher education. Available at http://78.158.56.101/archive/palatine/files/1024.pdf (accessed 20.07.15).

Jenkins, A. (2002) 'Designing a curriculum is like creatively "controlling" a ouija board', paper produced for the 'Imaginative Curriculum' project of the former Learning and Teaching Support Network (LTSN) established in UK higher education

Jenkins, A. (2009) 'Supporting student development in and beyond the disciplines: The role of the curriculum', in C. Kreber (ed.), *The University and its Disciplines: Teaching and learning within and beyond disciplinary boundaries*. London: Routledge, pp.157–68.

Jenkins, A., Healey, M. and Zetter, R. (2007) *Linking Teaching and Research in Disciplines and Departments*. York: Higher Education Academy. Available at www.alanjenkins.info/publications/LinkingTeachingAndResearch_April07.pdf (accessed 9.9.15).

Jonassen, D. H. (2010) *Learning to Solve Problems: A handbook for designing problem-solving learning environments*. New York: Routledge.

Jonassen, D. H. and Hung, W. (2008) 'All problems are not equal: Implications for problem-based learning', *Interdisciplinary Journal of Problem-Based Learning*, 2 (2): 6–28. Available at http://docs.lib.purdue.edu/ijpbl/vol2/iss2/4/

*Journal of Problem Based Learning in Higher Education*, a new interdisciplinary and international open access, online journal published since 2013. Available at http://journals.aau.dk/index.php/pbl/index (accessed 9.9.15).

Kahn, P. and O'Rourke, K. (2005) 'Understanding enquiry-based learning', in T. Barrett, I. Mac Labhrainn and H. Fallon (eds), *Handbook of Enquiry and Problem-based Learning*. Galway: National University of Ireland Galway. pp.1–12. Available at www.aishe.org/readings/2005-2/contents.html

Kemp, J. (1977) *Instructional Design: A plan for unit and course development*. Belmont: Fearon-Pitman.

Kentli, F. D. (2009) 'Comparison of hidden curriculum theories', *European Journal of Educational Studies*, 1 (2): 83–8. Available at www.ozelacademy.com/EJES_v1n2_Kentli.pdf (accessed 9.9.15).

Kirkpatrick, D. L. (2006) *Evaluating Training Programs: The four levels* (3rd edn). San Francisco, CA: Berrett-Koehler.

Knight, P. (2001) 'Complexity and curriculum: A process approach to curriculum-making', *Teaching in Higher Education*, 6 (3): 369–81.

Knight, P. (2002) 'A process approach to curriculum-making to support complex learning', paper produced for the 'Imaginative Curriculum' project of the former Learning and Teaching Support Network (LTSN) established in UK higher education: pp.5–6. Available at http://78.158.56.101/archive/palatine/files/1047.pdf (accessed 20.07.15).

Kolb, D. A. (1984) *Experiential Learning: experience as the source of learning and development*. New Jersey: Prentice-Hall.

Land, R., Cousin, G., Meyer, J. and Davies, P. (2005) 'Threshold concepts and troublesome knowledge (3): Implications for course design and evaluation', in C. Rust (ed.), *Improving Student Learning – Equality and Diversity. Proceedings of the 12th Improving Student Learning Conference*. Oxford: Oxford Centre for Staff and Learning Development, pp.53–64.

Land, R., Cousin, G., Meyer, J. and Davies, P. (2006) 'Implications of threshold concepts for course design and evaluation', in J. Meyer and R. Land (eds), *Overcoming Barriers to Student Understanding, Threshold Concepts and Troublesome Knowledge*. London: Routledge, pp.195–206.

Land, R., Rattray, J. and Vivian, P. (2014) 'Learning in the liminal space: A semiotic approach to threshold concepts', *Higher Education*, 67 (2): 199–217. Available at http://dro.dur.ac.uk/13381/1/13381.pdf (accessed 9.9.15).

Lee, J. S., Blackwell, S., Drake, J. and Moran, K. A. (2014) 'Taking a leap of faith: Redefining teaching and learning in higher education through project-based learning', *Interdisciplinary Journal of Problem-Based Learning*, 8 (2): 19–34. Available at http://docs.lib.purdue.edu/ijpbl/vol8/iss2/2/

Light, G., Cox, R. and Calkins, S. (2009) *Teaching and Learning in Higher Education: The reflective professional*. Thousand Oaks, CA: Sage.

Luckett, K. (2009) 'The relationship between knowledge structure and curriculum: A case study in sociology', *Studies in Higher Education*, 34 (4): 441–53.

Macdonald, R. (2005) 'Assessment strategies for enquiry and problem-based learning', in T. Barrett, I. Mac Labhrainn and H. Fallon (eds), *Handbook of Enquiry and Problem-based Learning*. Galway: National University of Ireland Galway. Available at www.aishe.org/readings/2005-2/contents.html

Margolis, E., Soldatenko, M., Acker, S. and Gair, M. (2001) 'Hiding and outing the curriculum', in E. Margolis (ed.), *The Hidden Curriculum in Higher Education*. New York and London: Routledge, pp.1–20.

Marton, F., Hounsell, D. and Entwistle, N. (eds) (1997) *The Experience of Learning*. Edinburgh: Scottish Academic Press.

McAlpine, L. (2004) 'Designing learning as well as teaching', *Active Learning in Higher Education*, 5 (2): 119–34.

McCarthy, M. (2008) 'Teaching for understanding for lecturers: Towards a scholarship of teaching and learning', in B. Higgs and M. McCarthy (eds), *Emerging Issues II: The Changing Roles and Identities of Teachers and Learning in Higher Education*. Cork: National Academy for Integration of Research & Teaching & Learning (NAIRTL), pp.101–113.

McMahon, T. (2010) 'Combining peer-assessment with negotiated learning activities on a day-release undergraduate-level certificate course (ECTS level 3)', *Assessment and Evaluation in Higher Education*, 35 (2): 223–39.

Merrill, M. D. (2002) 'First principles of instruction', *Educational Technology Research and Development*, 50 (3): 43–59.

Meyer, J. H. F., Knight, D. B., Callaghan, D. P. and Baldock, T. E. (2015) 'Threshold concepts as a focus for metalearning activity: Application of a research-developed mechanism in undergraduate engineering', *Innovations in Education and Teaching International*, 52 (3): 277–89.

Moon, J. (2002) *The Module and Programme Development Handbook: A practical guide to linking levels, outcomes and assessment criteria*. London: Kogan Page.

Moon, J. (2007) 'Linking levels, learning outcomes and assessment criteria – EHEA version'. Available at http://spectare.ucl.slu.se/adm/sus/2008/plagiarism_eng/ JennyMoonExercise.pdf (accessed 9.9.15).

Morgan, H. and Houghton, A-M. (2011) *Inclusive Curriculum Design in Higher Education: Considerations for effective practice across and within subject areas.* York: Higher Education Academy. Available at www.heacademy.ac.uk/resources/ detail/inclusion/Disability/Inclusive_curriculum_design_in_higher_education (accessed 9.9.15).

Norris, J. and Conn, C. (2005) 'Investigating strategies for increasing student response rates to online-delivered course evaluations', *Quarterly Review of Distance Education*, 6 (1): 13–29.

Norris, N. (1998) 'Curriculum evaluation revisited', *Cambridge Journal of Education*, 28 (2): 207–219.

O'Neill, G. (2010) 'Programme Design: overview of curriculum models', resource produced for University College Dublin. Available at www.ucd.ie/t4cms/ UCDTLP00631.pdf (accessed 9.9.15).

Ornstein, A. C. and Hunkins, F. P. (2009) *Curriculum Foundations, Principles and Issues* (3rd edn). Boston, MA: Allyn and Bacon.

Park, J. Y. (2014) 'Course evaluation: Reconfigurations for learning with learning management systems', *Higher Education Research and Development*, 33 (5): 992–1006.

Park, J. Y. and Son, J. B. (2010) 'Transitioning toward transdisciplinary learning in a multidisciplinary environment', *International Journal of Pedagogies and Learning*, 6 (1): 82–93.

Parlett, M. and Hamilton, D. (1972) 'Evaluation as illumination: A new approach to the study of innovatory programs', Occasional Paper 9. Edinburgh: University of Edinburgh, Centre in the Educational Sciences. Available at http://files.eric. ed.gov/fulltext/ED167634.pdf (accessed 9.9.15).

Perkins, D. (1993) 'Teaching for understanding', *American Educator: The Professional Journal of the American Federation of Teachers*, 17 (3): 28–35. Available at www. exploratorium.edu/ifi/resources/workshops/teachingforunderstanding.html (accessed 9.9.15).

Praslova, L. (2010) 'Adaptation of Kirkpatrick's four level model of training criteria to assessment of learning outcomes and program evaluation in Higher Education', *Educational Assessment, Evaluation & Accountability*, 22 (3): 215–25.

Pratt, D. (1980) *Curriculum Design and Development*. New York: Harcourt Brace Jovanovich Inc.

Quinlan, K., Male, S., Baillie, C., Stamboulis, A., Fill, J. and Jaffer, Z. (2013) 'Methodological challenges in researching threshold concepts: A comparative analysis of three projects', *Higher Education*, 66 (5): 585–601.

Rambe, P. (2012) 'Constructive disruptions for effective collaborative learning: Navigating the affordances of social media for meaningful engagement', *Electronic Journal of e-Learning*, 10 (1): 132–46.

Ramsden, P. (2003) *Learning to Teach in Higher Education* (2nd edn). London: RoutledgeFalmer.

Reynolds, M. and Trehan, K. (2000) 'Assessment: A critical perspective', *Studies in Higher Education*, 25 (3): 267–78.

Romiszowski, A. J. (1981) *Designing Instructional Systems*. London: Kogan Page.

Ross, A. (2000) *Curriculum: Construction and Critique*. London: Falmer Press.

Rowe, N. and Martin, R. (2014) 'Dancing onto the page: Crossing an academic borderland', *Waikato Journal of Education*, 19 (2): 25–36.

Savin-Baden, M. (2014) 'Using problem-based learning: New constellations for the 21st century, *Journal on Excellence in College Teaching*, 25 (3–4): 197–220.

Schweitzer, L. and Stephenson, M. (2008) 'Charting the challenges and paradoxes of constructivism: A view from professional education', *Teaching in Higher Education*, 13 (5): 583–593.

Sirotnik, K. A. (1991) 'Critical inquiry: A paradigm for praxis', in E. C. Short (ed.), *Forms of Curriculum Inquiry*. Albany, NY: State University of New York Press.

Smith, M. K. (2011) 'What is praxis?', *The Encyclopaedia of Informal Education*. Available at www.infed.org/biblio/b-praxis.htm (accessed 9.9.15).

Spiel, C., Schober, B. and Reimann, R. (2006) 'Evaluation of curricula in higher education: Challenges for evaluators', *Evaluation Review*, 30 (4): 430–50.

Sumsion, J. and Goodfellow, J. (2004) 'Identifying generic skills through curriculum mapping: a critical evaluation', *Higher Education Research and Development*, 23 (3): 329–46.

Swan, K. and Ice, P. (2010) 'The Community of Inquiry framework ten years later: Introduction to the special issue', *Internet and Higher Education*, 13 (1–2): 1–4.

Tam, M. (2014) 'Outcomes-based approach to quality assessment and curriculum improvement in higher education', *Quality Assurance in Education*, 22 (2): 158–68.

*The Interdisciplinary Journal of Problem-Based Learning*. Available at http://docs.lib.purdue.edu/ijpbl/ (accessed 9.9.15).

Tight, M. (2014) 'Theory development and application in higher education research: The case of threshold concepts', *International Perspectives on Higher Education Research*, 10: 249–67.

Tobin, T. J. (2014) 'Increase online student retention with universal design for learning', *Quarterly Review of Distance Education*, 15 (3): 13–24.

Toohey, S. (1999) *Designing Courses for Higher Education*. Buckingham: Society for Research into Higher Education and Open University Press.

Tran, N. D. (2015) 'Reconceptualisation of approaches to teaching evaluation in higher education', *Issues in Educational Research*, 25 (1): 50–61.

Trowler, P. (2009) 'Beyond epistemological essentialism: Academic tribes in the twenty-first century', in C. Kreber (ed.), *The University and its Disciplines: Teaching and Learning within and Beyond Disciplinary Boundaries*. London: Routledge, pp.181–95.

Turner, D. (2002) *Designing and Delivering Modules*. Oxford: Oxford Centre for Staff and Learning Development.

University of Birmingham (n.d.) 'Enquiry-Based Learning (EBL) case studies'. Available at https://intranet.birmingham.ac.uk/as/cladls/edudev/ebl/case-studies/index.aspx (accessed 9.9.15).

Warren, D. (2013) 'Arts-based inquiry as learning in higher education: Purposes, processes and responses', in P. McIntosh and D. Warren (eds), *Creativity in the Classroom: Case studies in using the arts in teaching and learning in higher education*. Bristol: Intellect, pp.257–69.

Winter, J. and Cotton, D. (2012) 'Making the hidden curriculum visible: Sustainability literacy in higher education,, *Environmental Education Research*, 18 (6): 783–96.

Wiske, M. S. (ed.) (1998) *Teaching for Understanding: Linking research with practice*. San Francisco, CA: Jossey-Bass.

Wiske, M. S., with Franz, K. R. and Breit, L. (2005) *Teaching for Understanding with Technology*. San Francisco, CA: Jossey-Bass.

Wright, S. and Jenkins-Guarnieri, M. A. (2012) 'Student evaluations of teaching: Combining the meta-analyses and demonstrating further evidence for effective use', *Assessment & Evaluation in Higher Education*, 37 (6): 683–99.

# 3

# Teaching by Leading and Managing Learning Environments

## Steven Cranfield

### Chapter overview

This chapter explores:

- what is meant by 'learning environments', including core principles
- different ways of leading and managing learning environments
- specific strategies for leading and managing learning in large group (lecture), small group and laboratory and practice-based settings
- some common concerns in managing learning environments with practical ideas distilled from current and emerging research into best practice
- implications of future advances in the design of learning environments

## Introduction

The aim of this chapter is to promote an understanding of how different environments or settings within which students are asked or required to learn, such as large groups, small groups and laboratory and practice settings, have an impact on how they approach their learning and hence on the design and delivery of teaching. It provides an overview of underpinning principles and concepts before exploring their application in practice. The focus is on face-to-face teaching and learning. Online learning environments are discussed in Chapter 5: Blended Learning.

## What is meant by 'learning environments'?

In its widest sense, a learning environment is anywhere that learning may conceivably take place: for example, a laboratory, a classroom, a library, the patient's bedside, an oil refinery, cyberspace, even outer space. Spaces not designated as learning environments may nonetheless be places of learning. Evidence shows that an effective learning environment, wherever it may be located, is likely to be interactive and learner-centred (Chickering and Gamson, 1999) and characterised by learner engagement, dialogue and activity-based learning (Mortiboys, 2010; Biggs and Tang, 2007; Savin-Baden, 2007). A multi-national survey of learning research identified a number of core principles for designing an effective learning environment, which can be summarised as its being learner-centred, structured, personalised, social and inclusive (Istance and Dumont, 2011).

## Core principles for designing learning environments

According to Istance and Dumont (2011), the learning environment:

1 recognises the learners as its core participants, encourages their active engagement and develops in them an understanding of their activity as learners;
2 is founded on the social nature of learning and actively encourages well-organised co-operative learning;
3 has learning professionals who are highly attuned to the learners' motivations and the key role of emotions in achievement;
4 is acutely sensitive to the individual differences among the learners within it, including their prior knowledge;
5 devises programmes that demand hard work and challenge from all without excessive overload;
6 operates with clarity of expectations and deploys assessment strategies consistent with these expectations; there is strong emphasis on formative feedback to support learning;
7 strongly promotes 'horizontal connectedness' across areas of knowledge and subjects as well as to the community and the wider world.

It has been argued that only a certain number of conditions are needed to establish the basis of a learning environment, namely: a subject (the learner), an object (experiences, knowledge, products) and a learning activity (Engeström, 2000). However, as the principles set out above imply, it is important to see learning environments in holistic rather than reductionist terms. A learning environment encompasses more than technical and practical knowledge such as managing resources, designing learning activities and deploying interpersonal skills. It requires the engagement of the learner as a person, a 'critical being', drawing on and fostering that person's capacity for critical action and critical self-reflection (Barnett, 1997). The extent and type of this criticality will naturally depend on the kind of learning involved and require interpretation by lecturers in their specific disciplines. Values and their underpinning educational philosophy are equally foundational to any learning environment and, arguably, these will transcend disciplines (see UKPSF, 2011). The educationalist Jack Mezirow contends that learning has an important emancipatory function: for this notion to become more than merely aspirational requires us to see learning environments as potentially transformative spaces that enable 'the individual [to] become a more autonomous thinker by learning to negotiate his or her own values, meanings, and purposes rather than to uncritically act on those of others' (Mezirow, 1997: 11). Considered from a holistic perspective, a learning environment should be seen as being about the individual lecturer leading (envisioning, inspiring, motivating, caring) as much as it is about managing (planning, organising, coordinating, controlling).

## Leading and managing learning environments

Learning environments are spaces that can serve different or complementary functions: for instance, for writing, reflection, practice, play, performance, discussion, argument and contestation (Savin-Baden, 2007). Hence the leading and managing approaches adopted in any learning environment need to be appropriate to the methods of teaching or instruction used as well as to the context, focus, level and content of the learning. These approaches may need to move deftly along a continuum of styles between more didactic or authoritative at one end to more facilitative and discreet at the other (Heron, 1975).

## Types of interventions in learning environments

### Authoritative interventions

- *Telling* – 'Cholera can be transmitted via ...', 'The class starts at 9.30 prompt ...'
- *Guiding* – 'If you apply this particular tool to the data you can expect ...'

*(Continued)*

*(Continued)*

- *Directing* – 'I want you to stop and reflect on the discussion we've just had ...'
- *Explaining* – 'There are three parts to this workshop, consisting of ...'
- *Clarifying* – 'What the assessment is specifically asking for here is ...'
- *Persuading* – 'This is a really useful method for ...'

**Facilitative interventions**

- *Delegating* – 'Please decide among yourselves on a rapporteur.'
- *Observing* – 'I noticed that when you used that particular dance technique you ...'
- *Monitoring* – 'Do people need more time to complete that exercise?'
- *Collaborating* – 'Can I share some ideas about what I have found useful?'
- *Encouraging* – 'You're doing fine. I mean that! It isn't easy.'
- *Participating* – 'I'm here as a resource. How do you want to use me?'

The decision-making style in any learning environment may also be:

- *participative* – lecturer and students make joint decisions, for example, agreeing the marking criteria for a group presentation;
- *consultative* – lecturer consults with group but takes responsibility for taking the decision, for example, asking students to suggest topics for seminars;
- *benignly authoritarian* – lecturer makes decisions in the best interests of the group, for example, ensuring classes start and finish on time, requiring students to follow health and safety procedures in a laboratory.

(see Likert, 1961)

When adopting an appropriate style or balance of styles it is important to look at your teaching role strategically and to map out in advance what is expected of you, from students, course team colleagues, institutional requirements and, of course, yourself, and manage expectations accordingly. 'Many new teachers get the balance wrong – partly because they have not learned how to organise their teaching activities and partly because everything takes a little longer in the early stages of teaching' (Debowski, 2012: 76). Running in tandem with these pragmatic considerations, and largely justifying them, is the value of authentic leadership; that is, leading by example, practising fairness and consistency, ensuring students understand what you expect from them, and generating enthusiastic support through honest, trusting relationships with colleagues and students (Katzenmeyer and Moller, 2009).

Having overall responsibility for leading a learning environment need not mean being centre stage, or directing the spotlights. In some learning environments the role of leader is likely to be delegated, distributed or rotated: team teaching and peer- and group-learning methods provide good examples of these approaches (Spillane and Diamond, 2007). Spaces for learning will have different lead actors at different times with different leading styles, whether consciously or not. Sometimes it will be appropriate to have no designated leader or to prevent one taking charge by default, for example in an online discussion forum. It is a misunderstanding of facilitation and online moderation that it entails not being in control or even abdicating control of the learning environment. The professional lecturer always has a certain amount of control over what is going on, even when in facilitative or moderating mode.

## Learning in lectures and large groups

Lectures are as effective as other methods, such as discussion or reading for transmitting information. In general, however, students capture only 20–40 per cent of a lecture's main ideas in their notes (Kiewra, 2002) and without reviewing the lecture material, students remember less than 10 per cent after three weeks (Bligh, 1998). While students' attention spans clearly vary during lectures there is little evidence for the often-cited figure of 10–15 minutes as the average attention span (Wilson and Korn, 2007). Attention spans can be extended by strategies such as improved note-taking. Even so, most lectures are not as effective as group discussion and debate, for example, for promoting critical thinking. They are also relatively ineffective for teaching behavioural skills. Changing students' attitudes should not normally be the major objective of a lecture either.

Nowadays, then, when many students have access to a range of knowledge resources, why continue offering lectures? Valid reasons include:

- To provide a focus for shared learning, where everyone gets together regularly.
- To whet students' appetites for learning or give them the chance to make sense of things they already know.
- To clarify or introduce important or contested areas of knowledge, as well as provide a common briefing on assignments and intended learning outcomes.

- To use the power of voice, facial expression and body language to communicate the significance and relative value of what is being discussed.
- To provide material for later discussion, exploration and elaboration.

(Adapted from Race and Brown, 2001: 107)

In particular, new technologies, for example question-response software, have increased awareness of the value of integrating interactive components to lectures and teaching large groups, moving away from the notion of the lecture as a didactic exercise (Dalrymple and Eaglesfield, 2013). (See Chapter 5: Blended Learning.)

Lectures and large group learning environments pose a number of challenges, however. Below are just three commonly identified challenges with suggested strategies.

### Students do not get the individual help they need

- Facilitate learning from peers, by encouraging interactions among students (Biggs and Tang, 2007).
- Provide follow-up seminar groups.
- Often problems stem from study skills: offer advice or refer to study skills support.

### Students find it hard to concentrate and pay attention

- Speak clearly and intelligibly. Check that students can hear and comprehend you, particularly if English is not your (and/or their) first language (Miller, 2007).
- Vary approaches and methods during lectures (Mortiboys, 2010).
- Assign engaging activities to encourage active learning (Brown and Race, 2002). It may be harder to encourage interaction among 200 rather than 40 students but interactive lectures certainly can work (Habeshaw et al., 1993). (See 'Ten basic ideas' in box below)
- Activities take more thought and preparation than straightforward lecturing. Introduce small activities gradually and increase them as you gain confidence. There doesn't have to be constant activity every lecture.
- Be alert to students' daily work and rest regimes and other factors impacting on their physical and emotional well-being. It is hard to concentrate without sufficient sleep or on an empty stomach. Some learning styles models (e.g., Dunn et al., 1984) provide user-friendly tools for discussing these factors with students.

## Students do not ask or answer questions

- Ask open questions. It is more important to know how to ask the right questions than to have all the answers (Exley and Dennick, 2009).
- Avoid answering your own question if it isn't answered quickly.
- Call at random and explain the advantage of contributions.

## Ten basic ideas for making lectures more interactive – none requiring technology

1  Include individual, pairs and small group activities.
2  (A variation on 1.) 'Think, pair, share'; pose a short question or a problem and get students to think individually, share with a partner and then with the group.
3  Pose a more substantial problem and get students working in small groups.
4  Punctuate the lecture with questions and wait for answers.
5  Introduce short writing exercises; for example, ask students to write down a key learning point so far and share this with a partner.
6  Use brainstorming; for example, ask students to recall and write a list of important terms, concepts and ideas from the material covered.
7  Use short tests and quizzes.
8  Ask students to do a calculation or complete a diagram.
9  Invite students to contribute to the whiteboard to write up their key points, questions or answers.
10  Get students to do a one-minute paper at the end of the lecture.

## Vignette: Managing disruptions in lectures

During an interactive lecture on historical skills given by Len, four students arrived individually around 25 minutes late. The rest of the students were underway with the tasks and Len's time was being spent on a small group basis dealing with queries and enabling each group to work at its own pace. When the new students arrived, Len was forced to go quickly through the initial mini-lecture with them again. Spending time trying to assist the latecomers meant that the last part of the session was not used

*(Continued)*

*(Continued)*

to gain student feedback and to discuss findings and comments generated from the task. Len failed to conclude the lecture, which frustrated him. In future he decided to minimise disruptions by not allowing students to arrive more than 15 minutes late, explaining that this impinged on the quality of learning for everyone. While this did not eliminate the problem entirely – some students simply did not like to follow rules – it enabled Len to arrange to speak with these students early on and discuss plans of action with them. Early detection of disruptive behaviour also let the rest of the class know that Len meant business.

**Points to explore**

- The subsequent decision about latecomers taken here was benignly authoritarian ('fair but firm'). Lecturers will need to weigh up the pros and cons of using different leading and decision-making styles: there is no 'one size fits all' rule.
- Lecturers can model good practice to encourage prompt attendance. They can, for example:
  - always start and end lectures on time;
  - indicate at the outset that punctuality is expected, explaining the benefits of this rule;
  - schedule an interesting or essential activity at the start of the lecture to practise positive reinforcement of being punctual;
  - draw attention to latecomers through a remark or non-verbal cue, while avoiding sarcasm, getting angry or issuing threats;
  - minimise disruptions by asking students present to move to the front and middle seats before starting.

(adapted from NUS, 2008)

# Vignette: Interactive lecturing using mobile devices

Anya arrived at her lecture on marketing for second-year undergraduates without the data stick containing her PowerPoint slides. She had a momentary panic when she realised they were not available online either. Then she recalled a recent seminar in which a colleague had presented research on interactive lecturing with the use of technology (see Graham et al., 2007), including the use of mobile devices in lectures (Gehlen-Baum and Weinberger, 2012).

Anya quickly decided to try something novel (for her and the class), taking cues from the seminar. She asked for a group of volunteers in the lecture hall with smartphones to act as 'research nodes' for small groups. Nearly all students had phones or other portable devices so finding sufficient volunteers was not a problem. Each group of five was randomly allocated a theme related to the lecture content, asked to research this online and to identify a rapporteur to feed back one key point to the plenary lecture: the 'node' or another volunteer was asked to take responsibility for uploading this and additional points discussed to a course blog. Anya circulated around the hall, acting as a resource and monitoring groups, some of which had decided to have a number of members research the same theme simultaneously and compare findings. Introducing, explaining and facilitating the activity took much longer than the PowerPoint presentation but the plenary discussion, though shorter than usual, was focused and lively. The blend of activities kept the majority engaged for the whole hour and materials and ideas sourced by groups were uploaded to the course virtual learning environment for further tasks and revision. Some students had also been introduced to ways to use portable devices to conduct research.

**Points to explore**

- Technology is but one way of promoting collaborative dialogue and learning in the classroom (Webb, 2009; Hmelo-Silver et al., 2013).
- Audio-visual aids can cater to a range of different learning styles (Coffield et al., 2004) but over-reliance on bulleted PowerPoint slides can inculcate a linear, stereotyped approach to teaching that yields diminishing returns (Kinchin et al., 2008).
- Lecturers can create, as well as exploit, opportunities that allow for improvisation and the unpredictable (Cvetek, 2008; McCarron and Savin-Baden, 2008; Debowski, 2012).

## Learning in small groups

There are several pedagogic benefits to having students working and learning in small groups. Collaborative learning can be a powerful tool for joint knowledge creation (Hakkarainen et al., 2013) and for encouraging critical thinking and 'deep' rather than 'strategic' or 'surface' learning (Entwistle, 1997; Prosser and Trigwell, 1999). It can foster communication, team building and other skills for personal effectiveness, skills that are increasingly linked to the employability agenda (Yorke and Knight, 2006). Some pedagogies such as problem-based learning and many of those shaping professional education programmes are predicated on small-group and peer learning (Fry et al., 2008). It is also becoming a progressively more important vehicle for formative and summative assessment (Boud et al., 2001). Small group learning can carry social benefits too; it may facilitate integration into university life and student diversity can be drawn on to bring different experiences to the group (Ho et al., 2004).

There is no agreed definition of how many members constitute a small group. It may range from anything between two (tutorial) and 20-plus members (seminar). While it is foolhardy to make hard-and-fast rules, evidence suggests that groups between seven and 15 participants are better suited to learning activities based on problem solving or decision making (Dillenbourg et al., 1995), and having odd numbers can help avoid deadlocks. Where in-depth discussion or exploration of sensitive issues is important, smaller-sized groups tend to be more conducive to harmonious working.

Despite being aware of the suggested benefits, lecturers will need little telling that much can go wrong with small group work to make it less than effective or even counterproductive. Students may exhibit various challenging behaviours and attitudes, prompted in part by the group method or group allocation process: for example, being silent, domineering, over-dependent or straying from the topic. Lecturers equally may undermine small-group work by talking too much, leaving struggling groups to their own devices, belittling students, ignoring feelings, or inadequately eliciting and processing feedback.

What can lecturers and groups themselves do to try to minimise or avert these and related problems? Below are some points and strategies to consider, by no means exhaustive.

- *Groundwork* – ensure that students are made aware of the importance and value of participation and co-operative learning, for example, through course literature and agreeing ground rules for group working.
- *Modelling behaviour* – set the example by adopting interactive methods from the start of the course or early in a session, to foster sustained participation. Lecturers who talk uninterruptedly for 40 minutes or who stay in authoritative mode for five lectures in a row can hardly be surprised if students are silent or fixed to their seats when suddenly asked to 'get into small groups and discuss'.

- *Leadership* – take yourself out of the equation to some degree – encourage students to talk to each other, rather than go through you. Allow the group to be its own problem solver before offering remedies if the group reaches an impasse.
- *Group size* – different sizes of group call for different types of behaviour and learning strategies and leadership styles (Jaques and Salmon, 2007). The larger the group the less likely that all members will share the same aims or be cohesive. As a group gets smaller the less likely people may be to share the same aims either, which can inhibit dialogue, joint work and generation of ideas. Groups of 6 and below tend to require less organisation and leadership tends to be fluid. Between 7 and 12 differentiation of roles begins and face-to-face interaction is less frequent. Between 12 and 25 structure and role differentiation become vital: sub-groups emerge, face-to-face interaction is difficult and stereotyping and avoidance behaviours occur. Emotional responses to what is going on in the group may go unnoticed.
- *Appropriate tasks* – set tasks that cannot be completed alone to encourage discussion and group participation (Fink, 2004; Dennick, 2007; Webb, 2009).
- *Layout and seating* – room layout has a direct effect on interpersonal communication, for example: '10 students seated round a rectangular table, at least 4 students on either side of the table have no eye contact with each other thus reducing participation' (Jaques, 2003: 492).
- *Group development and dynamics* – groups go through a lifecycle, a beginning, a middle and an end, which occurs in every group at some level and is independent of the group's task (Tuckman, 1965). Activities such as personal introductions can help break the ice, establish a comfortable and trusting working atmosphere, and set the agenda. Structured tasks, with clear roles and expectations, can help define and focus the issue being explored. Careful timings and tasks that participants regard as meaningful can allow for open exchange of ideas (including disagreements), recognition of other viewpoints, and creative problem-solving. Groups should be allowed time to end, wrap up and disengage, without being hustled to a conclusion (Jaques and Salmon, 2007).
- *Group allocation for projects* – various methods can be used to assign students to group-based projects, including randomly (e.g., electronically), by self-selection, psychological profiling (including learning styles questionnaires) or context-specific criteria, such as previous attendance or attainment. No one method appears to have more benefits than another (Huxham and Land, 2000).
- *Cultural competence* – how students behave and express themsel ⌐⌐ needs to be understood in context: behaviour will be affected

personal, professional and cultural factors. For example, different groups may have different ways of expressing disagreement, conflict and reconciliation. In some groups compliance may be seen as a cultural norm and attempts to probe beneath surface pleasantries may cause discomfort and embarrassment (Ho et al., 2004). Strategies for facilitating intercultural communication in small groups can include recognising differences as group strengths rather than liabilities, lecturers asking themselves whether students' behaviour might have a cultural origin, and their being willing to consider discussing intercultural differences openly and sensitively: 'All communications are to some extent intercultural but some much more than others' (Galanes et al., 2003: 134).

- *Be alert* – lecturers who are always aware of what is going on in their class are less likely to need to control it (Charles et al., 2014). Move around the class often and allow time to interact with students.

Involving more silent students in small group discussions may call for sensitive intervention. For example, if some students are habitually silent in small groups, the lecturer can ask the groups to stop briefly and to write down anything they don't understand, or find surprising or annoying. Comments are collected and reviewed (while students are continuing with the group task or going on to another). The lecturer picks out some good points and follows them up, encouraging the student who proposed it to identify themselves. Sometimes silent students have excellent points to make but are shy or self-conscious. If their point already has positive acceptance from the lecturer they will be encouraged to 'claim' it.

## Vignette: Small group learning in a design studio

Andrew had asked students to work on an assignment and bring this to the design studio for discussion and feedback in groups of 4–5 participants. Having introduced the task on the day and given students some prompt questions, he kept a sharp eye on groups in the studio, and there was a good buzz of activity. About half-way through he noticed one male student, Eteng, looking flustered and unhappy. Andrew was attentive but did not interfere. The group were making some clear criticism of Eteng's designs, but in a positive spirit. They identified the area to work on and gave him some practical tips about assignments. At the end of the session Andrew brought everyone together to elicit and summarise generic issues and points. Eteng was silent.

Afterwards Andrew approached Eteng in private and mentioned he had noticed that he seemed a bit uncomfortable with the feedback from the group. Eteng became quite tearful and said it was like a replay of many past issues. He had come to the programme via an access course: not having gained any formal qualifications, he felt the feedback brought back unhappy memories of school.

Andrew listened with empathy and clarified with Eteng that he could indeed get some practical help with structuring of assignments which would stand him in good stead, pointing out how positive it was that this issue had been bought up so early in his studies. He had time to work on this and get some help. Andrew made sure Eteng knew where to get additional study skills support should he need it.

**Points to explore**

- Group activities and processes can arouse powerful emotions. Judging if, when and how to intervene calls for the exercise of emotional intelligence: listening skills and attention to non-verbal communication are crucial (Mortiboys, 2010).
- Structuring activities initially in pairs may be less exposing for some students, make them feel less defensive about their work, and help prevent them losing face (Murray, 2012; Merry et al., 2013).
- 'Incidents' happen all the time in the classroom, but *critical* incidents are produced by the way someone looks at a situation. A critical incident only becomes critical because someone sees it as such. Critical incidents can offer important opportunities for learning and developing professional judgement, given that in teaching there is seldom one 'right answer' (Tripp, 2012).

## Learning in laboratories and practice settings

Educationalists have noted that in science laboratories, computer labs, field work (Morss and Murray, 2005), studios and performance spaces (Parncutt and McPherson, 2002; Stucky and Wimmer, 2002) and practice classes the up-front delivery tends to be much reduced: the lecturer usually moves or travels around seeing individual students, or groups of students, to mentor, demonstrate or model best practice. However, student-centred approaches outlined above remain applicable in such environments. In computer labs,

, some lecturers may still go straight into a teacher-focus mode at the terminal sorting out the problem. What, we might ask, happened to the student 'learning by doing'? Given an increasing student computer ownership it has been argued that computer labs are becoming passé (Kolowich, 2009). Others contend that, apart from the issue of ensuring equality of access to technology, labs have a continuing and sometimes under-utilised value for project collaboration, socialisation and computational research (Hawkins and Oblinger, 2007), as well as for developing critical thinking skills through virtual and simulated experiments (Simon, 2015).

Additional considerations will apply in highly regulated environments such as laboratories to ensure that everyone follows health and safety protocols. Educational institutions in the UK are required to have a health and safety policy that sets out the responsibilities in relation to risk assessments in the classroom and other learning environments. Policy guidelines may stipulate assessing physical and other hazards, who might be harmed, what the harm could be and existing measures to manage the risk effectively.

In some learning environments touch may be appropriate, indeed central to the learning, for example, in dance classes or physiotherapy practicals. In these and related contexts there will be institutional policies and guidelines governing physical contact with students which lecturers should familiarise themselves with.

## Vignette: Computer lab teaching

The unrefurbished computer lab Francine had been assigned to teach in was certainly a challenge: an awkward layout of 50 monitors and some poor sight lines blocked by pillars which made it difficult to see at a glance what the whole class was doing. She quickly realised that she needed to review and possibly adapt her teaching style to make use of this space to ensure the classes were a success.

- She opened each session ensuring she was as visible and audible as possible, which in this space was to the side rather than the front of the class. She explained or repeated any general rules and procedures, for example about health and safety, logging on, downloads and acceptable use, saving work, not personalising settings and not consuming food.
- Whenever the room was full to capacity, she asked some students to wheel their chairs towards her. She designed opportunities for

working in pairs to minimise students' isolation and to encourage peer learning and troubleshooting.

- She avoided hugging the lectern area or lurking in one corner and circulated around the room, monitoring actively, through frequent screen checks, to ensure that students were doing something purposeful and related to the class. She moved around and interacted rather than wait to be summoned, and spread her attention evenly.
- She tried to generalise from individual questions and problems: calling for the attention of all the students to get them to help solve a problem or to explain an issue to them that might be of common interest.
- Because of the confined space Francine was particularly sensitive to students' personal space. When demonstrating something at a student's monitor, she asked the student to get up, then sat in the chair or pulled a chair over if available and asked the student to shift sideways to a comfortable distance. She tried to avoid invading the student's personal space by leaning over the keyboard. If she did lean over she first asked permission.
- She concluded the class with a summary of what had been learned and a roundup of problems or solutions that had arisen. As the group progressed through the course and gained in confidence she invited students to perform this task.

**Points to explore**

- Lecturers will need to adjust their voice levels under different classroom acoustics conditions. Observing basic strategies for voice care can help prevent damage to the vocal cords (Voice Care Network, 2006).
- Personal space rules that apply at home, and in different cultures, are not necessarily the same that exist in the classroom environment and among sub-groups of students (Novelli et al., 2010). Lecturers need to be sensitive to these rules and cultural and group norms.
- Lecturers need to avoid unhelpfully 'hovering' over students, including those with disabilities (Giangreco et al., 1999). Students with a learning impairment, for example, autism or Asperger's syndrome, may have additional needs or issues about maintaining personal space (Ruble and Dalrymple, 2002).

# Linchpins of learning environments

In the UK and internationally a number of drivers at policy and strategic levels have had a direct impact on learning environments that lecturers will need to take account of in their teaching practice. These include notably the push to promote student engagement, progression and retention (Haselgrove, 1994; Lizzio et al., 2002; Johnson, 2010) and the complementary focus on being a more effective teacher in your chosen subject (Mortiboys, 2010; UKPSF, 2011). Senior managers, heads of faculties and departments, administrators and allied staff, including in library, IT and information services (Johnson, 2008), are increasingly involved in creating, maintaining and enhancing learning environments. Employers and community-based organisations continue to have an important role in providing access to work-based learning environments and lecturers often have a major liaison role here. Lecturers are thus increasingly likely to find themselves linchpins of these wider networks concerned with learning environments. Even those employed part-time or not centrally involved in curriculum design can still use steps to create effective learning environments in contexts where they can exert an influence (Beaton and Gilbert, 2013), including exercising authentic leadership through demonstration teaching, peer coaching and study groups (Katzenmeyer and Moller, 2009).

## Future horizons

We know that physical learning environments affect how students learn and that moreover there is a need for flexible learning spaces that provide access to technology and web connectivity and facilitate social learning – all combined with the need for more cost-effective, sustainable use of space and other resources (JISC, 2006). Advances in information technology, neuroscience, ergonomics, industrial design and green building technology continue to extend the possibilities of learning environments in ways that even a decade ago might have seemed improbable: the incorporation of social media into learning, the paperless classroom, surgical skills simulation centres, and classrooms with integrated physical and digital technologies, are just some of the examples of cutting-edge, often inspirational practice.

Yet as some horizons expand others appear to stay much the same: 'If you look at a classroom from a hundred years ago and compare [it] with one today, it's almost like a game of spot the difference. They are almost identical. In some ways, our current use of technology for education is actually a way for telling us how far we haven't come' (Bush, 2012). A case in point is the reliance in many settings on the traditional lecture despite the evidence pointing to its limitations as a pedagogic tool (Gibbs, 2013).

The drive to innovate that is changing the shape of many learning environments is not without its challenges. If, as argued earlier, learning environments are potentially transformative spaces then this entails a process of change that is inherently destabilising. Amid the flux lecturers need to be, and to provide, points of consistency for students, problematic as this undertaking may be when lecturers and their institutions are themselves buffeted by the winds of change. Barnett and Coate (2005:47) highlight the need to recognise that nowadays 'the student's learning environment … is characterized by many kinds of fragility', citing as examples shifts in educational infrastructures, staff mobility and changes to 'hard' physical resources. Realising a learning environment in any given context challenges us, new and more experienced lecturer alike, to articulate and possibly re-evaluate preferred ways of working and learning. Hence the emphasis in much recent research on seeing learning environments as a means of embodying a vision and values as well as of facilitating acquisition of knowledge and new or more skilled competencies. Some types of knowledge are rapidly out of date; principles and values seldom are. Amid change and uncertainty one thing seems certain: the learning environment, however we might imagine it, can no longer be taken for granted.

## Questions for reflective practice and professional development

1 How can you encourage students' active engagement as learners, enabling them to learn and work co-operatively? Specifically, what leadership and decision-making styles might you consider adopting, or trying out, and for what purpose? How will you notice any differences?

2 How can you take into account students' varying motivations and the role of physical and emotional well-being to create and maintain a thriving learning environment? What might need to change and how can your awareness of social and emotional learning help?

3 How can you build on your awareness of individual differences among students to devise learning environments that are inclusive and which both stretch and support participants?

4 How can you create or make use of opportunities to seek and use feedback to improve students' learning environments?

5 How can you best lead or manage learning environments authentically in ways that help students grasp or create 'the bigger picture' and thus promote a sense of 'horizontal connectedness'?

## Acknowledgement

I owe a particular debt in sourcing this chapter to Alison Britton, formerly of London South Bank University.

## Useful websites, further reading

In addition to the studies referenced above, the following online resources provide information on a wide range of materials related to learning environments.

### Centre for Effective Learning Environments (CELE), Organisation for Economic Co-operation and Development (OECD)

The Centre provides information on events, initiatives and resources globally on learning environments in their widest sense, from pedagogy to building design. While covering all sectors, not just higher education, it offers some stimulating and creative projects and ideas.
www.oecd.org/edu/innovation-education/centreforeffectivelearningenvironment
   scele/

### Higher Education Academy (UK)

This site provides a range of generic and discipline-based publications and resources related to leading and managing learning environments.
www.heacademy.ac.uk/

### JISC: Designing Spaces for Effective Learning

This website, developed from a UK project on how innovative technologies influence the design of physical learning spaces, provides several documents and videos of UK-based examples of innovative classroom design.
www.jisc.ac.uk/whatwedo/programmes/elearninginnovation/learningspaces.aspx

### Education Resources Information Centre (ERIC) (USA)

A comprehensive database of international research on education, teaching and learning with an excellent search engine.
http://eric.ed.gov/

## References

Barnett, R. (1997) *Higher Education: A critical business*. Buckingham: SRHE/Open University Press.
Barnett, R. and Coate, K. (2005) *Engaging the Curriculum in Higher Education*. Maidenhead: SRHE/Open University Press.

Beaton, F. and Gilbert, A. (2013) *Developing Effective Part-time Teachers in Higher Education*. London: Routledge.

Biggs, J. and Tang, C. (2007) *Teaching for Quality Learning in University*. Maidenhead: SRHE/Open University Press.

Bligh, D. (1998) *What's the Use of Lectures?* Exeter: Intellect.

Boud, D. J., Cohen, R. and Sampson, J. (eds) (2001) *Peer Learning in Higher Education: Learning from and with each other*. London: Kogan Page.

Brown, S. and Race, P. (2002) *Lecturing: A practical guide*. London: Routledge.

Bush, T. (2012) 'Exploring the future impact of technology on teaching and learning', *Guardian*, 10 September.

Charles, C. M., Charles, M. G. and Senter, G. W. (2014) *Building Classroom Discipline*, (11th edn). Harlow: Pearson Education.

Chickering, A. W. and Gamson, Z. F. (1999) 'Development and adaptations of the seven principles for good practice in undergraduate education', *New Directions for Teaching and Learning*, 80: 75–81.

Coffield, F., Moseley, D., Hall, E., and Ecclestone, K. (2004) *Learning Styles and Pedagogy in Post 16 Learning: A systematic and critical review*. London: The Learning and Skills Research Centre.

Cvetek, S. (2008) 'Applying chaos theory to lesson planning and delivery', *European Journal of Teacher Education*, 31 (3): 247–56.

Dalrymple, R. and Eaglesfield, S. (2013) *Teaching Large Groups*. York: Higher Education Academy.

Debowski, S. (2012) *The New Academic: A strategic handbook*. Maidenhead: McGraw-Hill Education/Open University Press.

Dennick, R. (2007) *Small Group Teaching, Tutorials, Seminars and Beyond*. London: Taylor and Francis.

Dillenbourg, P., Baker, M., Blaye, A. and O'Malley, C. (1995) 'The evolution of research on collaborative learning', in E. Spada and P. Reiman (eds), *Learning in Humans and Machine: Towards an interdisciplinary learning science*. Oxford: Elsevier, pp.189–211.

Dunn, R., Dunn, K. and Price, G. E. (1984) *Learning Style Inventory*. Lawrence, KS: Price Systems.

Engeström, Y. (2000) 'Activity theory as a framework for analyzing and redesigning work', *Ergonomics*, 43 (7): 960–74.

Entwistle, N. (1997) 'Contrasting perspectives on learning', in F. Marton, D. Housnell and N. Entwistle (eds), *The Experience of Learning: Implications for teaching and studying in higher education*. (2nd edn). Edinburgh: Scottish Academic Press.

Exley, K. and Dennick, R. (2009) *Giving a Lecture from Presenting to Teaching*. London: RoutledgeFalmer.

Fink, L. (2004) 'Beyond small groups: Harnessing the extraordinary power of learning teams', in L. K. Michaelson, A. B. Knight and L. D. Fink (eds), *Team-based Learning: A transformative use of small groups in college teaching*. Sterling, VA: Stylus.

Fry, H., Ketteridge, S. and Marshall, S. (2008) *A Handbook for Teaching and Learning in Higher Education* (3rd edn). London: Routledge.

Galanes, G. J., Brilhart, J. K. and Adams, K. (2003) *Effective Group Discussion: Theory and practice* (11th edn). Boston, MA: McGraw-Hill College.

Gehlen-Baum, V. and Weinberger, A. (2012) 'Notebook or Facebook? How students actually use mobile devices in large lectures', in A. Ravenscroft, S. Lindstaedt, C. D. Kloos and D. Hernández-Leo (eds), *21st Century Learning for 21st Century Skills: Lecture notes in computer science*, 7563. Heidelberg: Springer Berlin, pp.103–12.

Giangreco, M. F., Edelman, S. W., Luiselli, T. E. and MacFarland, S. Z. C. (1999) 'Helping or hovering? Effects of instructional assistant proximity on students with disabilities', *Exceptional Children*, 64 (1): 7–18.

Gibbs, G. (2013) 'Lectures don't work, but we keep using them', *Times Higher Education Supplement*, 21 November. Available at www.timeshighereducation. co.uk/news/lectures-dont-work-but-we-keep-using-them/2009141.article (accessed 23.7.15).

Graham, C. R., Tripp, T. R., Seawright, L. and Joeckel, G. (2007) 'Empowering or compelling reluctant participators using audience response systems', *Active Learning in Higher Education*, 8 (3): 233–58.

Habeshaw, S., Gibbs, G. and Habeshaw, T. (1993) *53 Problems with Large Classes: Making the best of a bad job*. Bristol: TES.

Hakkarainen, K., Paavola, S., Kangas, K. and Seitamaa-Hakkarainen, P. (2013) 'Sociocultural perspectives on collaborative learning: Toward collaborative knowledge creation', in C. E. Hmelo-Silver, C. A. Chinn, C. Chan and A. M. O'Donnell (eds), *The International Handbook of Collaborative Learning*. London: Routledge, pp.57–73.

Haselgrove, S. (ed.) (1994) *The Student Experience*. Buckingham: SRHE/Open University Press.

Hawkins, B. L. and Oblinger, D. G. (2007) 'The myth about the need for public computer labs: "Students have their own computers, so public labs are no longer needed"', *EDUCAUSE Review*, 42 (5): 10–11. Available at www.educause. edu/ero/article/myth-about-need-public-computer-labs (accessed 22.7.15).

Heron, J. (1975) *Six Category Intervention Analysis*. Guildford: Human Potential Research Project, University of Surrey.

Hmelo-Silver, C. E., Chinn, C. A., Chan, C. and O'Donnell, A. M. (eds) (2013) *The International Handbook of Collaborative Learning*. London: Routledge.

Ho, E., Holmes, P. and Cooper, J. (2004) *Review and Evaluation of International Literature on Managing Cultural Diversity in the Classroom*. Wellington, New Zealand: Ministry of Education.

Huxham, M. and Land, R. (2000) 'Assigning students in group work projects: Can we do better than random?', *Innovations in Education and Training International*, 37 (1): 17–22.

Istance, D. and Dumont, H. (2011) 'Future directions for learning environments in the 21st century', in H. Dumont, D. Istance and F. Benavides (eds), *The Nature of Learning: Using research to inspire practice*. Paris: OECD, pp.318–36.

Jaques, D. (2003) 'ABC of learning and teaching in medicine', *British Medical Journal*, 7387: 492–4.

Jaques, D. and Salmon, G. (2007) *Learning in Groups: A handbook for face-to-face and online environments* (4th edn). London: Routledge.

JISC (2006) *Designing Spaces for Effective Learning: A guide to 21st century learning space design.* Bristol: HEFCE.

Johnson, B. (2010) *The First Year at University: Teaching students in transition.* Maidenhead: McGraw-Hill Education/Open University Press.

Johnson, W. G. (2008) 'The application of learning theory to information literacy', *College and Undergraduate Libraries*, 14 (4): 103–120.

Katzenmeyer, M. and Moller, G. (2009) *Awakening the Sleeping Giant: Helping teachers develop as leaders.* London: Sage.

Kiewra, K. A. (2002) 'How classroom teachers can help students learn and teach them how to learn', *Theory into Practice*, 41 (2): 71–80.

Kinchin, I., Chadha, D. and Kokotailo, P. (2008) 'Using PowerPoint as a lens to focus on linearity in teaching', *Journal of Further and Higher Education*, 32 (4): 333–46.

Kolowich, S. (2009) 'U. of Virginia plans to phase out public computer labs', *Chronicle of Higher Education*, 23 March. Available at http://chronicle.com/blogs/wiredcampus/u-of-virginia-plans-to-phase-out-public-computer-labs/4590 (accessed 2.7.15).

Likert, R. (1961) *New Patterns of Management.* New York: McGraw-Hill.

Lizzio, A., Wilson, K. and Simons, R. (2002) 'University students' perceptions of the learning environment and academic outcomes: Implications for theory and practice', *Studies in Higher Education*, 27 (1): 27–52.

McCarron, K. and Savin-Baden, M. (2008) 'Compering and comparing: Stand-up comedy and pedagogy', *Innovations in Education and Teaching International*, 45 (4): 355–63.

Merry, S., Price, M., Carless, D. and Taras, M. (eds) (2013) *Reconceptualising Feedback in Higher Education: Developing dialogue with students.* London: Routledge.

Mezirow, J. (1997) 'Transformative learning: Theory to practice', *New Directions for Adult and Continuing Education*, 74: 5–12.

Miller, L. (2007) 'Issues in lecturing in a second language: Lecturer's behaviour and students' perceptions', *Studies in Higher Education*, 32 (6): 747–60.

Morss, K. and Murray, R. (2005) *Teaching at University: A guide for postgraduates and researchers.* London: Sage.

Mortiboys, A. (2010) *How to Be an Effective Teacher in Higher Education.* Maidenhead: McGraw-Hill Education/Open University Press.

Murray, N. (2012) 'Improving the way technical skills are taught in the creative studio – an exploration of student centred learning methods', *CEBE Transactions*, 9 (2): 30–58.

National University of Singapore (NUS) (2008) *Learning to Teach, Teaching to Learn.* Singapore: National University of Singapore. Available at www.cdtl.nus.edu.sg/handbook/ (accessed 23.7.15).

Novelli, D., Drury, J. and Reicher, S. (2010) 'Come together: Two studies concerning the impact of group relations on personal space', *British Journal of Social Psychology*, 49 (2): 223–36.

Parncutt, R. and McPherson, G. E. (2002) *The Science and Psychology of Music Performance: Creative strategies for teaching and learning.* Oxford: Oxford University Press.

Prosser, M. and Trigwell, K. (1999) *Understanding Learning and Teaching.* Buckingham: SRHE/OUP.

Race, P. and Brown, S. (2001) *The Lecturer's Toolkit.* London: Routledge.

Ruble, L. A. and Dalrymple, N. J. (2002) 'A parent–teacher collaborative model for students with autism', *Focus on Autism and Other Developmental Disabilities*, 17 (2): 76–83.

Savin-Baden, M. (2007) *Learning Spaces: Creating Opportunities for Knowledge Creation in Academic Life.* Maidenhead: McGraw-Hill Education/Open University Press.

Simon, N. (2015) 'Improving higher-order learning and critical thinking skills using virtual and simulated science laboratory experiments', in K. Elleithy and T. Sobh (eds), *New Trends in Networking, Computing, E-learning, Systems Sciences, and Engineering.* Cham, Switzerland: Springer International, pp.187–92.

Spillane, J. P. and Diamond, J. B. (eds) (2007) *Distributed Leadership in Practice (Contemporary Issues in Educational Leadership).* New York: Teacher College Press.

Stucky, N. and Wimmer, C. (2002) *Teaching Performance Studies (Theatre in the Americas).* Carbondale, IL: Southern Illinois University Press.

Tripp, D. (2012) *Critical Incidents in Teaching: Developing professional judgement.* London: Routledge.

Tuckman, B. W. (1965) 'Developmental sequence in small groups', *Psychological Bulletin*, 63 (6): 384.

UKPSF (2011) *The UK Professional Standards Framework for Teaching and Supporting Learning in Higher Education.* York: Higher Education Academy. Available at www.heacademy.ac.uk/sites/default/files/downloads/ukpsf_2011_english.pdf (accessed 9.9.15).

Voice Care Network (2006) *Notes on Voice Care for Lecturers.* Kenilworth: Voice Care Network. Available at www.voicecare.org.uk (accessed 23.7.15).

Webb, N. (2009) 'The teacher's role in promoting collaborative dialogue in the classroom', *Journal of Educational Psychology*, 79: 1–28.

Wilson, K. and Korn, J. H. (2007) 'Attention during lectures: Beyond ten minutes', *Teaching of Psychology*, 34 (2): 85–9.

Yorke, M. and Knight, P. T. (2006) *Embedding Employability into the Curriculum.* York: Higher Education Academy.

# 4

# Assessment for Learning

Helen Pokorny

## Chapter overview

This chapter explores:

- the formative and summative purposes of assessment and feedback
- a learning outcomes approach to assessment design
- dialogic approaches to sharing understanding of assessment standards and feedback
- avoiding plagiarism through education and assessment design
- issues and approaches to group work assessment
- assessment of prior learning

## Introduction

This chapter examines the role of assessment in the teaching and learning process. There is a general recognition that although learning outcomes, assessment criteria and detailed assessment briefs are an important part of the assessment process they are not a sufficient focus to produce a shared frame of reference around assessment and to ensure a consistent and equitable process (Price et al., 2012; Price, 2005). The QAA Code of Practice (2013), Chapter B6: Assessment of students and the recognition of prior learning, specifies that 'Staff and students should engage in dialogue to promote a shared understanding of the basis on which academic judgements are made' (indicator 6). This chapter is concerned with ways of promoting that dialogue in order that students can develop their assessment literacy, learn through the assessment process and better understand the expectations of the process and the standards applied.

## Assessment and feedback design

### The formative and summative roles of assessment

Assessment is at the heart of student learning. It drives the learning process, providing a focus for student attention and time. Models such as Biggs' (1999) model of constructive alignment are an attempt to capture this process and to use it to design effective teaching and learning (see Chapter 2: Course and Learning Design and Evaluation). The learning outcomes for a module set out what the students are asked to demonstrate at the end of the learning process at a threshold (pass) level. The assessment criteria provide the qualities of an assessment that the assessor will refer to in making a judgement and the assessment method is the means by which this learning is demonstrated.

Implicit in this model is an assumption that there is a shared frame of reference between teachers, students and other markers in relation to the nature of the learning to be demonstrated and the standards to be achieved. For Biggs (1999) this is primarily achieved by using the assessment of learning outcomes to drive the design of the teaching process. What is learned and how it is taught starts with the question 'What do I want students to be able to do at the end of this module?' The answer to this question, however, is always much more nuanced and complex than the learning outcomes might imply.

Learning outcomes encompass a range of skills and understanding of a topic and an immersion within a discipline and ways of thinking and being that come from the position of being a knowledgeable participant within the field of practice (see Chapter 8: Engaging with Academic Writing and Discourse). This challenge informs current thinking about improving student learning outcomes and provides a primary focus on formative assessment and feedback as the driver of learning and teaching design (Boud and Molloy, 2013; Sambell et al., 2013; Price et al., 2011). The distinction between *formative* and *summative* assessment and feedback is important because the terms formative and summative describe two very different purposes of assessment and yet the terms may be conflated or combined in practice.

## Summative assessment

Summative assessment refers to a summation of someone's achievement and its primary function is to provide a judgement on, and a description of, what has been achieved to provide 'feedout' to stakeholders or an assessment *of* learning. Traditionally essays and examinations have been the most commonly used assessment methods and remain so in some contexts. Even so an examination may take the form of open-book in which students can take written texts into an examination: *unseen* – where examination questions are not known in advance; *seen* – where examination questions are given in advance and students are expected to research and prepare for the topic(s) during this time or online multiple-choice options. Examination methods may also give rise to equality of opportunity concerns. For example, Smith (2011) provides evidence to suggest that for second-language speakers a time constrained examination prevents some students from being able to express their true learning. This may be due to the challenge of writing in a second language or the confusion that arises from questions than unfairly test the students' English language skills or cultural knowledge. Hoadley (2008) provides useful guidance for examiners writing examinations taking account of cultural and linguistic diversity.

Over time and across disciplines assessment methods have diversified (see Brown and Race, 2013, and O'Neill, 2011, for a range of assessment methods). The number of end-of-module examinations has fallen in favour of end-of-module assessment by coursework alone or a mixture of coursework and examination (Richardson, 2015). The drive to provide authentic assessments that reflect real-life contexts and to open up assessment to take account of students' different prior learning has resulted in a plethora of different summative assessment tools including projects, presentations, reviews, portfolios, case studies, reports, plans, performances and the development of artefacts. Gibbs and Dunbar-Goddet (2007) found that students were often confused and unclear about the demands of assessments when confronted by a range of methods (see the TESTA web link at the end of this chapter for a useful methodology for planning assessment regimes across courses).

E-assessment opportunities afforded by multiple choice software, wikis, blogs, audio and podcasts also provide creative ways to extend assessment methods. The process of drafting and producing assessments can also more easily be monitored through online methods providing further feedback opportunities. Blending of assessment methods is also more commonplace. Matheson et al. (2012) report on an assessment designed to promote critical thinking and collaborative working through combining a patchwork text portfolio and online discussion board. A patchwork text provides a disparate collection of texts that build up over time to support different styles of writing (in this case including online discussion boards) and the development of final synthesising piece of writing. Online marking of written work is now the norm in many institutions, offering both easier access to feedback and a means of identifying potential plagiarism through the use of detection software. The key criterion in selecting a particular assessment tool should be its fitness for purpose within a specific context that should include consideration of the student's wider experience of, and preparation for, the assessment demands across a course.

## Formative assessment and feedback

In contrast, formative assessment and feedback support the learning process by providing developmental comments or opportunities for dialogue that 'feedforward' to facilitate improvements in the final summative submission. It is key to the concept of assessment *for* learning. The essence of formative assessment is to provide timely feedback information to students so that they have real opportunities to improve their performance (Black and Wiliam, 1998). It may be *contributory* in terms of marks or grades, perhaps in the form of a required draft or interim document, or *non-contributory*, and feedback may be provided by peers, tutors or through self-assessment. An excessive focus on contributory or graded feedback with multiple small assessment points is likely to result in stressed and dissatisfied students and staff (Harland et al., 2015). Non-contributory feedback may include discussion, debate, marking and criteria setting exercises, peer feedback, quizzes or collaborative learning opportunities. Formative feedback opportunities are most effective when designed as an integral part of the learning and teaching strategy for a module. Central to this idea is that of dialogue and dialogic approaches to teaching that incorporate ongoing formative feedback. Nicol and Macfarlane-Dick (2006: 205) advocate that a teaching environment rich in formative feedback:

1 Helps clarify what good performance is (goals, criteria and expected standards).
2 Facilitates the development of self-assessment in learning.
3 Encourages teacher and peer dialogue around learning.
4 Helps deliver high-quality information to students about their learning.
5 Encourages positive motivational beliefs and self-esteem.
6 Provides opportunities to close the gap between current and desired performances.
7 Provides information to teachers that can be used to help shape teaching.

## Student self-assessment

Orsmond and Merry (2013) argue that such principles while important are insufficient by themselves as a means of promoting effective use of feedback by students. To achieve this goal, they argue, students' ability to develop the skills of self-assessment is of fundamental importance. Self-assessment in this context goes beyond a task-based process linked to a particular assessment to the design of curricula that provide a learning culture through which students seek out feedback and clarify for themselves what is good performance. This means making a definite shift away from reliance on tutor regulation of feedback, and using peer discussion to develop their thinking. Orsmond and Merry (2013) demonstrated that high-achieving students, although using tutor feedback, were very often much more mutually engaged with peer discussions which had a developmental nature, whereas non-high achieving students were inclined to rely on tutor feedback, which may not be sufficiently understood to be used effectively. They thus advocate strongly a genuinely student-centred approach to designing a learning environment in which students are actively encouraged to develop the skills of self-assessment, questioning what they know and what they want to find out by developing actions and strategies to support their own development. The aim is to promote a learning environment in which students become cue-seeking with respect to assessment standards (Miller and Partlett, 1974).

Similarly Boud and Molloy (2013) in their Feedback Mark 2 model of sustainable feedback argue for a conceptual shift towards an overarching notion of student self-regulation to frame the design of curriculum delivery, suggesting that this would reposition feedback:

1  from an act of teachers to an act of students in which teachers are a part (from unilateral to co-constructed; from monologue to dialogue);
2  from almost exclusive use of teachers to that of many others (from single sources to multiple sources);
3  from an act of students as individuals to one that necessarily implicates peers (from individualistic to collectivist);
4  from a collection of isolated acts to a designed sequence of development over time (from unitary items to curriculum).

(Boud and Molloy, 2013: 710).

Informal or non-contributory feedback delivered as part of the learning and teaching process is likely to be impactful because of the opportunities this provides for students to expose and address weaknesses. Such informal assessment may provide practice for summative assessments. An example is in Jacoby et al. (2014), in which students undertook weekly online formative tests, completion of which appeared to be directly related to attainment of higher grades. Race (2008), in advocating the use of non-contributory feedback, provides a number of useful strategies that have a 'high learning pay-off' for students including peer feedback and learners comparing work, discussion, online or in-class quizzes, constructive questioning within groups and self-marking. Similar activities were found to be perceived as particularly useful forms of generating feedback by final-year students (Pokorny and Pickford, 2010). They found that first-year students were still largely conceptualising feedback on their learning as tutor led and had not yet acquired the skills of self-assessment of their learning. Developing students' understanding of the university feedback environment is a key element of first year transition planning.

## Ideas for generating the skills of self-assessment through peer dialogue

Students may be resistant to the use of peer-feedback and such an approach requires careful scaffolding by the tutor. Some ideas are provided below:

- *Using students to generate and respond to questions* – ask students to write down a question they would need to have answered in order to understand a topic. Put the students in groups or pairs to try to answer each other's questions. The teacher circulates and listens to the responses. This will also provide feedback to the teacher that can be used to help to shape teaching.
- *Team tasks* – students working collaboratively in teams on a problem or issue will often help to correct each other and to adjust their own understanding of a topic through dialogue. The feedback can be shared more widely across the group with prompts about what was easy and what was hard about the task.
- *Criterion-based exercises* – in using sample work to deconstruct standards against pre-determined criteria in pairs or groups, students will start to articulate what it is that terms such as critical analysis mean in relation to a specific task; at the pass threshold standard and above. The teacher mediates the process to provide a focus on sharing with students tacit understandings of assessment standards (Price et al., 2003).

- *Students as teachers* – as students explain something to another student and are prompted by questions from their tutee both parties often become clearer about what it is that is under discussion.

### Evaluative feedback to shape teaching

Using student feedback to shape and inform teaching can help to close the feedback loop. Evaluative feedback on teaching by students is generally provided at the end of a teaching period in the form of a module-evaluation questionnaire. This is often completed by only a small number of students from within the cohort. Therefore these types of surveys are often criticised as being unhelpful in providing specific feedback on concepts and ideas as they are perceived and experienced during the teaching and learning process. Angelo and Cross (1993) developed 50 ideas for what they termed classroom assessment techniques (CATs). These are short in-class methods of getting feedback from students. These approaches have endured and are used effectively by tutors today. Stead (2005) surveyed the literature on the use of one of these CATs, the one-minute paper, and concluded that the benefits for both students and staff appeared 'sizable for such a modest amount of time and effort' (p.118). The 'one-minute paper' is a simple device using two questions at the end of a session:

- What have you learned today?
- What question remains for you?

Responses can be collected on paper, sticky notes or electronically and reviewed in-class, online or in subsequent sessions. These and other simple tasks provide a pause in the teaching for dialogue around issues and challenges students have in relation to the specific learning context.

## Designing written feedback

As academics we spend many hours providing feedback on summative assessments. In some end-of-module assessments this is largely for the use of second markers and external examiners and may not be shared with students, particularly in the case of examinations (Blair et al., 2014). However, even when timely contributory formative written feedback is provided within this process there is a large body of evidence that suggests it may not be read, understood or acted upon (Gibbs and Simpson, 2004) despite the fact that students often report that they have paid attention to any feedback they receive and have the opportunity to use it. These studies suggest that 'rather than the feedback *per se*, it is how students make sense of this which is important' (Crisp, 2007: 577). Making sense of feedback is a complex process. This has led to a number of studies investigating the barriers to learning from written feedback that suggest principles for good practice. Psychological research has explored the emotional impact of feedback on learning. Carole Dweck (1999) has written about individual differences in relation to self-efficacy; that is, the extent to which students perceive their performance in assessment to be within their own control. Students with an entity view of ability may see their intelligence and performance in assessment as fixed and their ability to improve as limited leading to defeatism in relation to feedback provided. This is in contrast to students with an incremental view of ability which treats intelligence as malleable, fluid and changeable. Examples of feedback practices such as that described by Prowse et al. (2007) – '... do that and I'll raise your grade' – challenge such ways of thinking and encourage an incremental view of ability by encouraging students to respond to feedback as part of the assessment design process and rewarding this with a higher grade where appropriate. There is also evidence to suggest that separating grades from feedback results in feedback being read and acted upon more effectively (Butler, 1988). Hughes (2011) notes that feedback, however carefully constructed, sends powerful messages which are often interpreted at a personal level leading some students to give up or feel overwhelmed by critical feedback.

Burke and Pieterick (2010) draw on a wealth of evidence and research to provide guidance in crafting written feedback to promote engagement and address the affective dimension. They suggest adopting a strategy of guiding the feedback towards the author's intentions, rather than making judgemental or corrective comments. This could perhaps be expressed as, 'I think here you meant to imply x, y, z and this would have been clearer if you had included a, b, c, or had you thought about x?'

They also suggest that concise written feedback has time-saving benefits and is more manageable for students than lengthy comments which may be confusing. Burke and Pieterick (2010) have developed this notion, suggesting a P(raise)Q(uestions)R(evise) system for giving relevant, focused feedback which takes account of the motivational and emotional impact of feedback on the reader.

> The first comment Praises what works and works well ... [and is] genuine, specific and usable, rather than a 'bad blow cushion' for any criticism that follows. The second comment presents gaps [in the form of Questions] ... for

further consideration ... The final comment encourages the student to Revise with specific advice about how to do this (e.g., 'Next time, check your paper in these ways ...'). (2010: 39).

# Marking

In marking and providing written feedback assessors will often refer to the assessment criteria by way of explaining their evaluations. The assumption behind this process is that students and tutors, markers and co-markers share an understanding of these criteria as they are written. However, there is no evidence that simply having assessment criteria and sharing these with students has any impact on the effectiveness of their learning nor on the reliability of marking. Price et al. (2003) have described how the process of defining assessment standards includes both explicit and tacit knowledge and that tutors vary in the tacit meanings they ascribe to common criteria such as 'critical analysis' leading to divergence in the meaning of comments attached to grading and sometimes, a mistrust among many students of written feedback. These terms are often prefixed with 'good' or 'poor' that students are often unable to deconstruct in relation to their own work. For this reason Norton suggests that students are often wary of assessment criteria and 'perceive a hidden curriculum where tutors say they want certain things in their coursework essays but actually students perceive that tutors reward other things as well' (Norton, 2004: 688). Consequently, O'Donovan et al. (2008) argue that students' understanding of assessors' tacit knowledge can only be addressed by actively engaging students with assessment criteria in relation to the standards to which they apply, and providing dialogue through exercises such as deconstructing marking exemplars, developing with students assessment criteria, providing peer feedback and self-assessment practise using criteria.

Similarly, assessors' judgements include both explicit and tacit knowledge and standards. For this reason it is important that teams and pairs of markers also have the opportunity to engage with assessment criteria and share their meaning with reference to standards. Orrell (2008) points to a wealth of research that suggests that grading is highly context dependent and influenced by some factors that pertain to assessors themselves, including a desire to be seen as a tough marker; their prior knowledge or expectations of students; the quality of preceding papers and the surface features of texts. Despite the claim that assessment criteria provide a neutral form of measurement, Orrell (2008) found that tutors drew on their knowledge of different students' work in order to make their judgements about grading. Bloxham et al. (2011) suggest that assessment criteria are often used retrospectively following holistic marking of work. They suggest that this is perhaps inevitable in making complex judgements and provides an important role for criteria in developing inter- and intra-marker reliability. In addition to formal methods for controlling the quality assurance of marking, such as moderation through second marking, which is a key component of grading reliability, there are a number of activities and processes that can help to achieve and maintain consistency across markers. These are all different aspects of one underlying principle – that of involving all staff who take part in the assessment of students as active members of a community of practice with a shared frame of reference with respect to the standard of work to which assessment criteria are applied (Price, 2005).

Activities that help to promote such communities of practice are:

- common involvement in the development and ownership of the formal assessment criteria;
- pre-meetings of markers, to discuss what is required of students and what markers should be looking for in their work, and to 'calibrate' markers' applications of the assessment criteria. this can be done with a small sample of work marked independently and with judgements shared before completing the remaining marking;
- developing a critical awareness of one's own marking practice through making the process less private and sharing judgements across teams of markers, including those on part-time teaching contracts.

## Group work assessment

Working in groups is a common feature of higher education (HE) assessment across all subject areas. Group work assessment encourages social integration, collaborative learning and the development of team-working skills. Such work typically involves researching into and reporting on a topic, problem or brief, or developing a joint activity or product, and often requires both collaborative and individual efforts. The end product can take various forms, such as a report, paper, design, oral/audio-visual presentation, poster, video, film, performance or exhibition. While there are benefits to group working and collaborative learning, there are some consistent issues that affect students' satisfaction with this as a form of assessment and paramount is that of workload distribution (Burdett and Hastie, 2009). This is often linked to issues of fairness and reports that suggest that group assessment does not accurately reflect each student's individual academic ability.

A number of studies suggest that weaker students achieve higher grades in group work assessment (Moore and Hampton, 2015; Plastow et al., 2010; Almond, 2009). There are also many published studies that aim to address the issue of what are termed 'free-riders', that is, students who appear to contribute little or nothing to the group work outcomes.

The quest for appropriate and 'fair' mechanisms often focuses on whether *the product* or *the process* of group work is to be assessed, or if both, what proportion of the assessment will focus on each. In addition, there is the question of how the marks will be distributed; for example, a *shared group mark* whereby each group member receives the same grade, an *individual mark* whereby each student submits an individual piece of work, derived from a group process, for which a mark is awarded, or *a combination of the two* whereby a group mark is awarded, which is adjusted in relation to the individual contribution, either a product, peer assessment or additional assessment such as examination or reflective piece.

Nordberg (2008) argues that while group work can benefit student learning and skills development it is probably inherently less fair than individual assessment. For example, students may be perceived as 'lazy' or 'free riders' by their peers but their lack of contribution may equally be a function of the nature of the assessment task set, the group dynamics or personal issues outside of the group (Pokorny and Griffiths, 2010). Sweeney et al. (2008) also suggest that some students may dominate, marginalising the contribution of others. This brings into question the accuracy of labelling the 'free riders' and the role of the tutor in managing the assessment process.

The issue of cultural differences appears repeatedly in the group assessment literature. One of the challenges is to provide an environment in which students appreciate the benefits and learning that can be gained from working with students from diverse backgrounds. There are numerous studies that point to the problems of intercultural group working, including the preference of domestic students to work in homogeneous groups due to concerns that intercultural working will lower their grade (Moore and Hampton, 2015; Strauss et al., 2011). International students may prefer to work in groups where they can use their first language for discussion and translate into English. Following a review of the literature, Cotton et al. (2013: 275) propose a set of principles to frame the design of effective multicultural groupwork:

1 Proactively encourage or engineer mixed cultural groups.
2 Explain clearly the learning outcomes of the exercise.
3 Place equal emphasis on social and well-being goals as well as academic goals.

4 Make explicit the benefits of having a group composed of various cultures, languages and ethnicity and connect this to social and well-being goals.
5 Ensure that the nature of the task is conducive to the group work element, building on the diversity of knowledge and abilities.

In an attempt to make the assessment process fairer tutors often introduce a form of peer assessment through which students' grade group members' participation in the assessment process. The criteria used for assessing group work may be defined by the lecturer, developed by the students or through consultation between the two. An advantage of involving students in negotiating criteria is an explicit discussion and sharing of their meaning. One rationale for a peer assessment process is that group members are better placed to assess their peers' contributions than the tutor, although the tutor may retain the role of final arbitrator. However, Nordberg (2008) points out that although the term 'peer marking or peer review' is used frequently in literature there is no common approach. A number of studies report issues arising from a lack of fairness with peer marking of group work contributions. Kennedy (2005) suggests that while some students may be reluctant to peer assess and mark down their peers, others may be very ready to do so and some may collude in the marks given to maintain grades across the group. So although peer assessment may appear to differentiate marks for individuals, and is often viewed positively by students (Grajczonek, 2009), it is no guarantee of fairness for the individuals involved. The tutor's role is key to providing positive learning outcomes from assessed group work through careful establishment and monitoring of the process.

## Managing group assessment processes

- *The group task* – students need to be clear about the aims, relevance and benefits of the task, how it relates to the intended learning outcomes and their personal development, how it will be assessed, and the criteria used for assessing the process and/or product; as well as receiving written information, students should have opportunities to clarify these issues in class before commencing the group work.
- *The group membership* – the choice is whether groups are student selected or tutor assigned; if the latter, the options are random allocation, or deliberate matching or mixing on the basis of certain

characteristics such as interests, learning styles, ability, age or background; much depends on the context, for instance, if importance is placed on learning about group dynamics, or redressing tendencies towards instrumental learning, then group formation should probably be decided by the lecturer; however, students will often prefer to work with friends and in groups they know to have performed effectively in the past.

- *The group roles and rules* - effective group work requires clarity about appropriate interpersonal conduct and roles or responsibilities in the accomplishment of the task; students may find it helpful to have explicit guidelines or to develop their own group ground rules on this. In any case, tutors need to monitor how groups are dealing with any issues. The role of the tutor and nature of tutor interventions requires clarity.

- *The group meetings* - although group work entails some sharing of responsibility, it can also add to the time and workload pressures that cause anxiety for students; hence, scheduled time should be allowed for the work and for students to discuss arrangements for future group meetings.

Commenting on role of the tutor in facilitating group work assessment, Reynolds and Trehan (2000: 275) conclude that the experience of many students 'underline the need for tutors to be prepared and able to work with the complex social processes which are generated. If not, retaining traditional practice may be preferable.'

## Plagiarism

Plagiarism is an equally complex issue, rooted within a western academic orthodoxy and not necessarily shared across other social, cultural, linguistic, ethnic and educational contexts. The vexed question of intentionality is often side-stepped by university policies that penalise the infringement of plagiarism as narrowly defined within the broader umbrella of academic misconduct. However, even narrow definitions of plagiarism are subject to different interpretations and actions by academics who make judgements about how much plagiarism constitutes sufficient infringement for referral to university authorities. These judgements are influenced by the values and perspectives of the academics involved. It has been noted by Sutherland-Smith (2008),

Carroll (2013) and others that university policies around plagiarism result in penalties and punishments for a disproportional number of international students.

Many academics would argue that unintentional plagiarism is not the same as cheating and should be handled differently (Johnston, 2003). For example, Howard (1999) argues that novice students use a textual strategy she calls 'patchwriting', 'copying from a source text and then deleting some words, altering grammatical structures or plugging in one-for-one synonym substitutes' (p.xvii) as they learn to write academically and that this is a strategy particularly used by international students that may be understood in cultural terms. She sees this as a natural stage in learning to write as an academic.

## Reasons for student plagiarism identified in literature

- Accessibility of texts via the Internet.
- Poor time management and fear of failure.
- Excessive assessment loads and bunching of assessments across courses.
- Lack of understanding of what constitutes plagiarism and why it is seen as a serious offence.
- Lack of skills in referencing and paraphrasing.
- Rote learning of texts and notes, poor note-taking skills.
- Lack of language skills or confidence in academic writing.
- A perception that the offence or consequences are not serious, or a belief that the individual will not be caught.
- Ease of plagiarism by setting the same or single solution assessments.
- Too much over-assessment and bunched deadlines.
- Lack of clarity: unclear briefs; not stressing what is valued and rewarding it with marks.
- Focus on end product only – not requiring or rewarding evidence of process.

(Rust, 2007)

Carroll (2013) argues strongly for teaching students 'the rules of the game' on entry to HE and providing strategies and approaches by which students can develop the skills to reference and write in a new academic discourse by providing guidelines and practice in academic writing. This might include exercises in note-making, summarising, paraphrasing, using evidence, reading and analysing texts as well as argumentation and critical analysis in addition to more generic support clarifying when, why and how to reference. This she suggests is an important approach to addressing plagiarism in addition to control methods such as the use of plagiarism detection software.

## Recognising prior learning

The agenda for HE in the UK and internationally promotes lifelong learning, widening participation and employer partnership working. Consequently universities are increasingly recognising, for the purposes of awarding credit or contributing formally to an award, the significant knowledge, skills and abilities which students bring with them to university (Werquin and Wihak, 2011). These may be acquired through work, volunteering and through an individual's activities and interests. This process of recognition is known in the UK as the Recognition of Prior Learning (RPL) although different terminology is used elsewhere. There is a body of evidence that RPL can support retention and attainment (Travers, 2011) through:

- recognising and awarding academic value to a diversity of learning experiences;
- avoiding repetition of learning previously acquired;
- contributing to curricula flexibility for the student;
- accelerating the student's rate of progress.

In the UK, RPL is covered by the QAA Code of Practice, Chapter B6: Assessment of students and the recognition of prior learning (2013). This identifies the need for clear signposting and guidance for students seeking to undertake assessment of their prior learning. The capacity of RPL assessment to value knowledge which is different to that developed through formal study presents a continual challenge to Higher Education (HE), a challenge that is both supported and hindered in equal measure through the use of learning outcomes to frame RPL assessment. The challenge hinges on the extent to which RPL assessment requires exact equivalency between the outcomes of informal and non-formal learning and those of formal learning or whether there is any leeway to recognise outcomes which are different but *comparable* to formal learning in terms of level, depth and breadth of learning. Providing this flexibility is key to facilitating the recognition of prior learning within courses. RPL has been a core part of work-based learning, and negotiated curricula for many decades (Armsby et al., 2006). These courses will explicitly value knowledge gained through practice through their learning outcomes (see Chapter 10: Work-related and Professional Learning). In a more tightly prescribed course opportunities for bringing this type of learning into the curriculum can be afforded by the development of modules where learning outcomes can be negotiated or where RPL claims are set against the more holistic programme or level descriptors rather than by individual module mapping (Pokorny and Whittaker, 2014). Where the mapping is to an individual module, doing so in relation to the overall aims of the module is likely to be more productive and less atomistic than mapping to individual module learning outcomes.

The assessment method for RPL should be appropriate for the experiential nature of the learning to be assessed. This will usually differ from the assessment method approved through validation which is aligned to the taught curriculum. As with any assessment design, RPL assessments may include oral as well as written methods. The most common form of RPL assessment in the UK is the portfolio in which students compile evidence of their learning from different contexts and relate this to the relevant learning outcomes for which they are claiming credit. Undertaking an RPL portfolio assessment requires students to reflect upon their experience and consider the skills and knowledge they have developed and how this might be evidenced. It is important that this is a dialogic process and that the assessor is able to explore with the candidate the relevance of practice and experience and to support them in relating this to learning outcomes designed for a different purpose (Pokorny, 2012). RPL assessment may be undertaken prior to, or alongside, formal study. Michelson and Mandell (2004) provide a range of different approaches and methods used within such courses, all of which aim to provide a bridge between academia and prior learning in order to promote the use of RPL.

A key issue appears to be that we often do not recognise RPL as a specialised practice and responsibility and it is added onto the already heavy workload of academics without specific training and development. In the UK the Quality Assurance Agency (2013) has recognised this issue and recommends that HE institutions provide staff development that promotes an understanding of the theory and practice of prior learning assessment.

## Conclusion

It is in the nature of the academy to compartmentalise and disaggregate subjects and activities. Assessment has suffered from this compartmentalisation and consequently so has the student learning experience. Traditionally assessment has been seen as distinct from the teaching process and as an (often opaque) summative process. The argument underpinning this chapter is that assessment for learning positions the assessment process as an integral part of the teaching and learning process. The ideas and practices described here are focused on developing staff and student assessment literacy through a joint exploration of what it means to be successful in the learning process. The premise is that assessment is *not* an exact science (although it is often presented as such) and therefore in the interests of fairness and equality it is important for us to take a critical approach to our own assessment practice and to develop a shared frame of reference around the process.

## Questions for reflective practice and professional development

1   How does your assessment support your module learning outcomes?
2   How does your assessment provide opportunities for promoting student learning and providing evaluative feedback into the teaching process?
3   How do your teaching and feedback strategies promote student self-assessment and dialogue around standards?
4   How do you maintain reliability in your marking practices with your fellow assessors?

## Useful websites, further reading

### The Assessment Standards Knowledge exchange (ASKe)

www.brookes.ac.uk/aske/index.html
ASKe is focused on developing an evidence base and good practice to support HE communities in sharing understandings of assessment standards.

### Assessing Group Work

www.cshe.unimelb.edu.au/assessinglearning/03/group.html
This website is maintained by the Australian Centre for the Study of Higher Education. It includes advice and guidance on setting up and implementing group work assessment.

### Transforming the Experience of Students through Assessment (TESTA)

www.testa.ac.uk/
The TESTA project approach works with academics, students and managers – and for students, academics and managers – to identify study behaviour,

generate assessment patterns to foster deeper learning across whole programmes, and debunk regulatory myths which prevent assessment for learning.

Merry, S., Price, M., Carless, D. and Taras, M. (2013) *Reconceptualising Feedback in Higher Education: Developing dialogue with students.* Abingdon: Routledge.
This book sets out to challenge established beliefs and practices through critical evaluation of evidence and discussion of the renewal of current feedback practices. It offers useful strategies at the classroom, programme and institutional level underpinned by a strong conceptual framework.

Boud, D. and Molloy, E. (2012) *Feedback in Higher and Professional Education: Understanding it and doing it well.* Abingdon: Routledge.
This book offers a range of theoretically informed practical approaches to developing feedback practice with a wide range of perspectives including feedback in digital contexts, clinical practice, the impact of emotions in feedback, trust and its role in facilitating dialogic feedback.

McDowell, L. and Montgomery, C. (2012) *Assessment for Learning in Higher Education.* Abingdon: Routledge.
This book provides an important and accessible blend of practical examples of Assessment for Learning in a variety of subject areas. The authors present practical, often small-scale and eminently 'doable' ideas that will make its introduction achievable.

Harris, J., Wihak, C. and Van Kleef, J. (2014) *Handbook of the Recognition of Prior Learning: Research into practice.* Leicester: NIACE.
This handbook, organised thematically, consolidates the major research findings of experienced RPL researchers from around the world, identifying future research directions and drawing together evidence-based implications for policy and practice.

# References

Almond, R. J. (2009) 'Group assessment: Comparing group and individual undergraduate module marks', *Assessment and Evaluation in Higher Education,* 34 (2): 141–8.

Angelo, T. A. and Cross, K. P. (1993) *Classroom Assessment Techniques: A handbook for college teachers.* San Fransisco, CA: Jossey-Bass.

Armsby, P., Costley, C. and Garnett, J. (2006) 'The legitimisation of knowledge: A work-based learning perspective of APEL', *International Journal of Lifelong Education,* 25 (4): 369–83.

Biggs, J. B. (1999) *What the Student Does: Teaching for quality learning at university.* Buckingham: Open University Press.

Black, P. and Wiliam, D. (1998) 'Assessment and classroom learning', *Assessment in Education*, 5 (1): 7–74.

Blair, A., Wyburn-Powell, A., Goodwin, M. and Shields, S. (2014) 'Can dialogue help to improve feedback on examinations?', *Studies in Higher Education*, 39 (6): 1039–54.

Bloxham, S., Boyd, P. and Orr, S. (2011) 'Mark my words: The role of assessment criteria in UK higher education grading practices', *Studies in Higher Education*, 36 (6): 637–55.

Boud, D. and Molloy, E. (2013) 'Rethinking models of feedback for learning: The challenge of design', *Assessment and Evaluation in Higher Education*, 38 (6): 698–712.

Brown, S. and Race, P. (2013) 'Using effective assessment to promote learning', in Hunt, L. and Chalmers, D. (eds), *University Teaching in Focus: A learning-centred approach*. Abingdon: Routledge, pp.74–92.

Burdett, J. and Hastie, B. (2009) 'Predicting satisfaction with group work assignments', *Journal of University Teaching and Learning Practice*, 6 (1): 62–71.

Burke, D. and Pieterick, J. (2010) *Giving Students Effective Written Feedback*. Maidenhead: Open University Press.

Butler, R. (1988) 'Enhancing and undermining intrinsic motivation: The effects of task-involving and ego-involving evaluation on interest and performance', *British Journal of Educational Psychology*, 58: 1–14.

Carroll, J. (2013) *A Handbook for Deterring Plagiarism in Higher Education*. Headington: Oxford Centre for Staff and Learning Development.

Cotton, D. R. E., George, R. and Joyner, M. (2013) 'Interaction and influence in culturally mixed groups', *Innovations in Education and Teaching International*, 50 (3): 272–84.

Crisp, B. R. (2007) 'Is it worth the effort? How feedback influences students' subsequent submission of assessable work', *Assessment and Evaluation in Higher Education*, 32 (5): 571–81.

Dweck, C. S. (1999) *Self-theories: Their role in motivation, personality, and development*. Philadelphia, PA: Psychology Press.

Gibbs, G. and Dunbar-Goddet, H. (2007) *The Effects of Programme Assessment Environments on Student Learning*. York: Higher Education Academy. Available at www.tlrp.org/themes/seminar/daugherty/docs/grahamgibbspaper.pdf

Gibbs, G. and Simpson, C. (2004) 'Conditions under which assessment supports students' learning', *Learning and Teaching in Higher Education*, 1 (1): 3–31.

Grajczonek, J. (2009) 'Exploring students' perceptions of peer assessment in group work allocation of individual marks in Higher Education', *The International Journal of Learning*, 16 (3): 105–125.

Harland, T., McLean, A., Wass, R., Miller, E. and Sim, K. N. (2015) 'An assessment arms race and its fall out: High stakes grading and the case for slow scholarship', *Assessment and Evaluation in Higher Education*, 40 (4): 528–41.

Hoadley, S. (2008) *How to Create Exams: Learning through assessment*. Sydney: Macquarie University. Available at http://staff.mq.edu.au/teaching/teaching_development/resources/ (accessed 28.7.15).

Howard, R. M. (1999) *Standing in the Shadow of Giants: Plagiarists, authors, collaborators*. Stamford, CT: Ablex.

Hughes, G. (2011) 'Towards a personal best: A case for introducing ipsative assessment in higher education', *Studies in Higher Education*, 36 (3): 353–69.

Jacoby, J., Heugh, S., Bax, C. and Brandfor-White, C. (2014) 'Enhancing learning through formative assessment', *Innovations in Education and Teaching International*, 51 (1): 72–83.

Johnston, W. (2003) 'The concept of plagiarism', *Learning and Teaching in Action*, 2 (1). Available at www.celt.mmu.ac.uk/ltia/issue4/johnston.shtml (accessed 28.7.15).

Kennedy, G. J. (2005) 'Peer-assessment in group projects: Is it worth it?', paper presented at the Australasian Computing Education Centre Conference, Newcastle.

Matheson, R., Wilkinson, S. C. and Gilhooly, E. (2012) 'Promoting critical thinking and collaborative working through assessment: Combining patchwork text and online discussion boards', *Innovations in Education and Teaching International*, 49 (3): 257–67.

Michelson, E. and Mandell, A. (2004) *Portfolio Development and the Assessment of Prior Learning*. Sterling, VA: Stylus.

Miller, C. M. I. and Parlett, M. (1974) *Up to the Mark: A study of the examination game*. Guildford: Society for Research into Higher Education.

Moore, P. and Hampton, G. (2015) 'It's a bit of a generalisation, but ... participant perspectives on intercultural group assessment in higher education', *Assessment & Evaluation in Higher Education*, 40 (3): 390–406.

Nicol, D. J. and Macfarlane-Dick, D. (2006) 'Formative assessment and self-regulated learning: A model and seven principles of good feedback practice', *Studies in Higher Education*, 31 (2): 199–218.

Nordberg, D. (2008) 'Group projects: More learning? Less fair? A conundrum in assessing postgraduate higher education', *Assessment & Evaluation in Higher Education*, 33 (5): 481–92.

Norton, L. (2004) 'Using assessment criteria as learning criteria: A case study in psychology', *Assessment and Evaluation in Higher Education*, 29 (6): 687–702.

O'Donovan, B., Price, M. and Rust, C. (2008) 'Developing student understanding of assessment standards: A nested hierarchy of approaches', *Teaching in Higher Education*, 13 (2): 205–17.

O'Neill, G. (ed.) (2011) *A Practitioner's Guide to Choice of Assessment Methods Within a Module*. Dublin: UCD Teaching and Learning. Available at www.ucd.ie/t4cms/Practitioners%20Guide.pdf (accessed 9.9.15).

Orrell, J. (2008) 'Assessment beyond belief: The cognitive process of grading', in A. Havnes and L. McDowell (eds), *Balancing Dilemmas in Assessment and Contemporary Education*. Abingdon: Routledge.

Orsmond, P. and Merry, S. (2013) 'The importance of self-assessment in students' use of tutors' feedback: A qualitative study of high and non-high achieving biology undergraduates', *Assessment and Evaluation*, 38 (6): 737–53.

Plastow, N., Spiliotopoulou, G. and Prior, S. (2010) 'Group assessment at first year and final degree level: A comparative evaluation', *Innovations in Education and Teaching International*, 47 (4): 393–403.

Pokorny, H. (2012) 'Assessing prior experiential learning: Issues of authority, authorship and identity', *Journal of Workplace Learning*, 24 (2): 119–32.

Pokorny, H. and Griffiths, D. (2010) 'Exploring the "myths" of enhanced learning through group work assessment', in R. Atfield and P. Kemp (eds), *Enhancing Learning through Assessment*. York: Higher Education Academy.

Pokorny, H. and Pickford, P. (2010) 'Complexity, cues and relationships in student feedback', *Active Learning in Higher Education*, 11 (1): 21–9.

Pokorny, H. and Whittaker, R. (2014) 'Exploring the learner experience of RPL', in J. Harris, C. Wihak and J. Van Kleef (eds), *Handbook of the Recognition of Prior Learning: Research into practice*. Leicester: National Institute of Adult Continuing Education, pp.259–84.

Price, M. (2005) 'Assessment standards: The role of communities of practice and the scholarship of assessment', *Assessment and Evaluation in Higher Education*, 30 (3): 215–30.

Price, M., Handley, K. and Millar, J. (2011) 'Feedback: Focussing attention on engagement', *Studies in Higher Education*, 36 (8): 879–96.

Price, M., Rust, C. and O'Donovan, B. (2003) 'Improving students' learning by developing their understanding of assessment criteria and processes', *Assessment and Evaluation in Higher Education*, 30 (3): 213–30.

Price, M., Rust, R., O'Donovan, B., Handley, K. and Bryant, R. (2012) *Assessment literacy: The foundation for improving student learning*. Headington: Oxford Centre for Staff and Learning Development.

Prowse, S., Duncan, N., Hughes, J. and Burke, D. (2007) '"… do that and I'll raise your grade": Innovative module design and recursive feedback', *Teaching in Higher Education*, 12 (4): 437–45.

QAA (2013) *Code Of Practice For The Assurance Of Academic Quality And Standards In Higher Education*, Chapter 6: Assessment of students and the recognition of prior learning. Available at www.qaa.ac.uk/en/Publications/Pages/Quality-Code-Chapter-B6.aspx#.ViZAKW6uqJV

Race, P. (2008) *Make Learning Happen: A guide for post-compulsory education*. London: Sage.

Reynolds, M. and Trehan, K. (2000) 'Assessment a critical perspective', *Studies in Higher Education*, 25 (3): 268–78.

Richardson, J. T. E. (2015) 'Coursework versus examinations in end-of-module assessment: A literature review', *Assessment & Evaluation in Higher Education*, 40 (3): 439–55.

Rust, C. (2007) 'Changing and rethinking assessment to design out plagiarism', workshop slides from conference on Institutional Management of Plagiarism, Oxford Brookes University, 2 April.

Sambell, K., McDowell, L. and Montgomery, C. (2013) *Assessment for Learning in Higher Education*. Oxon: Routledge.

Smith, C. (2011) 'Examination and the ESL student – more evidence of particular disadvantages', *Assessment and Evaluation in Higher Education*, 36 (1): 13–25.

Stead, D. R. (2005) 'A review of the one-minute paper', *Active Learning in Higher Education*, 6 (2): 118–31.

Strauss, P., Alice, U. and Young, S. (2011) 'I know the type of people I work well with: Student anxiety in multicultural group projects', *Studies in Higher Education*, 36 (7): 815–29.

Sutherland-Smith, W. (2008) *Plagiarism, the Internet and Student Learning: Improving Academic Integrity*. Abingdon, Routledge.

Sweeney, A., Weaven, S. and Herington, C. (2008) 'Multicultural influences on group learning: A qualitative higher education study', *Assessment and Evaluation in Higher Education*, 33 (2): 119–32.

Travers, N. L. (2011) 'United States of America: Prior Learning Assessment (PLA) research in colleges and universities', in J. Harris, M. Breier and C. Wihak (eds), *Researching the Recognition of Prior Learning: International perspectives*. Leicester: NIACE, pp.248–84.

Werquin, P. and Wihak, C. (2011) 'Organisation for Economic Co-operation and Development (OECD) research reveals "islands of good practice"', in J. Harris, M. Breier and C. Wihak (eds), *Researching the Recognition of Prior Learning: International perspectives*. Leicester: NIACE, pp.161–72.

# 5

# Blended Learning

## Charl Fregona with Agata Sadza

---

**Chapter overview**

This chapter explores:

- definitions of blended learning
- blended learning technologies
- the student experience of blended learning
- models of blended learning
- blended learning strategies for engaging students

---

## Introduction

This chapter focuses on the nature and practices of blended learning, what these are, and the issues that are raised as a result of combining face-to-face teaching with the use of educational technologies. Digital technologies have changed how we learn, teach, collaborate and communicate in fundamental ways and there is a significant shift from teacher-centred to learner- and learning-centred practice in the social collaboration that characterises online learning. Developments such as Massive Open Online Courses (MOOCs) and the ease of anywhere, anytime, bite-sized mobile learning are challenging higher education (HE) perspectives about why, how and where students learn (Conole, 2013). Rapidly evolving technologies are offering unprecedented opportunities to shift from tutor-centred teaching towards activity-led methods which support student-generated content and collaborative, participatory, exploratory learning. As a result, UK HE institutions are focussing on blended learning as a means of pedagogical transformation to support student diversity, enhancement of learning, flexibility of provision, and the improvement of assessment and feedback (see, e.g., the work of Beetham et al., 2009; De Freitas and Conole, 2010; and Sharpe, 2009). Such innovations have created opportunities for self-directed, personalised learning in interesting and challenging ways and call for digitally savvy educators who are confident enough to 'blend' the affordances of new technologies with best practice face-to-face teaching.

Many educators are using technology to enhance the learning of their students and to ease the workload of teaching and learning in ways that have not been possible until now. New, critical pedagogies are evolving at the same dizzy pace as the hardware and software that make them possible. Ecclesfield et al. (2012) report, as many others do, that the transformation of learning and teaching is more likely to come from professional teaching practice than from institutional design because digitally adept teacher practitioners, influenced by social media and Web 2.0 behaviour, are using this tapestry of diverse educational technologies confidently and innovatively.

However, while educators, learning and learners are changing in response to increasingly virtualised forms of learning, students continue to value face-to-face contact with tutors. They appreciate the option of being able to learn online at times and locations that suit their busy lifestyles and still expect real-life classroom interaction. A large-scale study by Paechter and Maier (2010), for example, found that students preferred online learning for independent, self-regulated study and for clearly structured learning material, but found also that they preferred face-to-face learning for collaboration and communication when acquiring conceptual knowledge or skills. It is likely that students will continue to value face-to-face contact and that educators will use virtual learning even more pervasively than at present. The ability to 'blend' face-to-face and virtual learning, then, is an essential skill for both educators and learners. It should be kept in mind, though, that many tutors may be conservative in their desire to use the technologies, particularly when university delivery structures and systems may still be catching up with new ways of accessing and delivering learning. In addition, the time lecturers need for continuing professional development to acquire the necessary digital literacy skills is at a premium.

## What is blended learning?

We use the term *blended learning* in this chapter to mean a mix of physical, face-to-face on-site classroom contact (which is of necessity synchronous) and virtual learning (which may be delivered either synchronously or asynchronously and/or either on-site or off-site). 'Blended' learning is also known as 'hybrid' or 'flexible learning' and should be seen as distinct from 'distance' learning which relies almost entirely on virtual means of contact with a minimum of face-to-face interaction. Both distance and blended learning fall within the spectrum known as 'distributed learning'. Margaret Rouse (2010) defines 'distributed learning' as a method of learning and teaching that occurs in multiple places and spaces, and thus it requires some or most of the learning to be online, or mediated in some way by information and communications technology (ICT). Distributed learning can include face-to-face classroom time, a mix of web-based instruction, streaming video conferencing, distance learning through television or video, or other combinations of electronic and traditional educational models. Rouse (2010) suggests that while distributed learning can be executed in different ways, it always accommodates a separation of geographical locations for part (or all) of the learning and teaching.

*Blended learning* thus combines the affordances of digital technologies, such as social networking, virtual interaction and collaboration, sharing and generation of online resources, with at least some measure of face-to-face teaching and real life social interaction. The use of technology may occur during a face-to-face learning event with the tutor and students present in a physical classroom, or before or after the learning event by virtual means. Virtual delivery can occur *synchronously* when participants are all present in real time, such as in the physical classroom or in an online webinar which happens in real time, or *asynchronously* when participants access the event at different times, such as in a blog, recorded webinar or a mobile learning app (e.g., Wordpress, Blackboard Collaborate or Bambuser). Using applications such as these a tutor may, for example, ask students to research a topic online before the session, then use a virtual learning environment (VLE) while being physically present with students in a classroom to explore the topic in detail, perhaps by setting up a synchronous electronic poll; and then ask students to write up reflections in an electronic portfolio or blog for later assessment and feedback after the face-to-face classroom session.

## What kinds of technologies are being used to blend learning?

Given the pace of technological change, universities will need to rethink their provision and role in preparing graduates for a very complex world quite rapidly with the caveat that a real case can be made for adopting and adapting what learners are used to and enjoy; and universities will need to ensure that the technology serves learning outcomes and intentions rather than the other way around.

A wide range of technologies are commonly used in HE institutions for the delivery of blended learning. Freely available mobile applications, easily accessed open source software and reusable learning objects which require little or no training provide a huge variety of opportunities to take learning into virtual spaces (Bradley and Holley, 2011). The use of learning and content management systems such as Blackboard and Moodle (known as VLEs or virtual learning environments) is almost routine in most HE institutions. These VLEs may incorporate hyperlinked websites and YouTube mash-ups (a web page or application created by combining functionality from different sources). University infrastructures offer both networked and wireless access to the Internet in just about every classroom, and the notion of centrally supported software and services in universities is being replaced by learner-generated choices about which software to use since browsers provide almost total inter-operability across diverse technical platforms. Educational technologies include 'hard' technologies such as smart phones, tablets and laptops used in mobile learning, handheld student response devices, and interactive whiteboards and 'soft' technologies, which include social learning and sharing applications or 'apps', such as YouTube and Twitter, and game-based learning environments (e.g., Second Life and Sim City). E-books, search engines (such as Google) and information sources (such as Wikipedia) allow students to work independently and/or collaboratively at times and places of their own choosing.

It is a rich, interesting time for learning technologies. However, the caveat remains that we need to avoid the 'mist' of technological determinism and keep a clear focus on the renewal of learning and teaching.

It is difficult to predict where the technologies are heading. The annual NMC *Horizon Report* (2014), which describes how technologies will affect education, sees key trends as the:

- growing ubiquity of social media;
- integration of online, hybrid and collaborative learning;
- rise of data-driven learning and assessment;

- shift from students as consumers to students as creators;
- agile institutional and organisational approaches to change;
- evolution of online learning as a viable alternative to some forms of face-to-face learning.

They list the following as among the technologies that are likely to be adopted as a routine part of HE within the next five years:

- *The flipped classroom* – in a flipped classroom, digital technologies are used to rearrange how class time is spent so that the ownership of learning shifts from the tutor to the student. Research and information gathering is done by learners outside of class hours via video lectures; listening to podcasts; reading enhanced e-book content; and collaborating with peers in online communities. Time in class is spent in active, project- and problem-based collaborative learning, rather than with the teacher dispensing and the learner passively receiving information (NMC, 2014: 36).
- *Learning analytics* – learning analytics can be used diagnostically to improve student engagement and to provide personalised experiences for learners. An example given in the report is the case of the University of Michigan, which uses a software application called Gradecraft that encourages risk-taking as learners progress through course material as well as multiple pathways for achieving mastery. The analytics gathered in the process are used to guide students throughout the process and inform instructors of student progress (see http://gradecraft.com/ for details – accessed 21.9.15).
- *3-D printing* – a 3-D printer 'builds a tangible model or prototype from the electronic file, one layer at a time, through an extrusion-like process using plastics and other flexible materials, or an inkjet-like process to spray a bonding agent onto a very thin layer of fixable powder ...' (NMC, 2014: 42). Case studies of the use of 3-D printing in the report include Finnish art students who collaborate with a local artist collective to create sculptural works for an exhibition, and a case where researchers at the University of Wollongong use a bio-plotter to print living human cells.
- *Games and gamification* – owing to the proliferation of digital technologies such as electronic tablets and smartphones, laptop computers, and gaming consoles, recreational gameplay has evolved to offer immersive problem-based simulations and games as a way of incentivising learning activity through rewards, leader boards and badges. For example, the Stanford University School of Medicine uses a web-based simulation game called SICKO in which students manage virtual patients and must make critical decisions in the operating room.

- *Quantified self* – wearable computer devices are enabling people to track their lives automatically, as can be seen in the use of such devices as the Narrative Clip, a camera worn around the neck which captures an image every 30 seconds. As more and more people begin to rely on their mobile devices to monitor their daily activities, their personal data can be used for research and learning.
- *Virtual assistants* – virtual assistants in education have developed from work being done with natural user interfaces (NUIs) in the disciplines of engineering, computer science and biometrics. Microsoft, for example, has developed a computer program that translates English into written and then spoken Mandarin, heard within seconds using the speaker's own voice (NMC, 2014: 47).

## How are students learning today?

A term that often appears in literature on online learning and teaching provision is that of *digital natives* (see, e.g., Bennett et al., 2008, and Jones and Shao, 2011); that is, someone who was born into the post-millennium digital world and who is at home using technologies of all kinds. Introduced by Marc Prensky (2001a, 2001b, 2012), the notion of the digital 'native' is based on the idea that as a result of 'the sheer volume of their interaction with [technology], today's students think and process information fundamentally differently from their predecessors' (2001a: 1). Digitally adept learners who were born before the idea of the 'knowledge' society was popularised are also seen as *digital adopters* (Vai and Sosulski, 2011: 15) or *digital immigrants*, meaning those who 'were not born into the digital world but have, at some later point in their lives, become fascinated by and adopted many or most aspects of the new technology' (Prensky, 2001a: 1–2). White and Le Cornu (2011) prefer the terms *digital residents* and *digital visitors* for the differences in modes of engagement with the web between those who have accommodated these technologies as a routine part of their lives and 'visitors' who may not be all that comfortable with them and who may use technology as a tool for a particular purpose but are unlikely to have any form of persistent profile online.

We need to keep in mind, therefore, the idea that while many students are using the abundance of access to information and social media to develop digital skills and knowledge deftly and aptly, there are constraining factors for students who do not have the means, the opportunity or sometimes even the desire to develop the digital literacies needed for modern life (Holley and Oliver, 2011). Of more concern, perhaps, is that even students who are familiar with digital technologies may not possess the critical and analytical skills they need to assess the information that they find on the Internet. Gilster's (1997) view that digital literacy is 'about mastering ideas, not keystrokes' springs to mind. A report commissioned by JISC and the British Library showed also that the research-behaviour traits usually associated with younger users, such as impatience in searching and navigating the web and a lack of tolerance for any delay in satisfying their information needs, are common to all age groups (Rowlands et al., 2008).

Contemporary learners use many technologies in different ways very casually and informally. However, that kind of acceptance of technology can throw up challenges, as well as benefits, for learners and tutors alike. Thus, students' experiences of digital technologies and expectations of e-learning may run counter to the intentions of teachers and the apparent ease and usefulness of ubiquitous access to information can mask a lack of critical research skills and 'digital scholarship' (Beetham et al., 2009). Students may not have developed the *heutagogical* skills needed for successful learning in this way; that is, students may not yet have learned *how* to learn and to do so independently. Blaschke (2012) describes heutagogy as a form of self-determined learning with practices and principles rooted in andragogy, saying: 'In a heutagogical approach to teaching and learning, learners are highly autonomous and self-determined and emphasis is placed on development of learner capacity and capability' (p.56). In addition, other problems associated with e-learning and e-assessment also have to be addressed, such as the need to protect students' online privacy, a sufficient level of student digital, information and computer literacy, and the problems of plagiarism and access. Nonetheless, in the hands of a knowledgeable tutor, the benefits far outweigh the costs. Fortunately, and perhaps serendipitously, the ability to make sense of, and effectively use, the Internet requires attributes such as trust, teamwork, communication, collaboration and open sharing – the very attributes which allow neophytes and experts to work together to solve complex problems in a complex, globalised world.

The emerging notion of heutagogy perfectly describes the new approaches to learning and teaching approaches evolving out of these innovations. Garnett and Ecclesfield (2011) show that a heutagogical approach is 'cognisant of the affordances of new, networked, Web 2.0 and later technologies for learning' (p.9). The case study described below shows how the use of technology skilfully blended with teaching and learning develops, as Garnett and Ecclesfield put it, good subject-based learning while enabling collaborative learning strategies and creative forms of assessment to be deployed.

# What does blended learning look like in a university classroom?

We know that blended learning works best with learning environments that engage students in problem-based, authentic and socially constructed forms of learning. In such environments, according to Kear (2011), learners actively construct their own knowledge and understanding through the intellectual and physical activities that they carry out in collaboration with one another.

The case study below is drawn from a BA Translation course and provides an example of blended learning in action and gives a good account of how learners responded to a particular blended learning design.

## Case study

**Blended learning in a translation course context,** *Agata Sadza*

I teach a blended learning module for second-year undergraduate students which aims to familiarise students with professional practices in the translation industry, including translation project management and quality assurance (QA). The blended mode of delivery includes a combination of classroom-based (synchronous) and online (asynchronous) sessions. BA Translation is a vocational course, focused on developing professional skills that students will be able to utilise successfully in their future careers. The main focus is thus on tasks resembling real-life activities and dilemmas. The learners already had some experience of translation and some familiarity with the professional practices in the industry; however, I wanted to help them consolidate their knowledge and their skills in a more systematic way. This general purpose was related to, for example, managing projects, translation revision, and collaborative work, in order to help them reflect on and possibly improve the procedures and practices they had been relying on so far, as well as to give them an opportunity to test new practices.

The blended mode proved to be particularly effective for delivering educational content through guided discovery and knowledge construction. This was confirmed by the students, who reported that they enjoyed the asynchronous (online) mode of delivery of some of the sessions where they were asked to conduct their own information research, assess and filter the results, and post these online, because it gave them the freedom to explore areas of interest to them individually, share resources, organise their time as they saw fit and work at their own pace.

Activities included using online resources to research professional practices (such as related to dealing with client queries) and posting a report from the results of the research on a class blog available within the University's virtual learning environment. Students were then asked to read peers' posts and comment on two posts themselves, and an in-class discussion followed where students discussed examples of real-life problems and ethical dilemmas on an online discussion forum before a classroom-based discussion. They then identified and implemented the main principles of project management by setting up a translation 'cooperative' to deliver a professional group translation project.

Here they were asked to emulate the professional environment as closely as possible and to make use of asynchronous liaison for project management and feedback purposes.

They were assessed based on a portfolio of three critical-reflective commentaries on the knowledge and practices they had developed throughout the module.

Ozer (2004) sees social constructivist approaches such as the one described above as involving real-world situations, interaction and collaboration where learners are considered to be central in the learning process. When learners exercise the 'will, determination, and action to gather selective information, convert it, formulate hypotheses, test these suppositions via applications, interactions or experiences, and to draw verifiable conclusions' classrooms become 'a knowledge-construction site where information is absorbed and knowledge is built by the learner' (Ozer, 2004). Learners become accountable for their learning and the teacher supports learners 'by means of suggestions that arise out of ordinary activities, by challenges that inspire creativity, and with projects that allow for independent thinking and new ways of learning information' (Ozer, 2004). Within this perspective, Ozer says, the focus is shifted from the teacher as the expert and central figure who transmits knowledge, to be almost uncritically accepted by learners and reproduced in assessment situations, to the learner as the one responsible for their own cognition and understanding. It follows then that new practices will challenge long-held perceptions about learning and teaching, particularly in the more didactic and positivist disciplines where learning *what* to learn may often take precedence over learning *how* to learn. Reassuringly, though, needs of the discipline, the context of learning and the kind of learner involved, as well as the technologies available, will all have a role to play in the digitised university.

## Social, cognitive and teaching 'presence' in blended learning

Students can find learning online an isolating and frustrating experience because the taken-for-granted cues found in face-to-face classroom interactions tend to disappear in the primarily textual nature of learning online. The absence of these non-verbal language cues in a virtual setting requires particular attention in blended learning. Garrison and Anderson's (2002) community of inquiry model identifies three useful elements in the design and delivery of blended learning that may make up for this 'absence of presence' in the online space. These are social presence, cognitive presence and teaching presence. Swan and Ice remind us that:

> Social presence is defined as the degree to which participants in computer-mediated communication feel affectively connected one to another; cognitive presence is conceptualised as the extent to which learners are able to construct and confirm meaning through sustained reflection and discourse; and teaching presence is defined as the design, facilitation and direction of cognitive and social processes to support learning. (2010: 1–2)

When the tutor is to all intents and purposes physically 'absent', designing in the social aspects of learning such as posting self-introductions and profiles, finding, generating or sharing new resources are key. Cognitive activities which allow discourse and reflection to take place online are crucial in providing a satisfying and successful learning experience, as are challenging and achievable online assessments. Providing such activities promotes the same level of taken-for-granted 'presences' that are found in successful face-to-face classroom interactions. Facilitators should participate in discussions, and actively mediate, facilitate and moderate virtual learning activities. A strong online teaching presence enables students to connect with one another, to understand what is required and to meet learning outcomes. Requiring learners to provide critical commentary on a video, to carry out a concept mapping exercise, or to do co-writing via blog are deeply engaging learning activities and are good examples of exercises that engage and connect students in their learning. If well facilitated, online discussions can serve to explore concepts, debate topics and raise issues connected with project work in ways that ensure that students are actively engaged in the processes of learning (see Wang, 2008, for more on facilitating online discussions and practical ideas for using blogs).

Among a number of interesting case studies on the Higher Education Academy website (see additional resources at the end of this chapter) is one by Anouk Lang (2010) in which reflective online learning journals were used to help students to engage with literary theory. He found that reflective journals enhanced seminar discussions and motivated students as well as improving students' writing as an effective tool for fostering deep learning. Halcro and Smith (2011) show how wikis can be used to extend the classroom to the world of work and engagement with employers. Gilly Salmon's (2011) work on welcoming and encouraging students and familiarising and providing bridges between cultural social and learning environments is a useful guide to providing the kind of 'e-tivities' that infuse online learning with a sense that the facilitator and other students are present in the online space (see Salmon, 2013, for guidance in designing active online learning). Personalising content by using 'ice breakers', such as asking students to put up profiles of themselves and commenting on the introductions of other learners or designing engaging collaborative activities such as a group task, establishes a sense of social presence. A welcome page, use of humour and cartoons, the choice of texts and careful use of images go a long way in helping the loneliness of the long-distance learner in online courses. A sense of isolation is often why online learners drop out of sight and why there is such a low retention rate in many MOOCs and other non-facilitated online learning environments (see Yuan and Powell, 2013; Reich, 2014). That said, however, MOOCs do hold promise and potential for engaging online learners when learning analytics become sophisticated enough to personalise learning.

## Conclusion

As we have seen, digital learners, and tutors, are finding the locus of learning outside the boundaries of formal education and beyond the walls of the university in increasing measures, primarily through using social media and freely available open source learning resources. HE educators are making good use of the opportunities that new technologies are providing for engaged, authentic forms of learning and there is a new focus by universities on how learners could engage with complexity and uncertainty in the face of exponential technological change. However, as Ryan and Tilbury (2013) point out, there are also exciting new possibilities for critical, emancipatory teaching and learning, free from technological determinism and with a clear focus on the renewal and transformation of learning and teaching. The flipped classroom described earlier in this chapter is just one example of how technology can be used to create an absorbing and creative blend of authentic face-to-face classroom interaction between peers and tutors and virtual communications, collaborations and shared learning. While blending learning in this way offers challenges to both students and their tutors, and to universities as they gear up old infrastructures to provide for the new technologies and the new forms of learning, there is no doubt we can 'blend' the richness and immersion of virtual learning with the living, breathing experience of face-to-face learning at its best. Well-designed blended learning supports autonomous and self-determined heutagogical learners. In the face of a world that is caught in a warp speed change, a new 'pedagogy of nearness' seems to be at hand in which online interaction and collaboration has the same value as face-to-face learning (Veletsianos, 2010). The twenty-first century is definitely an exciting time for higher-order learning and teaching.

## Questions for reflective practice and professional development

1 How would you define the benefits of blended learning within your own teaching context and discipline?
2 What learning technologies are you using currently, for what educational purposes?
3 How could you take advantage of new technologies to enhance critical self-determined learning (heutagogy), collaborative learning, assessment and feedback?
4 Which model(s) of blended learning design are best suited to your context of practice?

## Useful websites, further reading

### Higher Education Academy

www.english.heacademy.ac.uk/explore/publications/casestudies/technology/index.php
This is a link to a set of e-learning case study material submitted to the English Subject Centre.

**JISC (2015) Guide to Enhancing the Student Digital Experience**

www.jisc.ac.uk/guides/enhancing-the-digital-student-experience
Provides a strategic framework for supporting institutions to develop digital environments for student progression and employment

**JISC Change Agent's Network**

www.jisc.ac.uk/rd/projects/change-agents-network
Supports students working as change agents, digital pioneers, student fellows and students working in partnership with staff on technology-related change projects.

Beetham, H. and Sharpe, R. (2007) *Rethinking Pedagogy for a Digital Age: Designing and delivering e-learning.* Abingdon: Taylor & Francis.
This well-written scholarly book focuses on learning design, and delivery while providing an excellent view of current learning theory in relation to virtual learning and its relationship to learning and teaching in general.

Kear, K. L. (2010) *Online and Social Networking Communities: A best practice guide for educators.* London: Routledge.
An excellent text with many real-life examples of online teaching, as well as a superb introduction to the theoretical frameworks of online learning.

Rennie, F. and Morrison, T. (2013) *E-learning and Social Networking Handbook: Resources for higher education.* London: Routledge.
This book has many examples of using online tools in practice and through a series of case studies provides a comparison of the different social learning tools used.

Vai, M. and Sosulski, K. (2011) *The Essentials of Online Course Design: A standards-based guide.* London: Routledge.
A practical, straightforward, no-nonsense guide to designing virtual learning spaces.

# References

Beetham, H., McGill, L. and Littlejohn, A. (2009) *Thriving in the 21st Century: Learning literacies for the digital age (LLiDA Project).* Bristol: JISC.
Bennett, S., Maton, K. and Kervin, L. (2008) 'The "digital natives" debate: A critical review of the evidence', *British Journal of Educational Technology*, 39 (5): 775–86.
Blaschke, L. M. (2012) 'Heutagogy and lifelong learning: A review of heutagogical practice and self-determined learning', *The International Review of Research in Open and Distance Learning*, 13 (1): 36–71.

Bradley, C. and Holley, D. (2011) 'Empirical research into students' mobile phones and their use for learning', *International Journal of Mobile and Blended Learning*, 3 (4): 38–53.

Conole, G. (2013) *Designing for Learning in an Open World*. New York: Springer.

De Freitas, S. and Conole, G. (2010) 'Influence of pervasive and integrative tools on learners: Experiences and expectations of study', in R. Sharpe, H. Beetham and S. de Freitas (eds), *Rethinking Learning for a Digital Age: How learners are shaping their own experiences*. Abingdon: Routledge.

Ecclesfield, N., Rebbeck, G. and Garnett, F. (2012) 'The case of the curious and the confident – the untold story of changing teacher attitudes to e-learning and "technology in action" in the FE sector', *Compass: The Journal of Learning and Teaching at the University of Greenwich*, 5. Available at https://journals.gre.ac.uk/index.php/compass/article/viewFile/71/107 (accessed 28.7.15).

Garnett, F. and Ecclesfield, N. (2011) *ALT-C 2011 Proceedings Papers: 0199 A framework for co-creating open scholarship*. Oxford: Association for Learning Technology. Available at http://repository.alt.ac.uk/2177/ (accessed: 28.7.15).

Garrison, D. R. and Anderson, T. (2002) *E-Learning in the 21st Century*. New York: RoutledgeFalmer.

Gilster, P. (1997) *Digital Literacy*. New York: Wiley.

Halcro, K. and Smith, M. J. (2011) 'Wikis: Building a learning experience between academe and businesses', *Reflective Practice: International and Multidisciplinary Perspectives*, 12 (5): 679–93.

Holley, D. and Oliver, M. (2011) 'Negotiating the digital divide: Narratives from the have and have-nots', in R. Land and S. Bayne (eds), *Digital Difference: Perspectives on online learning*. Rotterdam: Sense, pp.101–13.

Jones, C. and Shao, B. (2011) *The Net Generation and Digital Natives: Implications for Higher Education*. Milton Keynes: Open University, HEA. Available at www.heacademy.ac.uk/sites/default/files/next-generation-and-digital-natives.pdf (accessed 18.9.15).

Kear, K. L. (2011) *Online and Social Networking Communities: A best practice guide for educators*. Abingdon: Routledge.

Lang, A. (2010) *Using Online Learning Journals to Enhance Students' Engagement with Literary Theory*. York: Higher Education Academy. Available at www.english.heacademy.ac.uk/explore/publications/casestudies/technology/journals.php (accessed 22.7.15).

NMC and ELI (2014) *NMC Horizon Report> 2014 Higher Education Edition*. Austin, TX: New Media Consortium. Available at http://cdn.nmc.org/media/2014–nmc-horizon-report-he-EN-SC.pdf (accessed 18.9.15).

Ozer, O. (2004) 'Constructivism in Piaget and Vygotsky', *The Fountain*, 48. Available at www.fountainmagazine.com/Issue/detail/CONSTRUCTIVISM-in-Piaget-and-Vygotsky (accessed 28.7.15).

Paechter, M. and Maier, B. (2010) 'Online or face-to-face? Students' experiences and preferences in e-learning', *The Internet and Higher Education*, 13 (4): 292–7.

Prensky, M. (2001a) 'Digital natives, digital immigrants: Part 1', *On the Horizon*, 9 (5): 1–6.

Prensky, M. (2001b) 'Digital natives, digital immigrants: Part 2: Do they really think differently?', *On the Horizon*, 9 (6): 1–6.

Prensky, M. (2012) *From Digital Natives to Digital Wisdom: Hopeful essays for 21st century learning*. London: Sage.

Reich, J. (2014) 'MOOC completion and retention in the context of student intent', *EDUCAUSE Review*. Available at www.educause.edu/ero/article/mooc-completion-and-retention-context-student-intent (accessed 28.7.15).

Rouse, M. (2010) 'What is distributed learning?', definition from WhatIs.com. Available at http://whatis.techtarget.com/definition/distributed-learning (accessed 28.7.15).

Rowlands, I., Nicholas, D., Williams, P., Huntington, P., Fieldhouse, M., Gunter, B., Withey, R., Jamali, H. R., Dobrowolski, T. and Tenopir, C. (2008) 'The Google generation: The information behaviour of the researcher of the future', *Aslib Proceedings*, 60 (4): 290–310.

Ryan, A. and Tilbury, D. (2013) *Flexible Pedagogies: New pedagogical ideas*. York: Higher Education Academy. Available at www.heacademy.ac.uk/sites/default/files/resources/npi_report.pdf (accessed 18.9.15).

Salmon, G. (2011) *E-moderating: The key to teaching and learning online*. Abingdon: Routledge.

Salmon, G. (2013) *E-tivities: The key to active online learning* (2nd edn). Oxford: Taylor & Francis.

Sharpe, R. (2009) 'The impact of learner experience research on transforming institutional practices', in *Transforming Higher Education Through Technology Enhanced Learning*. York: Higher Education Academy. Available at https://www.heacademy.ac.uk/resource/transforming-higher-education-through-technology-enhanced-learning

Swan, K. and Ice, P. (2010) 'The community of inquiry framework ten years later: Introduction to the special issue', *The Internet and Higher Education*, 13 (1–2): 1–4.

Vai, M. and Sosulski, K. (2011) *The Essentials of Online Course Design: A standards-based guide*. Abingdon: Routledge.

Veletsianos, G. (2010) *Emerging Technologies in Distance Education*. Edmonton: University of British Columbia Press.

Wang, Q. (2008) 'A generic model for guiding the integration of ICT into teaching and learning', *Innovations in Education and Teaching International*, 45 (4): 411–19.

White, D. S. and Cornu. A. Le (2011) 'Visitors and residents: A new typology for online engagement', *First Monday*, 16 (9). Online journal available at: http://firstmonday.org/htbin/cgiwrap/bin/ojs/index.php/fm/article/view/3171/3049

Yuan, L. and Powell, S. (2013) *MOOCs and Open Education: Implications for higher education*. Bolton: CETIS. Available at www.oerknowledgecloud.org/sites/oerknowledgecloud.org/files/MOOCs-and-Open-Education.pdf (accessed 18.9.15).

# 6

# Student Engagement

Kathy Harrington, Sandra Sinfield and Tom Burns

## Chapter overview

This chapter explores:

- staff engagement as an agency for student engagement
- the educational landscape of engagement: barriers and levers
- benefits of engagement for students and teachers
- principles and practices to foster engaged teaching and learning
- examples of engagement within and alongside the curriculum

## Introduction

There is extensive international literature on student engagement, comprising conceptual and theoretical approaches, empirical research, policy initiatives and numerous case studies of student engagement practice in a wide variety of contexts. This chapter draws on data from this substantial and diverse field to chart a path of particular relevance to any university teacher who takes an interest in thinking about and finding fresh ways to enable students' engagement with learning, both within and alongside the curriculum, with all of the benefits and challenges this brings within the social, cultural and economic complexity of contemporary higher education (HE). This chapter works with a broad understanding of 'curriculum' to encompass content and structures of a study programme as well as the dynamic and emergent processes of interaction between students and staff that enable relevant and meaningful learning (Fraser and Bosanquet, 2006), comprising academic, personal and professional dimensions. You may be involved with student peer mentoring, volunteering or community service learning programmes or with organising other co-curricular learning activities, alongside (face-to-face or virtual) classroom teaching and personal tutoring responsibilities. Models and principles of good engagement practice, as well as illustrative examples from across UK HE, are offered to enable you to reflect on, evaluate and take steps towards developing your own practice in thoughtful, manageable and fruitful new ways.

A central aim of this chapter is to encourage you to value the role of the teacher, as well as that of subject specialist. Other chapters in this book consider important aspects of the facilitation of students' learning in some depth. The focus here is more directly on the interface between teaching and learning, and on the relationship between teachers and students as a vehicle for engagement in all its diversity. The process of teaching involves a relationship of engagement: with students, with the subject matter, with oneself. The ways in which we as teaching staff approach this relationship can have an important influence on the nature and quality of students' engagement with their own learning and emerging academic and professional identities. Maintaining a reflective awareness of our own roles, beliefs and identities – as well as our limits – as teachers places us in a better position to make full use of ourselves as a resource that can contribute beneficially to students' experiences of HE.

Bryson (2014), influenced by Fromm (1978) and the idea of 'being' as more important than 'having', suggests that a notion of 'becoming' permeates a relational model of student engagement (Solomonides et al., 2012), and he connects this to Barnett's (2007: 70) notion of the 'will to learn' as foundational to a students' ability to engage 'without a self, without a will to learn, without a being that has come into itself, her efforts to know and to act within her programme of study cannot even begin to form with any assuredness'. We suggest that an understanding of student engagement as proposed in this chapter can help us to transcend a focus on the transmission of information and instead take an interest in processes that enable students to experience this more collaborative, complex and nuanced version of education, which at its heart is about engagement as learning, and learning as becoming.

## Student engagement: what is it and why does it matter?

As many scholars have noted (Bryson, 2014; Nygaard et al., 2013; Kahu, 2013), 'student engagement' is a broad and variously defined concept and collection of practices in HE, with the definition depending on the position one occupies in the educational system as well as one's motivating interests. For example, we can speak of student engagement with the process of learning and enquiry; with teaching enhancement and curriculum development; with fellow students and colleagues, including through peer mentoring and collaborative learning; with representational structures, institutional planning and policy development; with extra-curricular and community programmes; and with the socio-political process of the transformation of HE itself. Student engagement has been linked to a sense of belonging and academic and social integration, leading to retention and success (Thomas, 2012; Tinto, 2003); learning gains and improved educational outcomes (Kuh et al., 2008); critical thinking and grades (Carini et al., 2006); transformational learning (Bryson, 2014); employability and professional development (Montesinos et al., 2013; Summers et al., 2013); and preparedness for the complexity of the workplace and participation in civic life (Moxley et al., 2001). There are also benefits for staff of successful 'student engagement', not least with respect to a sense of reward and enjoyment in the work of teaching and transformations in our own understandings and professional practice as teachers in HE (Cook-Sather et al., 2014).

Graham Gibbs (2014) has recently suggested that 'student engagement' has become the latest educational buzzword, providing a catch-all phrase for 'so many different things that it is difficult to keep track of what people are actually talking about'. In this chapter, we take an approach to student engagement that encompasses students' academic and professional development as well as their social integration, and focuses specifically on the role that teaching staff can play in fostering students' engagement with the experience of learning both within and alongside the curriculum. Engagement from this perspective is a complex interplay of factors, including affective, cognitive and behavioural dimensions (Kahu, 2013; Wimpenny and Savin-Baden, 2013), for both students and teachers. It is contextual and situated, influenced by institutional structures, local cultures of practice and the wider socio-political climate, as well as shaped by the motivations, expectations, life experiences, attitudes and behaviours that both students and staff bring to HE and the processes of (facilitating) learning (Bryson, 2014).

Given the diversity of students and staff and the complexity of contemporary HE, there is no one method for fostering student engagement that will suit all contexts equally. Nevertheless, and particularly where differences amongst students are pronounced, such as with respect to family background, age, ethnicity, mother-tongue, prior educational and other experiences, assumptions and expectations of HE, it can be helpful to think about engagement from the perspective of inclusive teaching practices that value and actively work with such differences, and which avoid reinforcing an often unspoken yet powerful, and problematic, notion that 'difference' (and problem) resides with some students and not others. Embedding attentiveness to student diversity within curriculum design, particularly on courses where students come from a range of non-traditional academic backgrounds and may be more likely to struggle emotionally and practically, has been shown to lead to universally beneficial outcomes (Warren, 2002). (See Chapter 7: Embracing Student Diversity.)

## The contemporary educational landscape: barriers and levers to engagement

As outlined in the introduction to this book, substantial changes in the policy landscape of UK HE, including new funding structures that shift the fee burden much more towards individual students, an increase in providers and competition for students, and an overall trend towards greater marketisation, are linked to the growth of a consumerist approach to engaging with learning (Kandiko and Mawer, 2013). In this context, teaching staff committed to working in creative and innovative ways to support and challenge students academically can feel constrained by a sense – and a reality – that such work, which inevitably involves risk-taking and an openness to unpredictable learning experiences for both students and staff, is undervalued because it is not perceived as able to produce the kind of pre-determined, quantifiable educational outcomes that managers and fee-paying, employment-focused students (it is often assumed) expect. Under such pressure, it can be hard to resist the temptation to frame students as the 'problem', as seen, for example, in commonly heard complaint-explanations that 'students these days don't read', 'they can't write', 'they want to be spoon-fed'.

An alternative way of thinking about the current situation is to consider the academic terrain navigated by students before they enter HE, with a view to understanding the nature of the role they are often given within larger social and educational systems, and to consider the impact of this on student attitudes towards learning once they reach HE. For some students, the landscape of formal education will be experienced as a hostile one, in which they must learn to swim in swift educational currents shaped by powerful narratives of measurement and hierarchical comparison, embodied in standardised aptitude tests, league tables, school inspections and rankings, alongside moral panics about plagiarism and the 'dumbing-down' of education. Many students, perhaps particularly those who do not bring with them much of the cultural capital traditionally recognised and affirmed by academia (Bourdieu and Passeron, 1979), can find themselves as if set up to fail from the outset, and they can struggle to negotiate successfully through what is experienced as hazardous and punishing foreign territory (Sinfield et al., 2004; Leathwood and O'Connell, 2003). Thinking about (some) students' experiences from this perspective, we should not be surprised to discover that, particularly amongst those deemed 'weakest', contemporary students may strive to employ instrumental and strategic study practices that keep them afloat as a primary objective, which simultaneously, and deleteriously, prevent them from taking the risks to engage more meaningfully, creatively and unpredictably with their own learning at university.

Staff, too, swim in strong currents of monitoring and control, embodied in national benchmarking and league tables, quality codes, professional body requirements, research audits, and government and institutional policies and strategies that formally shape the direction and content of learning, teaching and assessment practice in the classroom. The sheer volume of paperwork and time spent preparing for quality and research audits alone has substantially undermined the academic's autonomy and capacity to engage with their students' learning and developing the quality of their teaching (Morgan, 2010). The role of the teacher can be experienced as disempowering by academics who may be accomplished and respected in their disciplinary or professional contexts but remain novices in areas of curriculum design, assessment and teaching development. Being a teacher, as well as an academic, is exposing: it makes us vulnerable to judgements from students as well as peers and managers; we regularly confront the unexpected in the classroom; and we are subject to the unrelenting and perhaps unforgiving gaze of our students as they demand value for money and expect their sometimes naive or conservative notions of 'good' teaching be fully met. Although successful teaching and learning encounters often contain elements of the messy, risky and unpredictable (Healey et al., 2014), especially for new teachers this can feel chaotic, unprofessional and very much like 'failure'. In this context, teachers can easily learn to see the fearful, recalcitrant or demanding student as the 'other', the one that creates an unsuccessful peer review, a poor probation year or inadequate module performance.

Acknowledging this tricky terrain is not to negate the potential for 'engagement' but to invite a focus on the relationship between staff and students as the site where engagement can be nurtured. Taylor (2012) examines prevalent notions underlying the way 'student engagement' is used in current discourse and suggests that there are three dominant, partly incompatible, ways of understanding it: 'student engagement' is variously about: 1) teaching and learning, and the means for enhancement, 2) accountability and transparency, or 3) dialogic and participatory practice. The first and, to an extent, the third meanings highlight the importance of the nature of the learning encounter between students and teachers, and the potential in this encounter for a transformational educational experience. The use of 'learning encounter' is understood to refer broadly to a relationship of learning and teaching, which can be between teachers and students but also between students where individual peers variously take on the different roles of 'teacher' and 'student'. Transformation could take the form of new understanding of a subject area, or a change in one's identity and self-knowledge, or a more differentiated awareness of others' perspectives and one's position in relation to them within a wider sphere of academic or disciplinary endeavour. However the transformation is manifest, the focus is on learning and on the co-created possibility for this through a relationship of engagement between teachers and students.

## Models of engagement

As a way into thinking about our own teaching and changes we may wish to implement with the aim of making it more engaging, it can be helpful first to reflect and take stock of how we are currently working. Informed by research into engagement amongst students with disabilities by May and Felsinger (2010), the UK National Union of Students (NUS) and Higher Education Academy (HEA) have developed a student engagement 'ladder of participation' (2011) that conceptualises different forms and processes of engagement as qualitatively different from one another, which can assist not only the evaluation of current practice but also identifying new ways of working that may feel more congruent with one's personal teaching values and goals.

## Forms of student engagement

- *Consultation* – opportunities are provided for students to express individual opinions, perspectives, experiences, ideas and concerns.
- *Involvement* – opportunities are provided for students as individuals to take a more active role.
- *Participation* – decisions are taken by students to take part or take a more active role in a defined activity.

*(Continued)*

*(Continued)*

- *Partnership* – there is a collaboration between an institution/faculty/department and student, involving joint ownership and decision making over both the process and outcome.

(Adapted from NUS and HEA, 2011)

Within the realm of curriculum development, consultation often takes the form of a 'feedback' mode of engagement, where students are asked for their thoughts about how they have experienced the teaching and learning processes designed and implemented by staff. While there are clear advantages to listening to student experiences in this way, so that where possible changes can be made to improve students' future learning experiences, the disadvantage of this approach is that too often it can feel, and in practice become, a predominantly managerial and superficial box-ticking exercise, for both students and staff. At the level of 'involvement', as defined by NUS and HEA, students are again invited by staff to participate, but the roles taken up involve a higher degree of agency and active participation in determining the shape of their learning experiences, for example in the roles of course representative or ambassador, where students are engaged with processes of curriculum review and enhancement and the induction of new students.

Participation involves a greater degree of student agency as decisions are taken by students about whether and the extent to which they wish to be involved, both within and alongside the curriculum. At this level of engagement, students may, for example, partake of a range of extra-curricular activities, including those designed and run by themselves and where participation is seen as enhancing their voice and authority to contribute meaningfully to their own learning processes (Sinfield et al., 2010). Engagement at the level of partnership works on the premise that staff and students actively engage with each other in a collaborative process that values the different perspectives and contributions each party brings to a shared activity.

The HEA foregrounds partnership as central to an understanding of student engagement and its potential benefits for enhancing both learning and teaching, with 'partnership' defined as:

> a relationship in which all involved – students, academics, professional services staff, senior managers, students' unions, and so on – are actively engaged in and stand to gain from the process of learning and working together.

Partnership is essentially a process of engagement, not a product. It is a way of doing things, rather than an outcome in itself. (Healey et al., 2014: 12)

This understanding of student engagement acknowledges the importance of teachers and students as different but equally valuable members of an inter-relational and transformational learning experience for all participants. The HEA offers a conceptual model for working with students as partners in learning and teaching, covering four overlapping areas (see Figure 6.1) of learning, teaching and assessment; subject-based research and inquiry; curriculum design and pedagogic consultancy; and scholarship of teaching and learning where teachers and students are variously

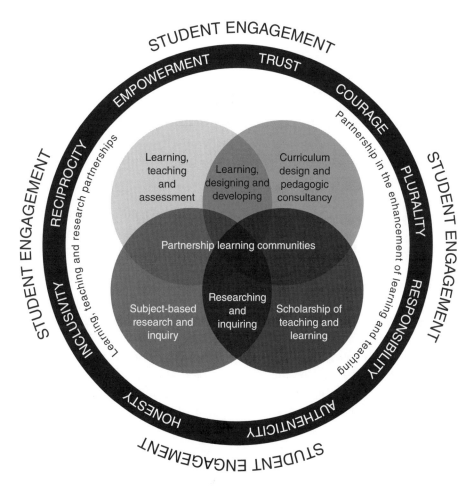

**Figure 6.1** Students as partners in learning and teaching in higher education – an overview model (taken from the publication *Engagement Through Partnership: Students as partners in learning and teaching in higher education*. Healey, Flint and Harrington. © The Higher Education Academy, 2014. All rights reserved).

involved in relationships of co-learning, co-designing, co-developing and co-researching (Healey et al., 2014). It is through the development of 'partnership learning communities', at the heart of the model, that principles and values of partnership – such as authenticity, honesty, inclusivity, reciprocity, empowerment, trust, courage, plurality and responsibility (HEA, 2014) – can be embodied and sustained in practice and lead to engaged learning and teaching.

Developing an ethos and culture of partnership in one's teaching practice requires adopting a questioning, reflective stance and a willingness to consider and challenge one's own assumptions and existing ways of thinking and working. Below are some principles to prompt reflection on attitudes and behaviours that can promote engaging practice.

## Principles for engagement

You may wish to reflect on the extent to which and in what ways you already put the following into practice, as well as areas you would like to prioritise and embody more strongly in your teaching. How can you make realistic and meaningful changes within the practical constraints of available time, class size and the turnaround time you have in which to get marking done?

- Get to know your students; for example, their cultural and family backgrounds, prior educational and other life experiences, expectations, understandings of the subject and learning generally.
- Find out how students perceive you, your role and their expectations of you.
- Recognise and value difference, and different 'ways of being a student' (Bryson, 2014), and let this influence the design and approach of your teaching.
- Engage with your students wherever they are in their learning process and provide the scaffolding to enable next steps (Vygotsky, 1978).
- Foster a relationship of trust and mutual respect that values agency, creativity, authenticity, critical dissent and collaboration.
- Facilitate dialogue and actively seek experiences of learning with and from students.
- Reflect on how knowledge is created in your discipline and the extent to which, and how, this aligns with the way knowledge is

created/reproduced in your teaching practice and the learning environments you create.

- Use the opportunity to see teaching not as second class to research but as an equally valuable though different aspect of the larger academic enterprise of inquiry.
- Be responsive to the moment of encounter.
- Maintain an openness to surprise and discovery.
- Create spaces for risk-taking – and take risks!

# Putting principles into practice

There is a wealth of existing case studies and other illustrative examples easily accessible in the public domain, and we point readers towards some of those we find most useful and current in the list of further resources below. There can be a tendency to regard 'student engagement' as if it were the sum of a collection of practices, across an institution or a department, for example; however, as Rachel Wenstone (NUS, 2012) persuasively argues, it is the *how* of the practices – the underlying principles, attitudes, ethos and ways of working – rather that the *what*, which enables practices to engage and benefit students in transformative and sustainable ways. Nevertheless, we hope offering some examples will help you to imagine possibilities for new ways of working and fostering engagement in your own context, and we draw attention to a selection below.

## Learning and enquiry

In her international review of research into student engagement, Vicky Trowler (2010) found that engagement with learning is enhanced by active participation, both in and out of class (see also 'Co-curricular activities' below); collaborative activity (see 'Peer mentoring and collaborative learning' below); and student involvement in the design, delivery and assessment of their learning (see 'Curriculum development' below). With respect to encouraging active participation, teaching and learning in a twenty-first century (virtual or physical) classroom is likely to include a mix of more traditional modes, such as lectures and seminars, alongside more participatory and experiential learning activities, such as role plays and simulations; inquiry and problem-based learning; rich pictures and drawing-to-learn activities (see: http://systems.open.ac.uk/materials/T552/

accessed 23.9.15); and research projects, including in partnership with academic staff (Healey and Jenkins, 2009). In addition, engaging teaching can include digital artefact development, blogging and other social network activities.

The underlying rationale for diversifying learning and teaching methods is to model purposive academic endeavour and create opportunities for students to engage actively in meaningful and authentic ways with the subject of their studies as well as their own learning processes (Davies, 2011). A flipped classroom approach – whereby subject matter traditionally delivered through lecturers is provided as preparatory work and in-class time is devoted to collaborative and highly participatory learning activities – can be an effective way to foreground and reap the unique benefits of experiential learning (Gerstein, 2012). The 'Student as Producer' initiative at the University of Lincoln takes this process of active, discovery-based learning further by positioning students as collaborators in the production of knowledge, creating opportunities for engaging with real research and the development of disciplinary and academic identities as guiding principles of the undergraduate curriculum (http://studentasproducer.lincoln.ac.uk/).

## Peer mentoring and collaborative learning

There are many peer mentoring and collaborative learning models operating in HE today, both as extra-curricular programmes and embedded within the formal curriculum and teaching timetable, from peer-assisted learning (PAL) and peer-assisted study sessions (PASS) (Keenan, 2014), to mentoring specifically in academic writing (O'Neill et al., 2009), to pastoral mentoring designed to support first-year students through the transition to HE (Andrews and Clark, 2011), to mainstream modules where mentoring principles are taught and opportunities to gain experience and practical skills are built into the formal curriculum (Abegglen et al., 2015). When done well, mentoring can aid students in building communities of practice, where mentor and mentee work together to articulate and grapple with academic questions. In this model, a reciprocal relationship (Kossak, 2011) between mentor and mentee is fostered, where each is encouraged to learn with and from the other, working to support each other's academic achievement as well as personal and social growth within new disciplinary and professional spheres.

## Personal tutoring

As with peer mentoring, personal tutoring offers a relationship that facilitates a sense of connection with the university or department and provides a supportive space that fosters students' engagement with their academic discipline as well as their own learning and development. In her final report from the multi-institutional What Works? Student Retention & Success programme, Thomas (2012: 43–4) found personal tutoring to be an important strategy for supporting students' engagement and belonging, and that when effective it displays the following characteristics:

- proactive rather than relying on students finding and accessing tutors;
- early meetings with students;
- students have a relationship with the tutor and the tutor gets to know the students;
- structured support with an explicit purpose;
- embedded into the academic experience and based at school or faculty level;
- strong academic focus;
- identifying students at risk and providing support and development;
- linked to student services, students' union and peer mentoring or similar peer scheme to provide pastoral and social support and referring students for further support where appropriate.

While there are times when the provision of specific information and advice is helpful (e.g., about assessment deadlines and extensions or other support services available), at its essence the personal tutoring relationship is one which empowers the student to set the agenda, explore concerns and questions they wish to bring, develop their own thinking and discover ways of responding that work best for them (Wisker et al., 2008).

## Curriculum development

Engaging students in processes of designing and enhancing the curriculum can feel risky and uncomfortable for both students and staff because it challenges traditional roles and expectations (Healey et al., 2014; Cook-Sather, 2013). While the degree and nature of student involvement will vary according to the teaching context, level of study, different attitudes and prior experiences as well as the influence of professional bodies (Bovill, 2013) – and there also are times when it may not be desirable or possible to work in a (fully) collaborative, co-creative way (Bovill and Bulley, 2011; Weller and Kandiko Howson, forthcoming 2016) – there is nevertheless evidence that involving students in the design, delivery and assessment of their learning can have a beneficial effect on engagement with their course and the experience of learning in HE generally, as well as providing challenge, reward and transformation for teachers themselves (Cook-Sather et al., 2014).

Sambell and Graham (2011), for example, describe an assessment partnerships model in which students on a Health, Community and Education Studies programme not only study the philosophy and principles of Assessment for Learning (AfL) but also produce enhancement materials which have then been used by staff and students to both interrogate and improve their own assessment and learning practice. An increasingly common model of student involvement in curriculum development is when they act as course design and pedagogic consultants to improve teaching and learning within specific modules, courses or departments (Jensen and Bagnall, 2015; Sheffield Hallam University, 2013; University of Sheffield, 2013). Some universities have implemented a partnership approach to educational change and development as a fundamental way of working across the institution, enabling students to lead and co-develop local projects that have resulted in improved teaching practice, re-designed curricula, new learning resources, enhanced graduate skills, as well as changes to policy and practice at strategic levels (Birmingham City Students' Union, 2015; Nygaard et al., 2013; Dunne and Zandstra, 2011; Dunne and Owen, 2013).

## Co-curricular activities

Engaging co-curricular activities can include service and community-based learning, volunteering and internships, all of which are identified as high-impact activities that have the potential to enhance student retention and performance (Kuh et al., 2008). Student development weeks, festivals and student-led conferences can also offer opportunities for engagement with learning and wider academic life, where the crucial ingredient is that student contributions to the design and delivery of such activities are valued by students as well as staff. In many institutions such activities may be initiated by 'third space' professionals such as widening participation or employability teams, or by institutional centres for academic development, learning and teaching. Where there are clear connections with the academic curriculum and discipline-based staff are actively involved in the support and implementation of such initiatives, students can be more likely to regard the activities as contributing to their academic development as well as the enhancement of civic responsibility and interpersonal skills (Hébert and Hauf, 2015). Increasingly, HE institutions are adopting processes such as the Higher Education Achievement Report (www.hear.ac.uk/ accessed 21.9.15) to formally recognise the valuable contributions co-curricular experiences can have on the quality of students' learning, development and employability.

# Conclusion

There are numerous avenues for improving student engagement, and ultimately responsibility for doing so lies with each party: student, teacher, institution and the government (Kahu, 2013). This chapter has focused on the responsibility of the teacher set within the context of the contemporary landscape of HE. We have sought to place emphasis on the lived experience of being a teacher – the unique perspectives, challenges, limits and potential capacities of the role – and to heighten awareness of how engaging with the complexity of the learning relationship can open up possibilities for reducing barriers to students' meaningful engagement with their learning. The underlying assumption is that student engagement is fundamentally linked to staff engagement: with students, with the process of teaching and with oneself as a teacher; and furthermore, that the way in which we as teachers engage, or do not, with students has a significant influence on how students engage with us and with their learning.

## Questions for reflective practice and professional development

1  Think of a particularly engaging learning experience you have had as a student. What made it so engaging? Now ask yourself, how engaged am I with my current teaching? What barriers and opportunities are there to develop my practice?
2  How well do I know my students? How can I find out more about them, and how can I build this knowledge into my teaching and student support so as to encourage an inclusive and engaging learning environment?
3  How can I design curricula and assessment in ways that foster students' increased engagement with their learning, with each other, with my teaching?
4  How can I enable students to play an active role not only in their own learning, but also in the process of curriculum and assessment design as well as the development of course content?
5  How can I foster an environment of active enquiry, where my students and I work together as partners in the pursuit of learning and new knowledge, within and alongside the curriculum?

## Useful websites

### Higher Education Academy – students as partners webpages

www.heacademy.ac.uk/workstreams-research/themes/students-partners (accessed
    28.7.15)

### Engagement Through Partnership: students as partners in learning and teaching in higher education

Scholarly publication including conceptual model, examples of partnership,
identification of tensions and challenges.
www.heacademy.ac.uk/engagement-through-partnership-students-partners-learning-
    and-teaching-higher-education (accessed 28.7.15).

### Framework for Partnership in Learning and Teaching in Higher Education

Short guide to inspire practice.
www.heacademy.ac.uk/students-partners-framework-action (accessed 28.7.15).

### Student Engagement Guidance in UK Quality Code for Higher Education (Chapter B5), Quality Assurance Agency

www.qaa.ac.uk/en/Publications/Pages/Quality-Code-Chapter-B5.aspx#.
VbfF7VRwbIU (accessed 28.7.15)

### Active Learning Case Studies, University of Gloucestershire

http://insight.glos.ac.uk/tli/resources/toolkit/resources/alcs/Pages/default.aspx
    (accessed 28.7.15).

### RAISE (Researching, Advancing and Inspiring Student Engagement)

Network of academics, practitioners, advisors and students in higher education discussing, researching and disseminating good practice in student
engagement
http://raise-network.ning.com/ (accessed 28.7.15).

## References

Abegglen, S., Burns, T. and Sinfield, S. (2015) 'Voices from the margins: Narratives
    of learning development in a digital age', *The Journal of Educational Innovation,
    Partnership and Change*, 1 (1). Available at https://journals.gre.ac.uk/index.
    php/studentchangeagents/article/view/148 (accessed 28.7.15).
Andrews, J. and Clark, R. (2011) *Peer Mentoring Works! How peer mentoring enhances
    student success in higher education*. Birmingham: Aston University. Available at
    www.heacademy.ac.uk/resources/detail/what-works-student-retention/Aston-
    What_Works_Final_Reports-Dec_11 (accessed 10.7.15).

Barnett, R. (2007) *A Will to Learn: Being a student in an age of uncertainty.* Maidenhead: Open University Press and Society for Research in Higher Education.

Birmingham City Students' Union (2015) 'Student engagement: A state of mind'. Available at www.bcusu.com/learning/academicpartnerships/saps/ (accessed 10.6.15).

Bourdieu, P. and Passeron, J. C. (1979) *Reproduction in Education, Society and Culture.* London: Sage.

Bovill, C. (2013) 'Students and staff co-creating curricula: An example of good practice in higher education?', in E. Dunne and D. Owen (eds), *The Student Engagement Handbook: Practice in Higher Education.* Bingley: Emerald, pp.461–75.

Bovill, C. and Bulley, C. J. (2011) 'A model of active student participation in curriculum design: Exploring desirability and possibility', in C. Rust (ed.), *Improving Student Learning (18), Global theories and local practices: Institutional, disciplinary and cultural variations.* Oxford: Oxford Centre for Staff and Learning Development, pp.176–88.

Bryson, C. (ed.) (2014) *Understanding and Developing Student Engagement.* Abingdon: Routledge.

Carini, R., Kuh, G. and Klein, S. (2006) 'Student engagement and student learning: Testing the linkages', *Research in Higher Education*, 47 (1): 1–32.

Cook-Sather, A. (2013) 'Student–faculty partnership in explorations of pedagogical practice: A threshold concept in academic development', *International Journal for Academic Development*, 18 (1): 1–12.

Cook-Sather, A., Bovill, C. and Felten, P. (2014) *Engaging Students as Partners in Teaching and Learning: A guide for faculty.* San Francisco, CA: Jossey-Bass.

Davies, J. (2011). *Don't Waste Student Work.* Video. Available at http://tedxtalks. ted.com/video/TEDxOttawa-Jim-Davies-Dont-Wast (accessed 28.7.15).

Dunne, E. and Owen, D. (eds) (2013) *The Student Engagement Handbook: Practice in higher education.* Bingley: Emerald.

Dunne, E. and Zandstra, R. (2011) *Students as Change Agents: New ways of engaging with learning and teaching in higher education.* Bristol: University of Exeter/ESCalate/Higher Education Academy. Available at http://escalate.ac. uk/8064 (accessed 10.4.15).

Fraser, S. and Bosanquet, A. (2006) 'The curriculum? That's just a unit outline, isn't it?', *Studies in Higher Education*, 31 (3): 269–84.

Fromm, E. (1978) *To Have or to Be?* London: Jonathan Cape.

Gerstein, J. (2012) 'Flipped classroom: The full picture for higher education'. Available at https://usergeneratededucation.wordpress.com/2012/05/15/flipped-classroom-the-full-picture-for-higher-education/ (accessed 10.4.15).

Gibbs, G. (2014) 'Student engagement, the latest buzzword'. *Times Higher Education* (online). Available at www.timeshighereducation.co.uk/news/student-engagement-the-latest-buzzword/2012947.article (accessed 10.4.15).

Healey, M. and Jenkins, A. (2009) *Developing Undergraduate Research and Inquiry.* York: Higher Education Academy. Available at www.heacademy.ac.uk/node/3146 (accessed 163.15).

Healey, M., Flint, A. and Harrington, K. (2014) *Engagement Through Partnership: Students as partners in learning and teaching in higher education.* York: Higher

Education Academy. Available at www.heacademy.ac.uk/sites/default/files/resources/Engagement_through_partnership.pdf (accessed 16.3.15).

Hébert, A. and Hauf, P. (2015) 'Student learning through service learning: Effects on academic development, civic responsibility, interpersonal skills and practical skills', *Active Learning in Higher Education*, 16 (1): 37–49.

Higher Education Academy (2014) *Framework for Partnership in Learning and Teaching in Higher Education*. York: Higher Education Academy. Available at www.heacademy.ac.uk/students-partners-framework-action (accessed 16.3.15).

Jensen, K. and Bagnall, D. (2015) 'Student teaching and learning consultants: Developing conversations about teaching and learning', *Journal of Educational Innovation, Partnership and Change*, 1 (1). Available at https://journals.gre.ac.uk/index.php/studentchangeagents (accessed 1.3.15).

Kahu, E. R. (2013) 'Framing student engagement in higher education', *Studies in Higher Education*, 38 (5): 758–73.

Kandiko, C. B. and Mawer, M. (2013) *Student Expectations and Perceptions of Higher Education: Final report*. London: King's Learning Institute.

Keenan, C. (2014) *Mapping Student-led Peer Learning in the UK*. London: Higher Education Academy. Available at www.heacademy.ac.uk/node/10208 (accessed 16.3.15).

Kossak, S. (2011) *Reaching In, Reaching Out: Reflections on reciprocal mentoring*. Bloomington, IN: Balboa.

Kuh, G., Cruce, T., Shoup, R., Kinzie, G. and Gonyea, R. (2008) 'Unmasking the effects of student engagement on first-year college grades and persistence', *The Journal of Higher Education*, 79 (5): 540–63.

Leathwood, C. and O'Connell, P. (2003) '"It's a struggle": The construction of the "new student" in higher education', *Journal of Education Policy*, 18 (6): 597–615.

May, H. and Feslinger, A. (2010) *Strategic Approaches to Disabled Student Engagement*. York: Equality Challenge Unit and Higher Education Academy. Available at www.heacademy.ac.uk/resources/detail/inclusion/Disability/StrategicApproachesFinalReport (accessed 8.4.15).

Montesinos, I. A., Cassidy, D. and Millard, L. (2013) 'Student employment and the impact on student motivations and attitudes towards university', in C. Nygaard, S. Brand, P. Bartholomew and L. Millard (eds), *Student Engagement: Identity, motivation and community*. Faringdon: Libri.

Morgan, J. (2010) 'Audit overload', *Times Higher Education* (online). Available at www.timeshighereducation.co.uk/features/audit-overload/410612.article [accessed 287.15).

Moxley, D., Najor-Durack, A. and Dumbrigue, C. (2001) *Keeping Students in Higher Education*. London: Kogan Page.

NUS (2012) *A Manifesto for Partnership*. London: National Union of Students. Available at www.nusconnect.org.uk/campaigns/highereducation/partnership/a-manifesto-for-partnerships/ accessed 16.3.15).

NUS and HEA (2011) *Student Engagement Toolkit*. York: National Union of Students and Higher Education Academy. Available at www.nusconnect.

org.uk/campaigns/highereducation/student-engagement/toolkit/ (accessed 8.4.15).

Nygaard, C., Brand, S., Bartholomew, P. and Millard, L. (eds) (2013) *Student Engagement: Identity, motivation and community.* Faringdon: Libri.

O'Neill, P., Harrington, K. and Bakhshi, S. (2009) Training peer tutors in writing: A pragmatic, research-based approach, *Zeitschrift Schreiben.* Available at www. zeitschrift-schreiben.eu/cgibin/joolma/index.php?option=com_content&task=view&id=75&Itemid=32 (accessed 10.4.15).

Sambell, K. and Graham, L. (2011) 'Towards an assessment partnership model? Students' experiences of being engaged as partners in Assessment for Learning (AfL) enhancement activity', in S. Little (ed.), *Staff-student Partnerships in Higher Education.* London: Continuum, pp.31–47.

Sheffield Hallam University (2013) 'Course design consultancy'. Available at www. heacademy.ac.uk/resources/detail/resources/detail/change/11_12_case_study_forms/SAP_09_SHU (accessed 10.6.15).

Sinfield, S., Burns, T. and Holley, D. (2004) 'Outsiders looking in or insiders looking out? Widening participation in a post-1992 university', in J. Satterthwaite, E. Atkinson and K. Gale (eds), *The Disciplining of Education: New languages of power and resistance.* Stoke-on-Trent: Trentham Books.

Sinfield, S., Burns, T., Holley, D., Hoskins, K., O'Neill, P. and Harrington, K. (2010) 'Raising the student voice', in J. Hilsdon, C. Keenan and S. Sinfield (eds), *Learning Development in Higher Education.* London: Palgrave.

Solomonides, I., Reid, A. and Petrocz, P. (eds) (2012) *Engaging with Learning in Higher Education.* Farringdon: Libri.

Summers, P., Pearson, D., Gough, S. and Siekierski, J. (2013) 'The effects on student engagement of employing students in professional roles', in C. Nygaard, S. Brand, P. Bartholomew and L. Millard (eds), *Student Engagement: Identity, motivation and community.* Faringdon: Libri.

Taylor, C. A. (2012) 'Student engagement, practice architectures and *phronesis-praxis* in the student transitions and experiences project', *Journal of Applied Research in Higher Education,* 4 (2): 109–25.

Thomas, L. (2012) *Building student engagement and belonging in higher education at a time of change.* Final report from the What works? Student retention & success programme. York: Higher Education Academy. Available at www. heacademy.ac.uk/workstreams-research/themes/retention-and-success/what-works-student-retention-and-success-change (accessed 9.6.15).

Tinto, V. (2003) 'Learning better together: The impact of learning communities on student success', Higher Education Monograph Series. Syracuse, NY: Syracuse University.

Trowler, V. (2010) *Student Engagement Literature Review.* York: HEA. Available at www.heacademy.ac.uk/resources/detail/evidencenet/Student_engagement_literature_review (accessed 13.6.15).

University of Sheffield (2013) 'Student ambassadors for learning and teaching'. Available at www.sheffield.ac.uk/als/students/salt (accessed 17.6.15).

Vygotsky, L. (1978) *Mind and Society: The development of higher psychological processes.* Cambridge, MA: Harvard University Press.

Warren, D. (2002) 'Curriculum design in a context of widening participation in higher education', *Arts and Humanities in Higher Education*, 1 (1): 85–9.

Weller, S. and Kandiko Howson, C. B. (forthcoming 2016) 'Defining pedagogic expertise: Students and new lecturers as co-developers in learning and teaching', in *Teaching & Learning Inquiry*, special issue on students as co-inquirers.

Wimpenny, K. and Savin-Baden, M. (2013) 'Alientation, agency and authenticity: A synthesis of the literature on student engagement', *Teaching in Higher Education*, 18 (3): 311–26.

Wisker, G., Exley, K., Antoniou, M. and Ridley, P. (2008) *Working One-to-One with Students: Supervising, coaching, mentoring and personal tutoring*. London: Routledge.

# 7

# Embracing Student Diversity

Susannah McKee and Matt Scandrett

---

## Chapter overview

This chapter explores:

- the context of diversity
- encouraging a sense of belonging
- an inclusive curriculum and classroom
- supporting diverse students through the student lifecycle
- inclusive assessment
- inclusion: institutional policy and practice

---

## Introduction

Universities are undeniably more diverse than in the past. Society is more multicultural and globally mobile, and knowledge creation cannot be nationally or socially confined. Advances in equality legislation in the UK and elsewhere require universities to be proactive in ensuring individuals are not discriminated against and that all have equal opportunity to participate and show their ability. Sector-wide widening participation initiatives have sought to make higher education (HE) accessible to under-represented groups and government policies promote access (Department for Business, Innovation and Skills, 2014).

However, student diversity is complex and in trying to advance equality and fair representation we can find ourselves using rhetoric which labels people into 'groups' and can be counter-productive to inclusion. This terminology, from 'non-traditional' to 'international' and 'disabled', is found across the literature, but in using it, its limitations and contested nature need bearing in mind. Students vary in any number of ways and should be seen first and foremost as individuals in all their diversity.

Embracing diversity calls not just for wider access, but also the creation of inclusive learning environments, prompting dialogue on some complex and important questions. To what extent do universities need to *adapt* to a diverse student body as opposed to expecting students to *assimilate* to the university? (See Zepke and Leach, 2005, for discussion of these two positions.) How can diverse students best be retained and supported to successful outcomes?

This chapter seeks to examine practical ways in which we might actively embrace diversity for positive change in student experience for all members of the university community through inclusive teaching, which Hockings refers to as:

> The ways in which pedagogy, curricula and assessment are designed and delivered to engage students in learning that is meaningful, relevant and accessible to *all*. It embraces a view of the individual and individual difference as the source of diversity that can enrich the lives and learning of others. (2010: 1)

## Encouraging belonging for diverse students

### Building relationships

Students are often understandably concerned about their new environment and research suggests isolation and not fitting in are two of the major reasons why students consider leaving HE (Thomas, 2012). Consequently, it is imperative that all students are helped to gain a sense of belonging and feel comfortable within their faculty and department and the university as a whole. Perhaps most importantly, students need to feel comfortable among their peers and within the classroom. Bamber and Tett (2000) highlight the benefits of establishing a community in which difference is positively valued, and in which there is opportunity for students to support each other and share experience and challenges, for example through learning clusters or collaboration. See Thomas (2012) for more on the importance of friendship and peer support to student retention, including case studies of peer guidance and mentoring schemes in which 2nd/3rd year students support new entrants.

Mortiboys (2005) makes the link between retention, belonging and using learner names and stresses the importance of acknowledgment as a key factor in developing a student's sense of belonging. Learning students' names can make them feel valued and accepted and help establish student–staff relationships, while not doing so can have a negative impact (Thomas, 2012; Mortiboys, 2005; Howle, 2004). This can also be an important step in avoiding excluding and stereotyping some students by calling on students with more familiar names. Learning names of entire classes can of course be challenging, but the benefits of trying cannot be understated when dealing with students who may feel excluded or are struggling to see how they belong. See Howle (2004) and Mortiboys (2005) for activities which can be used to learn student names. Stronger relationships can also be built by showing an interest in the students' lives and experiences and listening to and empathising with their concerns, such as balancing study with other commitments they may have (e.g., childcare, family or work).

## The classroom

A number of steps can be taken to make the atmosphere as welcoming and as conducive to learning as possible. Chairs and tables can be rearranged to suit the planned teaching activity, horseshoes being particularly effective arrangements for an inclusive group dynamic (see Scrivener, 2012, for further ideas).

Activities which allow students to get to know each other as individuals could be employed at the beginning of the semester. Students in Scandrett's (2012) study indicated that being a member of a minority group (whether relating to culture, class, ethnicity, age, gender, sexuality, disability or religion) may lead to feelings of discomfort and intimidation and that opportunities to familiarise themselves and collaborate with their classmates were key in creating a positive classroom dynamic. This is supported by research which found that students who experienced more cross-racial interaction were more confident and reported 'significantly larger gains made in their knowledge of and ability to accept different races and cultures … [and] … growth in general knowledge, critical thinking ability and problem solving skills' (Chang et al., 2006: 449).

## Inclusive curricula

Morgan and Houghton (2011: 7) define an inclusive curriculum as 'one where all students' entitlement to access and participate in a course is anticipated, acknowledged and taken into account'. They highlight the need, particularly in light of equality legislation, for universities and their staff to adapt their policy and practice to ensure access and inclusion for all, rather than expecting individual students to adapt. This is in keeping with the principle of 'universal design', common in the disability literature, whereby accessibility for all is considered and built into courses from the very start (Hockings, 2010; Hall and Stahl, 2006). Morgan and Houghton (2011) propose six key principles of inclusive curriculum design, namely that as well as being anticipatory, it should be flexible, accountable, collaborative, transparent and equitable. Consideration of inclusiveness needs to be given not just in relation to course content, but also a range of aspects from course delivery to assessment. Mighty (2001: 4) calls for inclusive teaching to address 'the 3 big Cs', namely Content (what we should include), Conduct (learning processes) and Context (learning environment).

It is generally acknowledged that curricula across HE, indeed all mainstream education across the UK, are largely constructed from a Western standpoint, often limited to perspectives which fail to address the interests of groups or people who do not fall into this category (see Parekh, 2000; Turney et al., 2002; Purwar, 2004). Module reading lists largely ignore scholarship from Africa, Asia and Latin America, while work from British writers from black and minority ethnic (BME) backgrounds also tends to be limited, which 'ultimately privileges the voices and perspectives of predominantly Western thinkers and practices whilst marginalising the voices and perspectives of those deemed "non-Western"' (Turney et al., 2002: 22). Coupled with realities such as the educational underachievement of many students from minority ethnic backgrounds (Amin et al., 1997; Gillborn, 2008; HEFCE, 2014) and the dearth of BME academics in senior positions – out of 14,000 university professors in the UK, only 50 are black (Shepherd, 2011) – it is not hard to see how accusations of institutional racism have been levelled at the academy (see Back, 2004; Pilkington, 2011; Singh, 2011).

Despite the drive to widen participation, working-class students continue to be under-represented in UK HE overall and participation is uneven across the sector (Archer et al., 2003; Reay et al., 2010). Some working-class students may encounter tensions around the academic norms of the institutions and behaviours that are expected of them (Casey, 2005). This is often seen in disciplines which involve teaching based around discussion and dialogue, with some academics having an 'idea of appropriate forms of classroom discourse … much closer to middle-class than working-class norms' (Brookfield and Preskill, 1999: 145). This in turn can have far reaching consequences and a reliance on 'academic conventions or forms of speech that are disorienting and even intimidating to working-class students' (Teaching Resource Center, 2007). This highlights the need for consideration of the accessibility of language used in course documentation and delivery. (See Chapter 8: Engaging with Academic Writing and Discourse.)

Research has shown the effectiveness of teaching that acknowledges students' social identities with international, BME and non-traditional students doing better in modules which embrace diverse cultures and interests and include subject matter they can relate to (Hermida, 2010; Van Dyke, 1998). If care is taken to avoid tokenism and stereotyping (see Cousin, 2006), creating class content and developing curricula that reflects the diversity of the student body should ensure 'the inclusion and integration of voices, perspectives, works and ideas that come from beyond a "white", "eurocentric" core' (Turney et al., 2002: 84).

Equivalent challenges and opportunities arise in creating inclusive learning environments and curricula for lesbian, gay, bisexual and transgender (LGBT) students (Evans, 2000). Studies have consistently shown that LGBT students in HE rarely see themselves reflected back in the curriculum and where this does occur it is often in a stereotyped or negative manner (Gunn, 2010). While some have argued that this is less to do with the content of the curriculum and more to do with student cultures (Ellis, 2009), others have advocated a range of strategies for promoting inclusivity in the classroom. These include awareness raising of the importance of non-discriminatory language and communication (including challenging derogatory remarks), integrating material relating to LGBT perspectives on a subject in a positive light, omitting negative material, and acknowledging that certain fixed notions of gender and sexual identity formation may not serve all students equally well (Gunn, 2010).

Allowing different voices and multiple perspectives is one way that social justice and global citizenship can be incorporated into the classroom. These can be incorporated via multimedia sources, from music, film, video clips, performance, documentary, photography, social media and online discussion forums. This acknowledges the wider range of discourses and narratives present in students' lives, and may be more accessible and accommodating to a range of learning styles as well as being engaging stimuli for critical discussion. One example with potential to encourage criticality and the inclusion of different world views is the pedagogical use of hip-hop. Considering its global appeal and position as a leading social and cultural movement (Chang, 2005), utilising hip-hop as a teaching tool can be powerful as a medium which speaks directly to young people. A key part of its potential lies in the 'influence of rap as a voice of resistance and the liberation … [that] proliferates through such artists as Lauryn Hill … Public Enemy … and Mos Def, who endeavour to bring an accurate yet critical depiction of the urban situation to a hip-hop generation' (Morrell and Duncan-Andrade, 2002: 89). There are a growing number of artists who have a huge online following and speak directly to the younger generation from which they come. Work by such musicians, poets and activists as Akala, Lowkey and Suli Breaks might be used to raise discussion of mainstream values and promote criticality, and social justice. For examples of how hip-hop can be used across academic disciplines, see Stovall (2006), Akom (2009) and Hill (2009).

It is important to stress that the suggestion is not being made that important, core topics should not be taught on the basis that they may not be immediately relatable to students of particular demographic profiles, nor that topic appropriateness is fixed or can be assumed. Rather that the curriculum might include some flexibility for negotiation or tailoring of content according to the lives and interests of the students. Mighty (2001) highlights the importance of courses including and validating students' own experiences, while also offering opportunities to engage critically with the wide-ranging experience and perspectives of others. Indeed, in the UK Singh (2011) stresses that acknowledging students' backgrounds and experience of life in Britain is vital to not only ensure inclusivity but also in addressing racism. Furthermore, allowing connections with the issues that students face is also key in fostering critical awareness, and helping them prepare to take their place in a complex contemporary world (Flores, 2004).

## Working collaboratively

Collaborative activities are not only useful for helping students to gel, but also for allowing the students themselves to engage with diversity and become accepting of difference. It is important to incorporate a wide variety of tasks and approaches that allow students to collaborate and interact in different ways: 'Teaching for inclusion means that we must foster non-threatening learning environments or contexts characterised by safety and trust that will allow students to heighten their awareness of "self", of their unique social identities as well as of others who are culturally different' (Mighty, 2001: 6).

A key strength of the multicultural and diverse classroom is the sheer range and depth of skills, knowledge and experiences which students have to offer. Tasks that draw on this enable students to see each other as valuable resources, and benefit from developing broader and more multicultural perspectives and awareness (Caruana, 2011). An example is provided by Hellmundt et al. (1998) who suggest an activity in which students work in mixed nationality groups combining linguistic and cultural knowledge to complete a task. Gudykunst et al. (1991) give examples of a number of assignments to encourage awareness and understanding of intercultural communication, including intercultural communication logs, interviews and journals.

Role play can be effective in a number of ways, but can be particularly useful as a strategy that encourages students to engage with multiple perspectives and viewpoints. One simple approach sees the class divided into groups with each provided with a position to defend. Groups are then given a set amount of time to both prepare their arguments (and anticipate counter arguments) before joining together for a debate. Of course, it is important for students to be given the opportunity to discuss and refine their own opinions; however, activities that allow them to express and support different opinions can increase their own criticality, along with providing a change of pace which can spark a completely new classroom dynamic. La Trobe University in Australia have provided guidance to support the discussion and debate of controversial issues, such as the inclusion of ethical issues and religious beliefs (La Trobe, 2015).

## Inclusive and supportive learning materials

Readings and reading lists can be daunting. To make them more accessible, course texts can be progressively introduced and overviews of texts and terminology given. Remembering that many students may be balancing their studies with other roles and time pressures, it may be worth using shorter, more readable texts, certainly in the first few weeks. A range of text types, including narratives and dialogue (see, e.g., Fevre and Bancroft, 2010) can serve to build bridges gradually towards more abstract academic concepts.

Seminar activities to deconstruct course texts can help students to process core reading more effectively and appreciate how different writers put forward and support arguments. This can counter the idea of 'one truth' and help students gain confidence in using similar processes to say what they want to say, within the conventions of their discipline. Students can be further encouraged to engage personally with their reading through tasks such as writing summaries or critical responses to texts or identifying questions for discussion.

Academic texts can also be supplemented with a range of relevant, engaging and accessible multi-media sources. Not only do digital materials offer great potential for improving accessibility for disabled students, they also acknowledge that a range of formats from visual to audio and video may be preferred by all (Hall and Stahl, 2006). A blended learning approach incorporating content delivered digitally also recognises the need for flexibility for students to fit study with other commitments.

## Inclusive course development

Developing an inclusive course is likely to be an ongoing process rather than a one-off intervention. If we see the process as engaging with students as individuals, we need some built-in flexibility to be responsive to the students we are teaching, being aware that what worked well for a previous cohort may need adapting for the next. Reflection on the appropriateness of course content and delivery in relation to the cohort is a logical first step. Ideally this would involve both course teams and the students themselves (May and Bridger, 2010). Curricula and pedagogy would therefore not solely be based upon assumptions of what students want and need, but more the result of informed decisions based on previous experience, reflection and student feedback (see Chapter 6: Student Engagement, for more on students as partners). Opportunities for choice or negotiation can help a diverse student body begin to have a transformative impact on courses.

# Supporting diverse cohorts through the student lifecycle

In addition to engaging current students, efforts to diversify the curriculum have been shown to help with the recruitment of diverse cohorts, by creating a sense that this will be a broad and non-elitist environment (Yorke and Thomas, 2003). Any new university student is likely to encounter challenges and uncertainties, and this may well be amplified in the case of, for example, a student newly arrived from another continent, a mature student juggling part-time work and childcare with a return to study or indeed any student who finds the 'institutional habitus' in Bourdieu's (1991) terms (Thomas, 2002; Reay et al., 2010) to be at odds with what they have previously experienced. While early support is essential, induction should not be seen as simply 'information giving' in the first few days (Thomas, 2012). Ongoing support is needed. Indeed the whole first year of study has been shown to be particularly important to creating the feeling of belonging critical to student retention (Yorke and Thomas, 2003). Engestrom and Tinto (2008: 46) point out that 'Access without support is not opportunity'. Students on transnational and exchange programmes may be equally challenged by their new environment (Bamford, 2015).

## A mainstream approach

Research suggests that a mainstream, inclusive approach to supporting students within their courses is beneficial for all and avoids stigmatising certain groups as 'in deficit' and in need of remedial support or special arrangements (Thomas, 2012; Thomas and May, 2010). If courses are set up with embedded support for all, no assumptions about students are made and there is a reduced need for special arrangements which can label students under problematic 'categories'. Many of the practices which can be particularly helpful, for example, for some disabled students (advance provision of lecture slides or seminar materials, well-prepared hand-outs, both written and oral instructions) can be beneficial to all students (Fuller et al., 2008). Embedded academic skills can also have the advantage of helping all students with the practices and discourses of their disciplines, seeing these as part of becoming operational in the discipline rather than independent skills to be learnt or remedied out of context (Warren, 2002). (See Chapter 8: Engaging with Academic Writing and Discourse.)

This is not to ignore that individuals may have particular needs, and may either want or require (and have a legal right to) specific support. Legislation, notably the Equality Act 2010, is clear on the responsibility to ensure equality of opportunity. In the case of disability, HE institutions are required to make anticipatory 'reasonable adjustments' to ensure individuals are not disadvantaged or discriminated against (Cavanagh and Dickinson, 2006; Felsinger and Byford, 2010; ECU, 2012). Useful resources, such as the Equality Challenge Unit website, which enable staff to familiarise themselves with this legislation and develop inclusive practice, can be found at the end of the chapter. These include further guidance on inclusion and support for disabled students on a range of issues from disclosure procedures to competence standards to awareness of accessible materials and assistive technologies. For guidance on support and inclusive practice for students with dyslexia, who constitute the largest percentage of those disclosing a 'disability' or 'specific learning difference' in HE, see Waterfield et al. (2006). See also Fuller et al. (2004), Rickinson (2010) and Waterfield and West (2006) for important insights from the voices of disabled students.

## Case study

### Profoundly deaf student working in studio context

This case study (Fell, 2005) outlines the experiences of a profoundly deaf student enrolled in an HEI studio-based 1-year Foundation Diploma in Art and Design studies. It highlights considerations which may be relevant to supporting students with other disabilities, and indeed to supporting the wider student body.

*(Continued)*

*(Continued)*

In particular it demonstrates the importance of:

- ensuring needs assessment and adequate support are in place from the outset (in this case, as the student's first language was British Sign Language (BSL), a communication support worker (CSW) with relevant subject specialism, as well as additional English language support and the support of the college's diversity officer, in particular, for an overseas field trip);
- staff training (in this case, deaf awareness training and introduction to BSL);
- consideration of social integration/peer awareness raising (here, improved via a deaf awareness/basic BSL session delivered with input from the student);
- assistive technology (in this case, hearing loops equipment, email/text communication, text minicom);
- supportive materials and tutorials (here, clear, simple bullet-point lists for project briefs, visual aids and early opportunity for one-to-one discussion with tutor/CSW to clarify understanding);
- consideration of the physical environment (adequate lighting, clear view of speakers' lip patterns, accommodation assessment).

For further details, see Fell (2005) and accompanying case studies.

## Inclusive assessment

Concerns about assessments can be heightened among diverse cohorts including, for example, students who have limited or less successful previous experience of academic assessment, or international students new to the UK system, trying to work out expectations. As Carroll (2005) points out, however, adjustments to make the unwritten expectations or 'rules' of academia more explicit are again likely to be welcomed by all. Academic practices have been shown to be far from transparent, with variation in expectations between and within institutions, disciplines and individual tutors, and complexities in articulating these to students (Lillis, 2001). Carroll (2005) urges tutors to become aware that their own practices are a product of culture, rather than the 'correct' way and to try to deconstruct these to make expectations clearer to themselves and students, and indeed see where flexibility may be increased. (See Chapter 4: Assessment for Learning, for ways of supporting students towards assessment success.)

Inclusive assessment means not just being more explicit, but also widening the parameters for students to produce different responses to a given assessment or indeed to have some choice of assessment. This might simply mean a choice of focus within an assessed task, chance to apply theory to a situation of the student's choice related to their own life or work or to present work in a range of formats, from work-based reports to case studies, web pages or reflective journals, alongside more traditional academic essays. In our own practice with diverse cohorts we have incorporated multimedia assessments such as digital stories, which give students time to prepare a series of images with their own voice-over to produce personalised and original outcomes that can be engaging for an audience of peers without the performance anxiety associated with presentations (see Gravestock and Jenkins, 2009 for more on digital storytelling).

Waterfield and West (2006) put forward a strong case, based on their 3-year research study, for an inclusive approach in which a flexible range of assessment types (from portfolios to viva voce exams, practical work to work placement reports, research projects to open book exams) are offered to allow all students to demonstrate the achievement of the learning outcomes. They propose this as a more sustainable and universally beneficial approach, encompassing different learning styles and preferences, in contrast with a 'contingent approach' of 'special arrangements' or an 'alternative approach' (Waterfield and West, 2006: 15) of a different assessment type only for disabled students. More varied and flexible assessment gives scope to credit students' diverse strengths and arguably to encourage more original and interesting outcomes, potentially in a range of formats relevant to varied post-university employment.

Embracing diversity may call for 'approaches that are more encompassing of students' linguistic repertoires' (Preece and Martin, 2010: 5), or at least greater willingness to see beyond surface academic discourse proficiency to focus on the content, that is, the student's thinking, learning and depth of understanding (Ryan, 2005). In a study among international students at a UK university, students expressed frustration that language may cloud evaluation of their other abilities (Sovic, 2008). Arguably if students have met stated entry requirements, institutions need to show some acceptance of linguistic range. Reflecting on assessments and assessment criteria can be a first move towards a greater focus on rewarding for achievement of learning outcomes rather than excessive penalising for 'non-standard' or 'non-native' English. Curzan (2013) proposes a pedagogy of working with students to raise their awareness of and ability to access more standard academic prose rather than deducting marks for so-called 'errors'.

Calls for greater acceptance can raise questions about fair marking and concerns over 'dumbing-down' of academic standards. Caruana (2011) counters this by pointing out that embracing multiple voices and perspectives is indicative of quality and rigour, and indeed in keeping with the principle of criticality. She recognises the need for a degree of balance: 'In effect inclusion involves negotiating a balance between affirming students' funds of knowledge and identities and bridging the gap in cultural academic capital to succeed' (p.3). Both supporting students and valuing their individual resources and backgrounds can maintain high expectations and increase the likelihood of their being achieved.

## Case study

### Choice in assessment

This study (Easterbrook et al., 2005) concerns a diverse cohort (10 per cent disabled students, 5 per cent mature students and 17 per cent international students) taking a Behaviour of Structures, Engineering module at the University of Plymouth. Students had not traditionally excelled in the module assessment, which had varied between labs, tests and exams and required both qualitative and quantitative skills.

Over a three-year period, an action research project was carried out whereby students were able to choose their preferred form of assessment on the module, rather than this being the same for all. Choices included an end-of-module test, coursework (including worked examples), a portfolio (including explanation of principles which could be visual/diagram-based) and weekly tests. Students were required to take responsibility for deciding which form would suit them best, taking into account, for example, learning style and strengths, time management considerations and performance under exam conditions.

As well as leading to an improvement in average marks, student feedback was 99 per cent positive. Whilst it was recognised that there were challenges in terms of time/resourcing to set up and mark the assessments, ensuring equity between the different assessments and clear examples of each, these benefits, together with the resources saved in not requiring special arrangements for any students, were felt to more than offset these.

## Institutions, departments and individuals

Individual practitioners actively seeking to engage with diverse student populations in their courses on a day-to-day basis can have a very real impact. However, since student experience generally includes different modules or courses, dealings with various professional services from libraries to career guidance, as well as social interactions in the university community, it is important to share best practice and engage with inclusivity within and across course teams, departments and the whole institution. Research supports the need for action at both individual and institutional level (May and Bridger, 2010). Institutions have a clear legal obligation to ensure equality. Commentators have criticised tokenistic 'tacking on' of additional measures to address racism (Turney et al., 2002) or to meet the needs of disabled students (Rickinson, 2010), calling instead for equality to be embedded within all activities from the outset, 'necessitating a shift away from supporting specific groups through a discrete set of policies or time bound interventions, toward equity considerations being embedded within all functions of the institution and treated as an ongoing process of quality enhancement' (May and Bridger, 2010: 2).

Examples of how institutions can start to make this shift include defining and auditing inclusive learning and teaching, including it in institutional strategy and in learning and teaching policy and carrying out equality impact assessments (see Thomas and May, 2010).

## Conclusion

Real engagement with diversity is clearly a crucial ongoing process, calling for action at all levels and sharing of best practice across the sector. Given the extent of this process, we have only been able to touch briefly on some of the issues here. Viewing this as an ongoing part of all mainstream activities of the institution and a responsibility of all members of the community rightfully prioritises equality issues and increases the likelihood of positive progress, transformation and enhancement for all.

## Questions for reflective practice and professional development

1  In what ways is your course curriculum inclusive to all? How do you embrace diversity and encourage students to do the same in your classes?

2  How inclusive is your course assessment? How much flexibility, choice and range is there? How are diverse students supported towards assessment success? How inclusive are your assessment criteria?

3  How is your institution engaging with equality and diversity in terms of policy and practice?

## Useful websites

### Equality Challenge Unit

www.ecu.ac.uk/
This website provides a range of resources and advice to support and further equality and diversity within UK HE, including legislative guidance.

### *Inclusive Curriculum Design in Higher Education*, Higher Education Academy

www.heacademy.ac.uk/resources/detail/inclusion/Disability/Inclusive_curriculum_design_in_higher_education
Provides links to a variety of sources of support for HE practitioners engaging with inclusive practice, including a number of research syntheses.

### *Cultural Diversity and Inclusive Practice*, Flinders University

www.flinders.edu.au/cdip/toolkit/teaching.cfm
The Teaching and Learning folios contain strategies and suggestions for enhancing inclusive practices in teaching environments. They offer self-assessment tools to assist the reader to reflect on and evaluate current practices and provide links to other resources available.

### *Learning to Teach Inclusively*, University of Wolverhampton (supported by JISC and the HEA)

www.wlv.ac.uk/about-us/internal-departments/centre-for-academic-practice/wolverhampton-learning-and-teaching-projects/learning-to-teach-inclusively/

An online 'tailor-able' open education resource focussing on inclusive practice, available to HEI staff through the Open University, OpenLearn website, for accredited professional development.

*Inclusive Teaching, Learning and Assessment*, **University of Plymouth**

Research-informed resources, guidance and videos.
www.plymouth.ac.uk/your-university/teaching-and-learning/inclusivity

# References

Akom, A. A. (2009) 'Critical hip hop pedagogy as a form of liberatory praxis', *Equity & Excellence in Education*, 42 (1): 52–66.

Amin, K., Drew, D., Fosam, B. and Gillborn, D., with Demack, S. (1997) *Black and Ethnic Minority Young People and Educational Disadvantage*. London: Runnymede Trust.

Archer, L., Hutchings, M. and Ross, A. (eds) (2003) *Higher Education: Issues of Inclusion and Exclusion*. London: RoutledgeFalmer.

Back, L. (2004) 'Ivory towers? The academy and racism', in I. Law, D. Phillips and L. Turney (eds), *Institutional Racism in Higher Education*. Stoke-on-Trent: Trentham Books, pp.1–6.

Bamber, J. and Tett, L. (2000) 'Transforming the learning experiences of non-traditional students: A perspective from higher education', *Studies in Continuing Education*, 22 (1): 57–75.

Bamford, J. K. (2015) 'A window to the world: The challenges and benefits of transnational joint Masters programmes for internationalising the curriculum in business', in W. Green and C. Whitsed (eds), *Critical Perspectives on Internationalising the Curriculum in Disciplines: Narrative accounts from business, education and health*. Rotterdam: Sense.

Bourdieu, P. (1991) *Language and Symbolic Power*. Cambridge: Polity Press.

Brookfield, S. D. and Preskill, S. (1999) *Discussion as a Way of Teaching: Tools and techniques for university teachers*. Buckingham: SRHE and Open University Press.

Carroll, J. (2005) 'Strategies for becoming more explicit', in J. Carroll and J. Ryan (eds), *Teaching International Students: Improving learning for all*. London: Routledge, pp.26–34.

Caruana, V. (2011) *Internationalising the Curriculum: Exploding myths and making connections to encourage engagement*. York: Higher Education Academy. Available at https://www.heacademy.ac.uk/resource/internationalising-curriculum-exploding-myths-and-making-connections-encourage-engagement

Casey, J. G. (2005) 'Diversity, discourse, and the working-class student', *Academe*, 91 (4): 33–6.

Cavanagh, S. and Dickinson, Y. (2006) *Disability Legislation: Practical guidance for academics*. York: HEA, Equality Challenge Unit. Available at www.ecu.ac.uk/wp-content/uploads/external/disability-legislation-guidance.pdf (accessed 18.9.15).

Chang, J. (2005) *Can't Stop, Won't Stop: A history of the hip-hop generation.* New York: Picador.

Chang, M. J., Denson, N., Sanex, V. and Kimberly, M. (2006) 'The educational benefits of sustaining cross-racial interaction among undergraduates', *Journal of Higher Education*, 77 (3): 430–55.

Cousin, G. (2006) 'Beyond saris, samosas and steel bands', *Academy Exchange*, 5: 34–5.

Curzan, A. (2013) 'Dinging for "grammatical errors"', *The Chronicle of Higher Education*, 14 August. Available at http://chronicle.com/blogs/lingua-franca/2013/08/14/dinging-for-grammatical-errors/ (accessed 18.9.15).

Department for Business, Innovation and Skills (2014) *National Strategy for Access and Student Success in Higher Education.* London: HEFCE and OFFA. Available at https://www.gov.uk/government/uploads/system/uploads/attachment_data/file/299689/bis-14-516-national-strategy-for-access-and-student-success.pdf

Easterbrook, D., Parker, M. and Waterfield, J. (2005) *Higher Education Academy Engineering Subject Centre Assessment Choice Case Study.* Plymouth: University of Plymouth, pp.1–9. Available at www.plymouth.ac.uk/files/extranet/docs/SWA/LTSN%20CS.pdf (accessed 18.9.15).

ECU (2012) *Equality Act 2010, Implications for colleges and HEIs* (revised). London: Equality Challenge Unit. Available at www.ecu.ac.uk/publications/equality-act-2010-revised/

Ellis, S. J. (2009) 'Diversity and inclusivity at university: A survey of the experiences of lesbian, gay, bisexual and trans (LGBT) students in the UK', *Higher Education: International Journal of Higher Education and Educational Planning*, 57 (6): 723–39.

Engestrom, C. and Tinto, V. (2008) 'Access without support is not opportunity', *Change*, 40 (1): 46–50.

Evans, N. J. (2000) 'Creating a positive learning environment for gay, lesbian, and bisexual students', in M. B. Baxter Magolda (ed.), *Teaching to Promote Intellectual and Personal Maturity: Incorporating students' worldviews and identity into the learning process*, New Directions for Teaching, 32. San Francisco, CA: Jossey-Bass, pp.81–7.

Fell, B. (2005) 'Profoundly deaf student working in studio context', in *Being Inclusive in the Creative and Performing Arts, Case Studies*, CADISE (The Consortium of Arts & Design Institutions in Southern England). York: HEA, pp.39–52. Available at www.incurriculum.org.uk/files/1236949230/cad016_case_study_final.pdf (accessed 18.9.15).

Felsinger, A. and Byford, K. (2010) *Managing Reasonable Adjustments in Higher Education.* London: Equality Challenge Unit. Available at www.ecu.ac.uk/wp-content/uploads/external/managing-reasonable-adjustments-in-higher-education.pdf (accessed 18.9.15).

Fevre, R. and Bancroft, A. (2010) *Dead White Men and Other Important People: Sociology's big ideas.* Basingstoke: Palgrave Macmillan.

Flores, B. (2004) 'Sheep in wolf's clothing: The paradox of critical pedagogy', *Racial Pedagogy*, 6 (1). Available at www.radicalpedagogy.org/radicalpedagogy8/Sheep_in_Wolfs_Clothing__The_Paradox_of_Critical_Pedagogy.html (accessed 22.8.13).

Fuller, M., Georgeson, J., Healey, M., Hurst, A., Kelly, K., Riddell, S., Roberts, H. and Weedon, E. (2008) *Disabled Students in Higher Education: Experiences and Outcomes*, TLRP Research Briefing 46. London: Institute of Education. Available at www.tlrp.org/pub/documents/Fuller%20RB%2046%20FINAL.pdf (accessed 18.9.15).

Fuller, M., Healey, M., Bradley, A. and Hall, T. (2004) 'Barriers to learning: A systematic study of the experience of disabled students in one university', *Studies in Higher Education*, 29 (3): 303–18.

Gillborn, D. (2008) *Racism and Education: Coincidence or conspiracy?* London: Routledge.

Gravestock, P. and Jenkins, M. (2009) 'Digital storytelling and its pedagogical impact', in T. Mayes, D. Morrison, H. Mellar, P. Bullen and M. Oliver (eds), *Transforming Higher Education through Technology-enhanced Learning*. York: Higher Education Academy. Available at https://www.heacademy.ac.uk/resource/transforming-higher-education-through-technology-enhanced-learning

Gudykunst, W., Ting-Toorney, S. and Wiseman, R. (1991) 'Taming the beast: Designing a course in intercultural communication', *Communication Education*, 40 (1): 1–14.

Gunn, V. (2010) *Lesbian, Gay, Bisexual, and Transgender (LGBT) Perspectives and Learning at University*. Glasgow: University of Glasgow. Available at www.gla.ac.uk/media/media_175529_en.pdf (accessed 18.9.15).

Hall, T. and Stahl, S. (2006) 'Using universal design for learning', in A. Adams and S. Brown (eds), *Towards Inclusive Learning in Higher Education: Developing curricula for disabled students*. Oxford: Routledge.

HEFCE (2014) 'New HEFCE analysis shows significant link between factors such as ethnicity, gender and school type on achievement in higher education'. Available at www.hefce.ac.uk/news/newsarchive/2014/Name,94018,en.html (accessed 18.9.15).

Hellmundt, S., Rifkin, W. and Fox, C. (1998) 'Enhancing intercultural communication among business communication students', *Higher Education Research & Development*, 17 (3): 333–43.

Hermida, J. (2010) 'Inclusive teaching: An approach for encouraging non-traditional student success', *The International Journal of Research and Review*, 5: 19–30.

Hill, M. L. (2009) *Beats, Rhymes, and Classroom Life: Hip-hop pedagogy and the politics of identity*. New York: Teachers College Press.

Hockings, C. (2010) *Inclusive Learning and Teaching in Higher Education: A synthesis of research*. York: Higher Education Academy. Available at https://www.heacademy.ac.uk/resources/detail/resources/detail/evidencenet/Inclusive_learning_and_teaching_in_higher_education

Howle, D. (2004) 'A way to learn names', *The Teaching Professor*, 18 (5): 2–6.

La Trobe University (2015) *Cultural Diversity: Teaching into practice strategies*. Melbourne: La Trobe University. Available at www.latrobe.edu.au/students/equity/equity-and-diversity-documents/Inclusive-Practices-for-Managing-Controversial-Issues.pdf (accessed 18.9.15).

Lillis, T. (2001) *Student Writing: Access, regulation and desire*. London: Routledge.

May, H. and Bridger, K. (2010) *Developing and Embedding Inclusive Policy and Practice in Higher Education*. York: Higher Education Academy. Available at https://www.heacademy.ac.uk/resource/developing-and-embedding-inclusive-policy-and-practice-higher-education

Mighty, J. (2001) 'Teaching for inclusion: The challenges and opportunities of diversity in the classroom', *Focus on University Teaching and Learning*, 11 (1): 1–8. Available at www.dal.ca/content/dam/dalhousie/pdf/clt/Focus/vol11no1.pdf (accessed 18.9.15).

Morgan, H. and Houghton, A. (2011) *Inclusive Curriculum Design in Higher Education*. York: Higher Education Academy. Available at https://www.heacademy.ac.uk/resources/detail/inclusion/Disability/Inclusive_curriculum_design_in_higher_education

Morrell, E. and Duncan-Andrade, J. M. (2002) 'Promoting academic literacy with urban youth through engaging hip-hop culture', *English Journal*, 7: 88–92.

Mortiboys, A. (2005) *Teaching with Emotional Intelligence: A step-by-step guide for further and higher education professionals*. London: Routledge.

Parekh, B. (2000) *The Future of Multi-Ethnic Britain: The Parekh report*. London: The Runnymede Trust.

Pilkington, A. (2011) *Institutional Racism in the Academy: A case study*. Stoke-on-Trent: Trentham Books.

Preece, S. and Martin, P. (2010) 'Imagining higher education as a multilingual space', *Language and Education*, 24 (1): 3–8.

Purwar, N. (2004) 'Fish in or out of water: A theoretical framework for race and the space of academia', in I. Law, D. Philips and L. Turney (eds), *Institutional Racism in Higher Education*. Stoke-on-Trent: Trentham Books, pp.49–50.

Reay, D., Crozier, G. and Clayton, J. (2010) '"Fitting in" and "standing out": Working-class students in UK higher education', *British Educational Research Journal*, 32 (1): 1–19.

Rickinson, M. (2010) *Disability Equality in Higher Education: A synthesis of research*. York: Higher Education Academy. Available at www.heacademy.ac.uk/resources/detail/evidencenet/disability_equality_synthesis (accessed 18.9.15).

Ryan, J. (2005) 'Improving teaching and learning practices for international students', in J. Carroll and J. Ryan (eds), *Teaching International Students: Improving learning for all*. London: Routledge, pp.92–100.

Scandrett, M. (2012) 'The student experience of seminars at London Metropolitan University and how to improve engagement and participation', MA Dissertation. London Metropolitan University, London.

Scrivener, J. (2012) *Classroom Management Techniques*. Cambridge: Cambridge University Press.

Shepherd, J. (2011) '14,000 British professors – but only 50 are black', *Guardian*, 27 May.

Singh, G. (2011) *A Synthesis of Research Evidence. Black and minority ethnic (BME) students' participation in higher education: Improving retention and success*. York: Higher Education Academy. Available at https://www.heacademy.ac.uk/resource/black-and-minority-ethnic-bme-students-participation-higher-education-improving-retention

Sovic, S. (2008) *Lost in Transition? The International Students' Experience project*. London: CLIP, CETL, University of the Arts. Available at www.adm.heacademy.

ac.uk/resources/features/the-international-students2019-experience-project-at-ual-issues-of-engagement-for-international-students-in-art-and-design/

Stovall, D. (2006) 'We can relate hip-hop culture, critical pedagogy, and the secondary classroom', *Urban Education*, 41 (6): 585–602.

Teaching Resource Center (2007) *Teaching a Diverse Student Body: Practical strategies for enhancing our students' learning*. Charlottesville, VA: Center for Teaching Excellence. Available at http://cte.virginia.edu/resources/teaching-a-diverse-student-body-practical-strategies-for-enhancing-our-students-learning/

Thomas, L. (2002) 'Student retention in higher education: The role of institutional habitus', *Journal of Educational Policy*, 17 (4): 423–32.

Thomas, L. (2012) *Building Student Engagement and Belonging in Higher Education at a Time of Change: Final report from the What Works? Student Retention and Success Programme*. London: Paul Hamlyn Foundation. Available at www.heacademy.ac.uk/resource/building-student-engagement-and-belonging-higher-education-time-change-final-report-what

Thomas, L. and May, H. (2010) *Inclusive Learning and Teaching in Higher Education*. York: Higher Education Academy. Available at https://www.heacademy.ac.uk/resource/inclusive-learning-and-teaching-higher-education

Turney, L., Law, I. and Philips, D. (2002) *Institutional Racism in Higher Education, Building the Anti-racist University: A toolkit*. Leeds: Centre for Ethnicity & Racism Studies. Available at http://cers.leeds.ac.uk/files/2013/05/the-anti-racism-toolkit.pdf (accessed 18.9.15).

Van Dyke, R. (1998) 'Monitoring the progress of ethnic minority students: A new methodology', in T. Acland and T. Modood (eds), *Race and Higher Education*. London: University of Westminster.

Warren, D. (2002) 'Curriculum design in a context of widening participation in higher education', *Arts and Humanities in Higher Education*, 1 (1): 85–99.

Waterfield, J. and West, B. (2006) *Inclusive Assessment in Higher Education: A resource for change*. Plymouth: University of Plymouth. Available at www.plymouth.ac.uk/uploads/production/document/path/3/3026/Space_toolkit.pdf (accessed 18.9.15).

Waterfield, J., West, B. and Chalkley, B. (2006) *Developing an Inclusive Curriculum for Students with Dyslexia and Hidden Disabilities*. Gloucester: Geography Discipline Network, University of Gloucestershire. Available at www2.glos.ac.uk/gdn/icp/idyslexia.pdf (accessed 18.9.15).

Yorke, M. and Thomas, L. (2003) 'Improving the retention of students from lower socio-economic groups', *Journal of Higher Education Policy and Management*, 25 (1): 63–75.

Zepke, N. and Leach, L. (2005) 'Integration and adaptation: Approaches to the student retention and achievement puzzle', *Active Learning in Higher Education*, 6 (1): 46–59.

# 8

# Engaging with Academic Writing and Discourse

Julian Ingle

## Chapter overview

This chapter explores:

- the challenges of teaching and learning academic writing and discourse
- students' perspectives on writing at university
- approaches to academic writing development
- writing intensive approaches
- co-teaching writing in the discipline

## Introduction

This chapter examines some of the challenges of teaching academic writing in higher education (HE), as well as the difficulties students encounter when learning how to write in their disciplines or subject areas. Although it takes a multilayered view of university-level writing and the ways it can be understood (Ivanič, 2004), the argument of the chapter is that teaching and learning about writing are most effective when situated within the discipline or subject area. One of the outcomes of a more discipline-based writing approach is that it enables students to become participants in their disciplinary or subject area communities.

After a brief outline of some of the challenges presented by academic writing, we consider students' attitudes to writing. Next is a meta-study that shows how writing has been addressed at an institutional level. The accounts of practice that follow the meta-study illustrate how some of the challenges can be addressed; how and why we might expand and use the resources and range of texts available to students and staff; and ways that discussions on writing and conceptual development, speech and dialogue have been incorporated.

# What are the challenges of 'academic writing'?

Written assignments, outputs, texts, however we characterise the different forms of writing that students produce, are widely thought of as the main institutional index of the quality of students' education at the level of the module or programme, department and even the university as a whole. The position of writing is key, because for most students it is predominantly the measuring of these grades that, on aggregate, constitute their final degree classification. What follow are some of the key challenges of teaching and learning academic writing.

## Teaching academic writing – some challenges for staff

1 Differences in educational cultures and backgrounds, experiences of and attitudes to writing mean that students bring with them a huge range of abilities and assumptions about writing (Monroe, 2003). For example, students who have taken a UK GCE A-level route through the sciences (such as many medical students) at age 18 may have done no extensive writing since their UK GCSE examinations at age 16 (Ivanič and Lea, 2006). Others with strengths in numeracy may have chosen a particular degree intending to avoid writing, such as engineering, only to discover that it is unavoidable. The progressive internationalisation of HE brings students with a wealth of experience and ability, who also provide valuable opportunities for new insights and perspectives on teaching and learning. For example, Western stereotypes about Chinese learning approaches, that they are rote learners and therefore lack critical approaches to their writing, were recently challenged by researchers at Durham University, who found that Chinese students' motivation was to learn for understanding not memorisation (Matthias et al., 2013). Although this is a complex and contested area, the research identified students' main difficulties as cultural and linguistic, that is, acculturation to Western university life and discourse.

2  The valued forms of writing students' produce at university are often tightly prescribed. This can be problematic and in some cases, disabled students for example, we are legally required to provide assessment methods that are equivalent, but different, to writing. Addressing student diversity can mean adapting the curriculum, in this case around writing, adaptations that frequently benefit all students. For example, how might you think about an alternative assessment to writing for a physically disabled student who has limited fine and gross motor control and uses a keyboard and voice recognition software?

3  Progressively larger intakes, shrinking resources and new and emergent digital technologies (e.g., distance learning courses, MOOCs, virtual learning environments) may result in higher student: staff ratios. The amount of time and attention academic staff have to devote to writing can therefore be limited.

4  Academic staff may feel that it is not their job to teach writing but to teach content (Bean, 2011). They may feel that they do not have the time and space in the curriculum for improving students' disciplinary writing or giving early feedback on written drafts, for instance.

5  Most academics' understanding of writing is gained through a lengthy process of study, research and teaching in their discipline and enculturation into their specialist areas. Much of this knowledge is tacit and is not easily explicable or taught (Turner, 2011).

## Learning academic writing – some challenges for students:

a  Learning to negotiate the complex, often unwritten codes of writing in a discipline takes time and practice (Monroe, 2003; Lea and Street, 1998; Clark and Ivanič, 1997). Students therefore need explicit guidance and time to practice. Time is also a factor in managing the simultaneous assessment demands of a range of modules or units, possibly across the disciplines, which requires excellent organisational abilities. This organisational burden can be lessened if tutors take a whole programme or course approach to scheduling assessments.

b  Academic writing may appear mysterious to students (Lillis, 1999); and tutors' expectations of writing are often unclear to students. While a drive for explicitness was in response to the opacity of certain educational practices, the relentless focus on learning outcomes, rubrics and criteria for evaluating writing may not be helpful if students do not understand the disciplinary differences and meanings of concepts such as 'critical analysis', structure and evidence, nor the ways in which certain knowledge and values are privileged in the disciplines

(Becher, 1981; North, 2005). For these reasons much of the feedback students receive on their writing can seem vague or indistinct.

c   Students may well have moved on to new areas of study by the time they get feedback on their work, may not read it and therefore are unable to take forward the comments into new work. There is little currency in the idea that you can learn to write as a decontextualised academic skill and then transfer this ability to any context or discipline (Lea and Street, 1998; Russell, 2000; Monroe, 2003). Academic Literacies research argues against the misconception 'that writing is a single universally applicable skill, largely unrelated to "content"' (Russell, 1990: 53), or that language is a transparent medium (Lillis, 2001) or conduit of meaning. Meanings are located in contexts and while certain strategies and writing activities may be transferable across contexts, the resulting forms of making meaning remain context specific.

While there are students who enjoy writing, the following section concerns a majority, who struggle for a variety of reasons, not the least of which is the very intimate nature of writing; for example, that something often experienced as very personal then becomes a public record.

## Students' attitudes to and experiences of writing

Research with undergraduate students reports that pain, dread, confusion and misery are frequently how students describe the experience of writing (Ivanič, 1998; Leedham, 2014; Murray, 2012). Ingle and Yakovchuk (2015) used freewriting as a technique to explore students' attitudes to writing (in this case medical students who as novice academic writers and researchers working towards possible publication are also future medical practitioners, possibly future academics). One student commented, 'There is no room to breathe or express yourself. You could say this is typical of medicine as a whole subject, not just research' (p.49).

When it comes to students' views about written feedback on their writing, there is sometimes a sense that a mysterious lexicon is being used that only tutors understand, which limits the value of feedback to students: 'The essay doesn't flow' is a comment I get frequently. I still don't know what they mean. Red pen on your work or just exclamation marks; what's the message? If there is no more explanation, students just leave it and move on' (Bailey, 2009: 5).

Although in Leedham's (2014) study 90 per cent of students said that they had received some teaching about academic writing, this was often felt to be too vague or minimal to be of use: 'I'm surprised how little help we get with writing our assignments at university, especially considering the fact that we had a whole module in a semester on how to use a PC' (p.4). Leedham reported that it isn't until Masters level that many students feel they get to grips with writing: 'I have never been taught how to write academically, I'm slowly learning during the Masters course, learning through the mistakes I make' (p.5).

There are many ways in which students can be supported in their academic writing and understanding of disciplinary discourse. Some of these are illustrated through the following case study, which discusses certain ideas and approaches that inform the work of an institution-wide initiative: Thinking Writing at Queen Mary University of London. Thinking Writing's role is fairly unique in the sector. While there have been similar initiatives in UK HE (and many of the ideas are widely used elsewhere), these have tended to be focused on one particular discipline (examples of different institutional approaches to academic writing can be found in Thaiss et al., 2012 and Deane and O'Neill, 2011). In contrast, the scope of Thinking Writing's work is across the whole university, supporting the professional development of teaching staff; finding ways to use writing to develop disciplinary thinking and to 'develop graduate level writing'; and, in partnership with academic staff to review and challenge practices and support change in order to respond to and meet students' needs. Additional accounts of the work, such as case studies, discipline-specific resources, reflections, accounts of the projects can be found on the website listed at the end of this chapter. (I am currently a member of Thinking Writing and while I broadly represent their work and ideas, I make no particular claim on the work or ideas. Although we work very much as a team, individual members, past and present, bring their own perspectives, concerns and interests to Thinking Writing).

## Case study

### Thinking Writing as institutional practice

The case study proposes:

- that writing is used as a pedagogical device to learn disciplinary content, thinking, concepts and discourse;
- that learning to write does not equate to learning to write essays;
- that students' writing is not a (or their) problem but is 'usefully problematic'. (Mitchell and Evison, 2006: 79)

'No one approach to writing or its development is advocated by Thinking Writing' (McConlogue et al., 2012: 205). The focus is more about the collaborative and negotiated nature of the work that has, as its main aim, improved student learning. We therefore work closely with staff, often over long periods of time (sometimes several years or more). This might entail any combinations of the following: observations of teaching, co-teaching with academic staff, working together on a particular project, or simply conversations about the work academics are involved in. In addition to the work itself, what usually comes out of these collaborations is greater insight into each other's practices that then inform our and their pedagogy.

For example, what might start as a conversation about the poor standard of essays on a particular module, students' inability to punctuate, or use appropriately formal language, might shift to questions about the syllabus, or group dynamics or graduate attributes. What may emerge from these conversations are ways of reframing curriculum design, assessment and teaching and learning and how writing could be used to learn, question and explore subjects students are studying. The emphasis is more on how writing can be used to engage students more fully with course content rather than with the surface features of their writing. A more detailed picture of this kind of development work, in this case in geography, can be found in Horne and Peake (2011).

Here are typical examples of how writing can be used as a pedagogical device:

- Designing short, formative writing tasks into the curriculum of a module to explore particular concepts or key themes.
- Designing written assessments that have more than one stage (an iterative approach) to create opportunities for feedback that will help improve the next stage.
- Providing opportunities for peer review or peer assessment of writing.
- Designing reading into writing tasks to strengthen the connections between reading and writing.

What these ideas look like in practice depends on the intention and focus of the staff, module or curriculum. Short tasks might range from writing for three or four minutes before, during or at the end of a lecture on a question about the previous lecture; initial ideas about the

*(Continued)*

*(Continued)*

topic, concept or areas that are unclear; to more scaffolded tasks such as defining, identifying or exploring key concepts. In mathematics, for example, students might be asked to write explanations of mathematical notation, or are given a plot of a function, followed by the question 'Describe accurately the behavior of the following function'. It is worth noting that many of these short tasks can also be adapted for developing academic reading (indeed many of the ideas and approaches described throughout this chapter would apply equally well to reading).

Here is a brief example of this approach in a module on global change biology, where the curriculum was redesigned to include iterative and peer review stages. In the module, students design an experiment to test for an increase in decomposition rates of organic matter in different ecosystems. Before the experiment ends they have to write the introduction and methods section of a scientific report on the experiment. The students then peer review each other's drafts, which are also reviewed by the tutors. To scaffold the process, students are given a set of questions to work through to help with the peer review. Students learn a great deal from scrutinising the work of their peers as it helps them to better understand assessment requirements and to think and respond critically to their work (O'Gorman et al., 2014). It may also be less intimidating for students to get feedback from a peer than an 'expert' academic, and they may be more inclined to listen and share thoughts about writing with someone at their level.

While it may seem that designing in formative writing opportunities simply creates more work for staff, this is frequently not the case. Students often engage more attentively with content and gain a sharper understanding, which results in better quality work that is easier to mark because of the tutor's greater familiarity with the work in progress.

Underlying some of the work described so far is a change in emphasis from the finished product or text to supporting the learning and writing processes.

## Forms of academic writing

The essay is traditionally viewed as the main vehicle for presenting an academic argument. Over time, however, this vehicle and argument have become conflated, such that the essay as a form now equates to an argument (Mitchell, 2010). Therefore when reductive ways of teaching the essay form are introduced (e.g., 'You should say what you're going to say, then say it, and then say what you said') what can emerge is very distorted writing and a lack of argument; this is perhaps one of the reasons why academic staff complain about their students' lack of critical thought. This is not to say that the essay, or rather the essayistic, is not of value. Two examples of teaching practice that try to reconnect with the idea of the essayistic can be found in discussions of their work by Catherine Maxwell and Kirsteen Anderson; the former based on her course on nineteenth-century aesthetic prose and the latter a course on twentieth-century French literature (Maxwell, 2010; Anderson, 2010). Critical self-commentaries, portfolios, short reflective or creative texts and a logbook were designed into the curriculum to try to recapture the critical consciousness, style and voice that were typical of the great essay writers like Montaigne, Hazlitt and Barthes (Maxwell, 2010; Anderson, 2010; Mitchell, 2010). At the same time students were 'learning through writing' in ways that enabled staff and students 'to question and explore established practices of disciplinary knowledge-making' (Mitchell, 2010: 188).

Dependence on the traditional essay may seem anachronistic given the ways that new technologies have altered the topographies of writing. Blogs, wikis, websites (e.g., tagging, social bookmarking, the semantic web) incorporate a range of audio-visual media, texts, style and genres or modalities of representation. Social media and other digital interfaces are part of the fabric of contemporary life; and the impact of digital technologies within HE are one of the reasons why writing has become an expanded and more complex term (Lillis, 2011). What writing, particularly writing at university, has therefore become is increasingly vague and insecure (Kress, 2010). Students already draw on this growing hybridity of texts and technologies in their work, using a range of media when preparing for assessment (Lea and Jones, 2011). Paradoxically, when it comes to written assessment, partly as a result of its regulatory role, what counts and is counted in HE can be quite a limited range of resources (Lillis, 2011).

What these new modes of representation offer are opportunities to expand the range of texts available for learning and assessment. This does not preclude the more normative, traditional essay, but opens up the possibility of including modes of communicating knowledge that could be adapted to 'the greater diversity of the student population' (Lillis and Turner, 2001: 66). However, implicit in the use of these new forms of digitally, aurally and visually mediated texts is the need to determine how we evaluate them in terms of assessment, and in terms of the kinds of thinking they generate.

To take an example, the School of Electronic Engineering and Computer Science (EECS) at Queen Mary University of London had for some time offered a first-year study skills course for over 250 students which included a surfeit of writing assignments (curriculum vitae, essays, reports, profile statements etc.), usually taught as a series of guest lectures by staff from across the university. What the inclusion of all these different tasks signal is a decontextualised view of writing: students are asked to write for lots of different readers without situating the writing in any purposeful context. In response to concerns about retention, attendance on the course, and the need to develop students' ability to communicate science to a range of audiences as a purposeful activity, a team of EECS and Thinking Writing staff, supported by colleagues at the universities of Birmingham and Leicester with expertise in these areas, designed and piloted a new curriculum (funding for which was secured from the National HE STEM Programme as part of the Transfer Practice Adopters scheme). Assessment included a three-minute video (a group task) on an area of science or technology and an article for a series of magazines used for outreach in secondary schools (for examples of the magazines, see www.cs4fn.org/ accessed 21.9.15). Key to the curriculum design was to link assessment to the discipline. A series of mini-lectures by researchers in EECS and people from industry (to reflect the need to meet accreditation by industry) provided the topics for the articles and videos.

The work continues and to date, student satisfaction and attendance have increased, some of the videos produced were exemplary and the best articles were published in the magazines and online. What we learned and valued were:

- The importance of purposeful communication (Ivanič, 2004) and situating writing in context.
- Contrasting visual and verbal modes of communication can shed light on both. When making videos lots of valuable writing happens (planning, scripting and storyboarding) and it is easy to overlook or undervalue these texts.
- Group work in the first year as a way of building relationships and a sense of belonging.
- Collaboration across the sector and with colleagues in the university allows you to share expertise and thinking, which give staff opportunities for reflection on practice.

If we acknowledge that 'the quality of writing and the quality of intellectual inquiry are inseparable from each other' (Monroe, 2007: 66), then it follows that as students grapple with new ideas, troubling concepts and unfamiliar terminology, this struggle will sometimes be reflected in their writing. It could be argued that as students strive to understand and make sense of complex ideas and then represent them in the unwritten codes and conventions of their discipline that we should expect to see signs of this struggle, and should respond with appropriate guidance. Rather than say that a student has a problem with writing, as if this is something specific and inherent in them as individuals, we need to look beyond the text and recognize that there may be other things happening. As Haggis (2003: 95) argues in her critique of the overused metaphor of deep and surface learning, '"understanding", like "meaning", is non-specific, and therefore inherently problematic'. In other words, not only is understanding specific to each discipline or subject area, but this often remains a tacit understanding among the academic staff in their discipline. Therefore, when we assess students for their understanding (manifest, for example, in written coursework) it can sometimes be viewed as some kind of reified state that they should all attain without struggle (Haggis, 2003).

The so-called problem of student writing therefore points us in interesting directions. If we understand academic writing as complex, bound up within the 'site specific features of the local educational and disciplinary contexts' (Kelly and Bazerman, 2003: 32), and reflecting the values and beliefs of these contexts, then we situate the problem in a more comprehensive frame. The traditional essay is a case in point. For many students despite (and perhaps because of) the explicit criteria and guidelines surrounding an essay, it remains 'an act of hopeful but uncomprehending compliance with a set of external and ... "mysterious" rules' (Winter, 2003: 118). The following more specific ideas address different aspects of this struggle to understand the complexities of academic writing:

- *Clarifying assessment requirements* – teaching staff may know the features of a good piece of work (when they see it) in response to an assignment, but this may be a tacit understanding that is not reflected in explicit assessment criteria. For example, what are the specific features of a good argument in your discipline or subject area?
- *Dialogue* – different kinds of dialogic 'interactions around texts' (Lillis, 2006) provide valuable insight for students and staff. Therefore we should make space in the curriculum for discussions (and writing) with students about the kinds of judgements being made about the qualities of texts (using either previous or current students' writing), or analyse what feedback means within disciplinary contexts.

- *Exploratory writing* – using and valuing the differences between 'casual speech and careful writing' (Elbow, 2012: 141) in activities such as free-writing, reading essays aloud to oneself and others, varieties of conversations with oneself that can happen in journal writing (or using smartphone recordings), are examples of powerful tools that can open up writing practices. Encouraging looser ways of writing can help over-come anxieties around painfully slow, polished writing practices through a more iterative approach. Valuing this work can be done through assignments that create a patchwork text, that is, an incremental assem-blage of short and varied pieces of writing that are eventually 'stitched together' (Winter, 2003: 112).

The two accounts that follow, one from the humanities and the other from the sciences, are designed to bring together some of the ideas and approaches described so far and illustrate what these might look like in practice. It is worth remembering that these are not fixed and complete solutions to particular problems but rather describe particular points in the evolution of these courses.

## Account of practice: Catalan culture – history, language, art

The first account is based on work that draws on a Writing in the Dis-ciplines (WiD) approach at Queen Mary, University of London. The module concerned provides an overview of twentieth-century Catalan history, art, cultural movements, sociolinguistics and politics.
   This account of practice outlines:

- what is often referred to as a writing-intensive approach to cur-riculum design that devotes time and space to writing in the discipline;
- ways of using writing to engage with and learn content;
- the use of a variety of forms and genres of writing.

The course leader initiated the work partly as a result of attending the annual consortium of WiD at Cornell University, an institution at the heart of developing this particular approach. Prompted by this experi-ence but also by a strong sense that despite having a well-organised and interesting course, 'students didn't seem to be learning what [he] was teaching' (Mitchell and Evison, 2006: 75), the course leader decided to include additional writing activities into the module.

However, simply inserting more writing activities into a course is no guarantee that students' thinking or writing will improve. This is what was discovered after the first iteration. So while it was clear to the course leader that writing and content should go together, putting this into practice was not so easy. In this case, and more generally with these ways of working, what is often required is to redesign the curriculum in such a way that opportunities for different kinds of writing are coherently integrated in the curriculum (Mitchell and Evison, 2006: 75) so that it becomes, in effect, a writing-intensive course.

So from a broad framework, and in collaboration with writing and curriculum developers, the course was redesigned from scratch to ensure that the possibility of fully exploring the potential for *writing as a means of thinking and learning* was at the centre. In practice, this involved careful staging and sequencing of writing activities. These ranged from 'warm-up exercises ("what do you want to find out today?") to analytical summaries – one sentence, one paragraph, one page. It means short homework assignments – say a 300 word account of the seminar to be shared in the next session. It means a writing journal' (Mitchell and Evison, 2006: 76). Assessment was by coursework only and consisted of: a 2,000-word essay, independently produced (50 per cent); a 1,250-word essay, peer-reviewed, re-drafted and re-submitted (20 per cent); a critical review of another student's essay (15 per cent); a writing journal and selection of short writing tasks (15 per cent).

All of which sounds like a lot, and provokes concerns about, first, the amount of marking involved, and second, the amount (or lack) of content coverage of the course. First, not everything is formally marked and many of the writing activities are very short, but more importantly, according to the course leader, because the quality of the work is higher, 'more focused' and well-argued, the marking is 'less onerous ... and above all, it's more fun for me and more fun for the students' (Mitchell and Evison, 2006: 76). Second, the reality was that while it may appear that students are covering less, because they are engaging more critically with the literature and their own writing, they are actually learning more.

In contrast to what is often thought of as a remedial position (and practices) in which writing is taught only to those problematic students

*(Continued)*

*(Continued)*

by specialists in units outside the discipline or as a separate module bolted on to a course, the ethos of a WiD approach is that writing and thinking are best taught and evaluated by academic staff in the disciplines or subject areas where this takes place (Monroe, 2007). Writing does not have to be confined to assessment. Rather, there can be a degree of flexibility in which the processes of writing are foregrounded, providing scope to understand the complex connections between thinking, writing and learning. Writing then becomes a means for students to learn disciplinary content, to gain a more explicit understanding of what is required, to practise and rehearse their writing in a controlled, safe environment. In this way the somewhat false dichotomy of the procedural and conceptual aspects of the subject area are brought together.

## Account of practice: Co-teaching in the sciences

The second account discusses an approach to writing and discourse in the sciences, in this case medicine, that is more typical of a semi-integrated approach to teaching writing (for an outline of different institutional models of writing development in UK universities, see Warren, 2002). The work comprises a series of co-taught research writing sessions (writing development tutors with disciplinary tutors) embedded into a number of intercalated degrees at the Barts and the London School of Medicine and Dentistry. Although nominally co-teaching, all aspects of the writing sessions are done jointly, from designing the writing syllabus, planning the sessions and teaching to the evaluation and review. Part of the rationale for co-teaching is that the presence of an academic member of staff with a writing tutor signals to students that writing is being taken seriously, and is not an add-on activity.

The main purpose of this account is to exemplify:

- the role of dialogue when collaborating and co-teaching writing;
- the need to look beyond language to discourse and identity;
- ways of making the tacit explicit.

Students in the third or fourth year of a five-year medical degree can opt to study for an additional year (an intercalated BSc Hons degree) and gain an additional award. Questions raised by external examiners and staff about disparities between some students' lack of ability to write research projects and their much greater fluency in vivas and presentations was one of the prompts for a collaboration between Thinking Writing and intercalated teaching staff. Some of the challenges were high expectations of the staff, a range of research supervisors and the students' lack of familiarity with research writing, all of which was compounded by the fact that the majority had taken a science route through A-level, and although they had been reading and writing on the medical degree many had done little extensive writing.

In the first instance a series of writing sessions were co-designed, the focus of which was primarily the assessed research project and, in particular, the literature review. The staff were keen that research projects and literature reviews were published, so assessment requirements mirrored the author guidelines of the *British Journal of Sports Medicine* (BJSM), a key journal in their field. Based on discussions about what makes good writing for this kind of journal, and using analysis of the language and style of articles from the target journal, a framework of four sessions was agreed.

The possibility of publication was important for the students (and for the University, as it augmented their research profile) because it could be added to their educational record, improve their standing in the job market and set them on an academic training pathway. In terms of their identities, therefore, students had to negotiate the transition from writing for assessment to writing for publication. Although the research project ostensibly covered the same content, the project for assessment was presented as a single author piece, with acknowledgements to research staff involved. Once the project had been submitted for assessment, it was then up to the research staff and students to decide if they wanted to aim for publication. At this point the report then becomes a co-authored piece with the research staff. As one of the co-authors, the student is then involved in the lengthy re-drafting process and the negotiations that surround the politics of publication, such as the order in which the authors appear on co-authored papers, which has particular significance in the sciences (Ingle and Yakovchuk, 2015).

*(Continued)*

*(Continued)*

Class time was devoted to exploratory writing activities, such as freewriting or short bursts of timed writing that used prompts to explore identity and power relations within their field. Discussions were consciously opened up around these themes with the students and co-teachers. The presence of an outsider (the writing advisor/ co-teacher with a background in the humanities) may also have enabled more explicit discussion of questions around knowledge, meaning making, power and identity. Not that it is possible to step outside one's own particular disciplinary discourse or identity and assume another's (Gee, 1990), but the contrast between different disciplinary cultures can help put each discipline in sharper relief. The intention was that by making explicit some of the 'values, beliefs and practices' (Ivanič, 1998: 344) of their subject area, students would gain more 'complex insider knowledge' (p.344) about the research writing cultures of their discipline.

What is particularly interesting when analysing journal articles in the classroom context (e.g., noticing rhetorical devices or linguistic moves), is that the collaboration of a discipline specialist, who brings their expertise to bear on the content, and a writing advisor who brings their understanding of discourse and writing, results in a much closer focus on meaning. Not only is there more balance in the attention given to the text but the artificial separation between language and content often becomes blurred and disappears. This blurring reflects the ways that writing and language are not distinct from the meaning and knowledge being represented.

The opportunities for dialogue that co-teaching offer (in the joint planning, teaching and evaluation) between the tutors themselves and with the students open up the potential for a rich exchange of ideas about the way knowledge is constructed or meaning made within a discipline, and the ways that this can be taught and learned. Discovering some of these tacit understandings and practices around writing and discourse is yet another way to challenge the mysterious practices of academic writing (Lillis, 1999).

At first glance, it may seem that co-teaching within the discipline is a resource-intensive and time-consuming approach to academic writing development. However, the conversations, dialogue and reflection that these kinds of collaboration enable can benefit all those involved. Although a lot of co- and team-teaching happens on courses and programmes, this tends to be by discipline or subject-area teams. There is a small but significant shift when co-teaching with somebody from a different field, who is at a remove from our normal practice, a difference that can open up a space for critique and reflection.

# Conclusion

To return to an earlier point about resisting an approach to writing development that is detached from the curriculum, there are grounds for why this resistance should be sustained:

- Teaching writing should reflect the complex of connections between, writing, knowing and doing (Schulman, 2005; Reynolds, 2010).
- The changing topography of writing outside and inside the university presents new challenges to this complex, as well as opportunities to extend the repertoire of modes of communication for students.
- The changing topography of writing can provide a range of modes for students to engage meaningfully with, learn about and represent their understanding of a discipline or subject area, and consideration of these modes can help meet the needs of an increasing diversity of students.

Many of the principles and ideas that inform this chapter assume that writing and discourse are completely entangled within the ways of knowing and being of a discipline; that is, their epistemologies (and ontologies). Therefore, if students are to learn and acquire this discourse, a good place to start is in the discipline itself, perhaps working collaboratively with either educational/learning developers or academic staff with expertise in curriculum development and writing to enable students to make these ways of knowing more explicit, to use writing (and reading) as devices to not only learn content but also to provide time and opportunities to practice and get feedback. That there can therefore be some kind of textbook for disciplinary writing that definitively captures these peculiar languages is unrealistic (Reynolds, 2010). This is not only because academic disciplines and subject areas are substantially different from each other, but also because they are not static, circumscribed categories. From time to time, for example, inter- and cross-disciplinary drives emerge, come and go, such as more recently the resurgence of the life sciences. If students are to negotiate their way through these communities, learn to speak and write in their peculiar languages, learn the ways of knowing and being of these singular discourses (Bartholomae, 1985), then this needs to happen within these contexts.

The influences of digital media and learning technologies are altering the ways that students write and the landscapes of academic writing. The compulsory use of virtual learning environments (VLEs) and web-based interactions pose useful challenges to assessment and the ways that we evaluate what is produced. What areas of learning and thinking can we explore in these new media? The challenge is how we make these changes and new requirements explicit to students and explore the opportunities that digital media provide in teaching and learning the ideas and discourse of these disciplinary communities.

'Who we are affects how we write, whatever we are writing' (Ivanič, 1998: 181) and therefore with the increasing diversity of students in HE, what the proliferation of new modes of communication offers is the possibility of reflecting and valuing these different identities. Many, but by no means all, students bring in considerable expertise or experience of digital media, expertise that they can not only share but which teaching staff could learn from and use in, for example, a more co-created curriculum.

## Questions for reflective practice and professional development

1 What do you want students to learn about thinking in the discipline? (e.g., processes of enquiry, experimentation, observation, reading, analysis, argument).
2 What do you want students to learn about the disciplinary ways in which thinking is expressed (e.g., aspects of genre, style, structure, references to authority, integration of quotations)?
3 What kinds of writing would it be possible or desirable for your students to do (e.g., convergent with disciplinary norms or challenging of/alternative to disciplinary norms)?
4 How could you adapt writing tasks and assessments to reflect the diverse needs of your students?
5 How will you evaluate whether students have learned features of the disciplinary thinking and writing of your discipline?

(Adapted from Mitchell and Evison, 2006)

# Useful websites, further reading

**Thinking Writing**

www.thinkingwriting.qmul.ac.uk.
Provides a resource for teachers in HE, exploring connections between thinking and writing.

**Association for Learning Development in Higher Education**

www.aldinhe.ac.uk/home.html
ALDinHE is the Association for Learning Development in Higher Education. Their website has a wealth of resources and networking opportunities with a common desire to empower students in their learning through helping them make sense of academic practices within HE.

Bean, J. (2011) *Engaging Ideas*. San Francisco, CA: Jossey-Bass.
John Bean's book is not only an excellent resource for ideas and approaches to developing writing tasks that can be adapted to the disciplines, it also gives useful guidance on assessing writing, and much more.

Ganobcsik-Williams, L. (ed.) (2006) *Teaching Academic Writing in UK Higher Education*. Basingstoke: Palgrave Macmillan.
A helpful overview of approaches and practices based on the work of practitioners and researchers from UK Higher education.

# References

Anderson, K. (2010) The whole learner: The role of imagination in developing disciplinary understanding, *Arts and Humanities in Higher Education*, 9 (2): 205–21.

Bailey, R. (2009) Undergraduate students' perceptions of the role and utility of written assessment feedback, *Journal of Learning Development in Higher Education*, (1): 1–14.

Bartholomae, D. (1985) Inventing the university, in M. Rose (ed.), *When a Writer Can't Write: Studies in writer's block and other composing process problems*. New York: Guilford, pp. 273–85.

Bean, J. (2011) 'Backward design: Towards an effective model of staff development in writing in the disciplines', in M. Deane and P. O'Neill (eds), *Writing in the Disciplines*. Basingstoke: Palgrave MacMillan., pp.215–35.

Becher, T. (1981) 'Towards a definition of disciplinary cultures', *Studies in Higher Education*, 6 (2): 109–122.

Clark, R. and Ivanič, R. (1997) *The Politics of Writing*. Abingdon: Routledge.

Deane, M. and O'Neill, P. (eds) (2011) *Writing in the Disciplines*. Basingstoke: Palgrave MacMillan.

Elbow, P. (2012) *Vernacular Eloquence: What speech can bring to writing*. New York: Oxford University Press.

Gee, J. (1990) *Social Linguistics and Literacies: Ideology in discourses*. Basingstoke: Falmer.

Haggis, T. (2003) 'Constructing images of ourselves? A critical investigation into 'approaches to learning' research in higher education', *British Educational Research Journal*, 29 (1): 89–104.

Horne, D. and Peake, K. (2011) 'Writing hazards', in M. Deane and P. O'Neill (eds), *Writing in the Disciplines*. Basingstoke: Palgrave MacMillan, pp.103–19.

Ingle, J. and Yakovchuk, N. (2015) 'Writing development, co-teaching and academic literacies: Exploring the connections', in K. Harrington, T. Lillis, S. Mitchell and M. Lea (eds), *Working with Academic Literacies: Research, theory, design*. Fort Collins, CO: Colorado State University, WAC Clearinghouse.

Ivanič, R. (1998) *Writing and Identity: The discoursal construction of identity in academic writing*. Amsterdam: John Benjamins.

Ivanič, R. (2004) 'Discourses of writing and learning to write', *Language and Education*, 18 (3): 220–45.

Ivanič, R. and Lea, M. (2006) 'New contexts, new challenges: The teaching of writing in UK higher education', in L. Ganobcsik-Williams (ed.), *Teaching Academic Writing in UK Higher Education*. Basingstoke: Palgrave Macmillan, pp. 6–14.

Kelly, G. J. and Bazerman, C. (2003) 'How students argue scientific claims: A rhetorical–semantic analysis,' *Applied Linguistics*, 24 (1): 28–55.

Kress, G. (2010) *Multimodality*. London: Routledge.

Lea, M. and Jones, S. (2011) 'Digital literacies in higher education: Exploring textual and technological practice', *Studies in Higher Education*, 36 (4): 377–93.

Lea, M. and Street, B. (1998) 'Student writing in higher education: An academic literacies approach', *Studies in Higher Education*, 23 (2): 157–72.

Leedham, M. (2014) '"Enjoyable", "okay", or "like drawing teeth"? Chinese and British students' views on writing assignments in UK universities', *Journal of Academic Writing*, 4 (1): 1–11.

Lillis, T. (1999) 'Whose "common sense"? Essayist literacy and the institutional practice of mystery', in C. Jones, J. Turner and B. Street (eds), *Students Writing in the University: Cultural and epistemological issues*. Amsterdam: John Benjamins, pp.127–47.

Lillis, T. (2001) *Student Writing: Access, regulation, desire*. Abingdon: Routledge.

Lillis, T. (2006) 'Moving towards an "academic literacies" pedagogy: Dialogues of participation', in L. Ganobcsik-Williams (ed.), *Teaching Academic Writing in UK Higher Education*. Basingstoke: Palgrave Macmillan, pp.30–43.

Lillis, T. (2011) 'Legitimizing dialogue as textual and ideological goal in academic writing for assessment and publication', *Arts and Humanities in Higher Education,* published online 25 July.

Lillis, T. and Turner, J. (2001) 'Student writing in higher education: Contemporary confusion, traditional concerns', *Teaching in Higher Education*, 6 (1): 57–68.

Matthias, J., Bruce, M. and Newton, D. (2013) 'Challenging the Western stereotype: Do Chinese international foundation students learn by rote?', *Research in Post-Compulsory Education*, 18 (3): 221–38.

Maxwell, C. (2010) 'Teaching nineteenth-century aesthetic prose: A writing-intensive course', *Arts and Humanities in Higher Education*, 9 (2): 191–204.

McConlogue, T., Mitchell, S. and Peake, K. (2012) 'Thinking writing at Queen Mary, University of London', in C. Thaiss, G. Bräuer, P. Carlino, L. Ganobcsik-Williams and A. Sinha (eds), *Writing Programs Worldwide: Profiles of academic writing in many places*. Fort Collins, CO: Colorado State University, WAC Clearinghouse, pp.203–11.

Mitchell, S. (2010) 'Beyond the schooled form and into the discipline: An introduction to writing-intensive courses in UK Humanities', *Arts and Humanities in Higher Education*, 9 (2): 185–9.

Mitchell, S. and Evison, E. (2006) 'Exploiting the potential of writing for educational change at Queen Mary, University of London', in L. Ganobcsik-Williams (ed.), *Teaching Academic Writing in UK Higher Education: Theories, practices and models*. Basingstoke: Palgrave Macmillan, pp.68–84.

Monroe, J. (2003) 'Writing and the disciplines', *Peer Review*, 6 (1). Available at www.aacu.org/publications-research/periodicals/writing-and-disciplines (accessed 18.9.15).

Monroe, J. (2007) 'Writing, assessment, and the authority of the disciplines', *Educational Studies in Language and Literature*, 8 (2): 59–88.

Murray, R. (2012) 'Social writing', in L. Clughen and C. Hardy (eds), *Writing in the Disciplines: Building supportive cultures for student writing in UK higher education*. Bingley: Emerald, pp.187–210.

North, S. (2005) 'Disciplinary variation in the use of theme in undergraduate essays', *Applied Linguistics*, 26 (3): 431–52.

O'Gorman, E., Ingle, J. and Mitchell, S. (2014) 'Promoting student participation in scientific research: An undergraduate course in global change biology', *Double Helix*, 2: 1–13. Available at http://qudoublehelixjournal.org/index.php/dh/article/view/18/148 (accesssed 23.7.15).

Reynolds, J. (2010) 'Writing in the discipline of anthropology – theoretical, thematic and geographical spaces', *Studies in Higher Education*, 35 (1): 11–24.

Russell, D. (1990) 'Writing across the curriculum in historical perspective: Toward a social interpretation', *College English*, 52 (1): 52–73.

Russell, D. (2000) 'Learning to write and writing to learn across the university: The US experience', in M. Graal and R. Clark (eds), *Writing Development in Higher Education: Partnerships across the curriculum*. Leicester: University of Leicester, Teaching and Learning Unit, pp.1–13.

Schulman, L. (2005) 'The Signature Pedagogies of the Professions of Law, Medicine, Engineering, and the Clergy: Potential Lessons for the Education of Teachers', speech delivered at the Math Science Partnerships (MSP) workshop *Teacher Education for Effective Teaching and Learning* hosted by the National Research Council's Center for Education, 6–8 February, in Irvine, California.

Thaiss, C., Brauer, G., Carlino, P., Ganobcsik-Williams, L. and Sinha, A. (2012) *Writing Programs Worldwide: Profiles of academic writing in many places*. Fort Collins, CO: Colorado State University, WAC Clearinghouse.

Turner, J. (2011) 'Rewriting writing in higher education: The contested spaces of proofreading', *Studies in Higher Education*, 36 (4): 427–40.

Warren, D. (2002) 'Curriculum design in a context of widening participation in higher education', *Arts and Humanities in Higher Education*, 1 (1): 85–99.

Winter, R. (2003) 'Contextualizing the patchwork text: Addressing problems of coursework assessment in higher education', *Innovations in Education and Teaching International*, 40 (2): 112–22.

# 9

# Effective Supervision

## Dave Griffiths and Digby Warren

### Chapter overview

This chapter explores:

- the complexity of the supervision process
- what makes a good supervisor
- themes and elements of good supervision
- new challenges for supervision
- the supervisor as navigator

## Introduction

Academic supervision is a complex and multi-layered process that operates at a variety of academic levels and within a variety of learning spaces, the purpose of which is to support learners along a path of sustained, independent work. At its core, the driver of the process, is an interpersonal relationship that has the potential to enable and validate learning or, conversely, to hinder and subdue it.

Typically, those who occupy the role of academic supervisor either acquire it as a general academic duty or, in the worst cases, may simply have had the role thrust upon them. Either way, the practice of supervision is far more complex than the generic guidance commonly found in 'supervisor's handbooks' could ever hope to support.

This chapter outlines what this complexity means for the practice and process of academic supervision, explores some new perspectives on the different elements that constitute the process and suggests some practical responses to the many challenges generated by the complexity of supervision today. It will be particularly useful if you are new to the supervision role, although experienced supervisors are also invited to read what follows and engage in some reflection on their own relationship to the supervision process.

## Questions for reflection

From your own understanding and experience of academic supervision:

- How does it feel for a student to be meeting a supervisor for the very first time?
- Do you think that feeling would be different if the student was preparing for an undergraduate or Master's dissertation, or for a doctoral thesis? If so, in what way would it be different?
- As a supervisor, would you prepare differently if the student you were meeting was preparing for an undergraduate or Master's dissertation, or for a doctoral thesis? What would you do differently?
- Would it make any difference to your preparation if you knew the student was an international student?

When asked to think about supervision, the model that springs most readily to mind is likely to be the one-to-one and face-to-face relationship between an academic member of staff and a student who is undertaking some substantial piece of research work generally leading to the award of a PhD. This 'Oxbridge' or 'British' model of the supervision relationship (Kiley, 2009: 294; Leonard et al., 2005: 136) is, of course, a stereotype and one that is becoming increasingly outmoded as newer approaches to the supervision relationship are being crafted such as online, communities-of-practice, coaching, mentoring and combinations of those approaches (Manek, 2004; Dysthe et al., 2006; Crossouard, 2008; de Beer and Mason, 2009). As Johnson (2007: 259) says, these are approaches and relationships that are 'connected, collaborative, and increasingly reciprocal[ly] developmental'.

If the nature of the supervisory relationship is changing, then so too is the idea that the expected product of research work for which supervision is required is a doctorate taken on a full-time basis. These days, student-focused, largely independent and sustained work, of which there is often a 'substantial research component' (Todd et al., 2004), is now a feature of many undergraduate and Masters' degree programmes (Healey et al., 2013; Boud and Costley, 2007; Anderson et al., 2006; Dysthe et al., 2006). These extended pieces of independent work (Boud and Costley, 2007: 120), often known as 'dissertations' or 'projects', nevertheless require some element of academic supervision which is 'now a ... pervasive aspect of academic work in virtually every department' (Delamont et al., 2004: 6).

While these pieces of work may not involve the kind of protracted time-scale imposed by the completion of a PhD, they often mirror many of the intellectual and emotional challenges inherent in higher degree research work. They also represent, for the student, the opportunity to engage in what Kamler and Thomson refer to as 'identity work' (2006: 56). Through their studies, students engage in processes of meaning creation and sense-making that serve to reshape their beliefs, values and sense of 'self'. In this way, they often 'undergo a change in the way they understand their learning and themselves as learners ... which can be a challenging experience ... as they transform their ways of viewing knowledge and themselves' (Kiley, 2009: 293, Noble, 2011: 2), for 'as in any creative endeavour, the work of research is transformative – of the researcher as of the work itself' (Salmon, 1992: 9–10). The support of this kind of personal and professional development is also a feature of the domain of supervision.

So a new supervision landscape is emerging, one within which entirely novel forms of practice are developing. There is a reshaping taking place in the logistical processes of research as supervisors are also being required to 'service' their students, squaring their supervision practices with a variety of technical and resource demands to do with 'matters of accountability, performativity, and instrumental rationality [wherein] there is debate about completion rates ... financial assistance and other forms of support, infra-structural provision, ethics, examination protocols and procedures' (Green and Lee, 1995: 40).

What once seemed a relatively simple role that could be learned expe-rientially (Halse, 2011), a role that was played within a 'secret garden' (Park, 2007: 28–9) or 'private space' (Manathunga, 2005), has now become a highly complex set of roles that must be learned quickly and then played out within a multi-featured landscape that is also patrolled and moulded by a variety of influential close and distant stakeholders. Anyone undertaking such a role (or roles) should be prepared for a bumpy ride!

## In search of the good supervisor

However, if there is no easy ride, it may be of some comfort for you to know that the single, most consistent finding of research is that it is the *quality* of systems, structures and processes of academic supervision that is central to the achievement of agreed and intended outcomes (Abiddin, 2007; Armitage, 2006; Deuchar, 2008; Vilkinas, 2008). What is less comforting may be that the role of 'good supervisor' 'has also been compared to other roles ranging from God to mum, shaman, master craftsman [and] counsellor' (Wisker et al., 2003b). Yet to be a good and effective supervisor, you need to possess and exhibit 'quality'. The only problem is that there are many and different views as to what constitutes that 'quality', and needless to say it is complicated, as explained below,

The implied student (Ulriksen, 2009) at the heart of much research into the supervision process has been the doctoral student and so it has been 'predicated upon a stereotype of research students as young people, with little work experience, who study full time' (Leonard et al., 2005: 136).

As outlined earlier, such early career researchers are now no longer the norm when it comes to the requirement for academic supervision of work. The recipients of supervision these days are just as likely to be mature, part-time, first-degree students with considerable work experience and domestic or personal relationship responsibilities who, for the greater part of their supervised work, may be off-site and possibly remote from the institution through which they receive supervision. As Murphy et al. illustrate:

> The more traditional supervisory model was once relatively easily adapted from the full-time to the part-time student's needs. However, when part time supervision takes place at a distance (perhaps overseas), maybe electronically, perhaps within the workplace or within a complex collaborative arrangement, both the operational and the pedagogical aspects need to be reconsidered to ensure that they are fit for purpose. (2007: 14)

This has had inevitable consequences for academic staff who may be asked to take on a supervisory role focused on these less traditional kinds of student, particularly when they have had little by way of preparation for that role, other than a memory of how they themselves were supervised.

Consequently, academic staff these days are likely to find themselves supervising participants at all levels, in a variety of settings, aiming to be that 'good' supervisor who enables each and every student to achieve what they intend to achieve. Finally, they have to marry that with what the academic department, institution, professional body, employer or other stakeholders wants them to achieve, and all within disciplinary and national quality standards.

## Taking stock

Given that the territory of supervision is this complex, what should our response be to that complexity which we, as supervisors, are required to manage? Perhaps we could begin to orientate to the question by taking a look at some very different attitudes towards 'good supervision' and the purpose of supervision generally.

## Questions for reflection

Here are three perspectives on supervision:

a  The Dean of a Business Faculty nominated 12 supervisors who were classified as being 'excellent' in their supervisory skills because they achieved high completion rates; had candidates submit within the normally expected time frame; engaged in multiple supervisions; and received excellent supervisory reports. (Adapted from Gatfield, 2005: 319)

b  '[T]he outcome of supervision is not only to teach the student skills but to teach the student how to be someone – a researcher, a scholar, an academic.' (Grant, 2003: 180)

c  '[There is a] need for a dynamic alignment of supervisory style with the student's degree of development ... as a student undergoes academic growth during candidature, the supervisory style needs to be adjusted to a more hands-off approach in order to allow competent autonomy to be developed.' (Gurr, 2001: 81, 86).

- Which, if any, of those attitudes towards supervision most appeals to you – and why?
- What do you see as the key differences between those points of view?
- Do you think that the type of 'home discipline' (such as science, arts, humanities) might influence what is considered to be good supervision?

The quotations in the box above represent some of the more common approaches to managing the complexity of supervision. A difficulty when engaging with complex processes is that to take any one perspective is to miss the substance of others and, consequently, the benefits that the 'bigger picture' brings. The trick is to see what, if anything, the different approaches might have in common or what may either underpin them or connect them in some way, bearing in mind that for staff and students 'the single word "supervision" obscures a great and sometimes troublesome diversity in values, beliefs, assumptions and practices' (Grant, 2005: 2).

From research there are some themes that run through a variety of approaches and Tables 9.1–9.4 set out, in more detail, just some of those key themes:-

# Themes and key elements of approaches to supervision

**Table 9.1**   Differing expectations of supervisor and student

| *Supervisors are expected to:* | |
| --- | --- |
| Woolhouse, 2002: 139–40 | ensure that the student knows the timeframe |
| | act as general advisor |
| | make sure students are clear about what they are doing |
| | give guidance on e.g., timescale, feasibility, what to read, correct structure |
| | read student work well in advance of tutorial |
| | be available when needed |
| | be constructively critical |
| | have good knowledge of research area |
| | take sufficient interest in research to put more information in student's path |
| | be sufficiently involved in their success to help get a good job at the end |
| Vilkinas, 2008: 298 – summarising a range of research by other authors | have research knowledge and related skills |
| | possess management and interpersonal skills |
| | be able to coordinate the activities of the research programme |
| | mentor the students |
| | develop supportive relationships among the research students themselves |
| *Students are expected to:* | |
| Woolhouse, 2002 | be independent even though some aspects demand conformity |
| Phillips and Pugh, 2000 | produce written work that is not just a first draft |
| | be honest when reporting on their progress |
| | follow the advice [supervisors] give, especially when it has been given at the request of the student |
| | be excited about their work, able to surprise [their supervisor] and [be] fun to be with! |

**Table 9.2** Roles and styles of supervisors and students

---

*Supervisor as, for example:*

| | |
|---|---|
| Polonsky et al., 2011 | information source |
| | educator |
| | motivator |
| | evaluator |
| | methodology expert |
| | process expert |
| | business manager |
| Deuchar, 2008 | facilitator |
| | director |
| | critical friend |
| Hasrati, 2005: 558 | more knowledgeable other (MKO) |
| Brown et al., 1988: 120 | director (determining topic and method, providing ideas) |
| | facilitator (providing access to resources or expertise, arranging field-work) |
| | adviser (helping to resolve technical problems, suggesting alternatives) |
| | teacher (of research techniques) |
| | guide (suggesting timetable for writing up, giving feedback on progress, identifying critical path for data collection) |
| | critic (of design of enquiry, of draft chapters, of interpretations or data) |
| | freedom giver (authorises student to make decisions, supports student's decisions) |
| | supporter (gives encouragement, shows interest, discusses student's ideas) |
| | friend (extends interest and concern to non-academic aspects of student's life) |
| | manager (checks progress, monitors study, gives systematic feedback, plans work) |

*Student as:*

| | |
|---|---|
| Armitage, 2006 | 'hare' - self-reliant students |
| | 'tortoise' - supervisor-directed and support-seeking students |
| | 'ostrich' - students who lose contact with their supervisor |
| Lee and Green, 2009: 622–5 | author |
| | disciple |
| | apprentice |

---

**Table 9.3** Supervision as a dynamic process

---

| | |
|---|---|
| Armitage, 2006 | starting out – relationship forming: establishing the 'supervisory/student contract' |
| | keep going – relationship norming: managing the 'supervisory/student contract' |
| | the end is nigh – relationship maturing: advancing the 'supervisory/student contract' |
| Anderson et al., 2006 | clarifying the objectives of the project |
| | coming up with an appropriate, detailed and practicable research design |
| | maintaining an appropriate conceptual direction, within overall aims of the project |
| | analysis and writing up |

---

*(Continued)*

**Table 9.3** (Continued)

| | |
|---|---|
| Malfroy and Webb, 2000 | from unstructured to semi-structured, to structured |
| Cullen et al., 2009 | helping the student choose a viable topic and initiate data collection (intensive) |
| | monitoring student progress (less intensive) |
| | terminating data collection and writing up (intensive) |

**Table 9.4**    Relationship and attitudes to supervision

| | |
|---|---|
| Grant, 2005 | technical rationality vs negotiated process/order (and/or professional artistry) |
| Acker et al., 1994: 485 | |
| Hasrati, 2005; Dysthe et al., 2006: 303 | supervision as situated learning (legitimate peripheral participation) |
| Murphy et al., 2007 | *thesis orientation*: the focus of the supervisor is on helping students produce their theses in an efficient and scholarly manner |
| | *professional orientation*: supervisors see the process as a kind of apprenticeship for induction into academic life |
| | *person orientation*: the supervisor's focus is on the whole person, being sympathetic and supportive of academic and non-academic aspects of the students' lives |
| Lee, 2007: 691 | functional |
| | enculturation |
| | critical thinking |
| | emancipation |
| | relationship development |

These perspectives, approaches and orientations to the supervision process are simply attempts to theorise the specific, individual elements. While each of them holds valuable 'truths' about particular supervision instances, what is needed now is a model or framework of, and for, the practice of supervision that is able to deal with the kind of complexity outlined earlier.

When faced with complexity the solution is not to take any particular perspective or adopt one fixed position, for it is certain that no single perspective will ever offer a comprehensive solution. A better approach is to have available for practice a framework that envisages, and supports the use of, navigation through and around different, theorised, perspectives of the kind outlined in the tables above. This is a flexible framework that can accommodate elements of expectation, style, phases and differing orientations to, or conceptions of, academic supervision. Such a framework, given the weight of research on the point, should also have the supervisory relationship at its core, and, by extension, no matter what the form of relationship envisaged (one-to-one, group supervision, online supervision etc.), supervision being a human encounter, have dialogue and dialogic processes as the central dynamic. Clearly, this will place the major responsibility on supervisors to be the navigators of such individualised pathways through their supervisory encounters.

## Creating good supervision – the challenges

Light and Cox make the point that

> supervision … is essentially about dialogue. There is a need for constant adjustment to what each participant is saying and the balance between giving and taking, listening and talking is crucial … the dialogue is not simply a friendly conversation … There is a more active, searching process involved whereby you become clearer about what the other is saying but also about the hidden assumptions and misconceptions. It is essentially an exploratory process … [that] involves a wider involvement in the student's personal and social life. (2001: 143)

### Questions for reflection

- What do you think of the quotation from Light and Cox above, does it tally or conflict with any of your ideas about supervision?
- If you think that supervision is 'an exploratory process … [that] involves a wider involvement in the student's personal and social life', do you think any boundaries should be set for that involvement and if so, what might those boundaries be?

This suggests some new possibilities for how supervisors might approach the navigation task. Take the following, for example: 'successful supervision depends to a significant extent on relationships that are founded in trust, warmth and honest collaboration' (Armstrong, 2004: 601). It is also absolutely clear from research that the presence of empathy in an academic supervision relationship builds such foundations (Emilsson and Johnsson, 2007: 171; Robinson, 2011: 221–2; Kilminster et al., 2007: 2). As Hampes (2001: 241) says, 'developing empathy with someone makes it easier to trust them since you are more likely to know what to expect from them emotionally and otherwise'. Unfortunately, there are very few definitions of what is meant by 'empathy' in an academic supervision context but most people would understand it as 'the ability to communicate understanding of another person's experience from that person's perspective' (BACP, 2013: 3). So empathy is not just a cognitive appreciation of someone else's experience, being able to take their perspective, it is also an appreciation of how it *feels* to 'stand in their shoes'. The importance of this definition is that it also includes communication of that understanding, back to the person whose experience is being understood, in such a way that the recipient senses it is an accurate understanding.

Now if anyone is concerned that by use of the definition above we are straying into the territory of counselling or therapy, you need not be concerned, supervision is neither. However, as Daniel Goleman (2007), famous for his work on emotional intelligence, suggests 'empathic concern' is a key social relationship skill and particularly important for anyone in supervisory roles, whether in business or in academia. Empathic concern, he says, is not 'living the feelings of another' but rather the supervisor (in this case) being able to accurately evaluate how someone else is perceiving or experiencing a situation, so that appropriate action can be agreed. That thoughtful and practical use of empathy is certainly what this context requires.

In previous sections, the importance of dialogue has also been flagged as foundational to good academic supervision. Light and Cox (2001) suggest that supervision is 'essentially dialogue' and others, notably Wisker et al. (2003a) and Dysthe et al. (2006), develop that notion further. Yet the term 'dialogue', as will be seen elsewhere in this book, implies more than good communication or discussion; it also entrains notions of mutuality, reciprocity, equality of voice and, to allow that to take place, particular attitudes towards the relationship itself. So, it is not just that dialogue takes place, what is important is the kind and quality of dialogue. Who, for example defines the topic, the field, the extent and form of the research and the responsibilities of the participants in the research? Who 'authorises' what is discussed, written or published. How does dialogue take place, face to face, online, in supervised groups and peer groups, and what is the quality of that dialogue, formal or informal, supportive or dismissive, directive or non-directive? Each of those elements – and the list is not exhaustive – has implications for the kind of relationship that is established and for the resulting impact of the supervision process.

Finally, the research summarised in Tables 9.1–9.4 also demonstrates the differences in attitude to the supervision task that generate 'tensions', characterised as 'technical rational' versus 'professional artistry', or 'negotiated order'. The term 'technical rationality' comes from the work of

Donald Schön, who characterised it as an attitude that places a value on instrumental problem solving (1991: 21), in this context 'the supervisor acts as a manager or director and the student is a passive recipient' (Acker et al., 1994: 485). This attitude is also characterised by a supervision process determined by 'milestone reports, public confirmations of candidature sessions, biannual progress reports, annual oral presentations of research and – in some universities … a form that must be signed off at the conclusion of every supervisory meeting' (Brabazon, 2013).

By contrast, 'professional artistry' in supervision is an attitude that values: 'creativity, innovation and exploration of alternative and sometimes contradictory perspectives … It thus sees quantity and quality indicators as more than a technical exercise; more than a set of defined regulations and procedures and, above all, more than the sum of its definable parts. It accepts that it is not possible to know everything' (Gore et al., 2000: 77).

Similarly, 'negotiated order' is a model of supervision, 'where the expectations between supervisor and student are open to change' (Acker et al., 1994).

This is a contrast that presents supervision in the same dichotomous, tension-generating, 'either/or' way, and it is very clear that supervision in this time of complexity requires supervisors to confront challenges that arise from the kind of technical aspects of research outlined by Brabazon above and the kinds of challenge thrown up by needing to orientate students from taught programmes or professional practice (Watts, 2009) to the research environment, where different rules apply.

## Technical and adaptive challenges

Heifetz talks about the complex challenges faced by business leaders (Heifetz and Linsky, 2002; Parks, 2005) and in so doing he makes a distinction between what he calls 'technical challenges' and 'adaptive challenges'. Technical challenges can be solved by the application of routine, known solutions, formats, procedures and processes whereas adaptive challenges are those, for example, where it becomes obvious, gradually or suddenly, that new and different sets of skills, knowledge and understanding, new mental models, are required in order to meet them. In supervision, an example of a technical challenge might be how the supervisee gets access to the specialist databases and instruments which are necessary for the conduct of the project. An adaptive challenge might be how well the supervisee adapts to a research environment when all or most of their experience has been as a 'taught' student. Another distinction he makes (Heifetz and Linsky, 2002) is that while technical challenges can be resolved by individuals who have particular expertise and particular knowledge, adaptive challenges can only be resolved through collaborative exploration, to coin a phrase, where solutions are not in people's heads but in a collaborative space 'between their noses'.

Academic supervision crosses and re-crosses each and both of those kinds of challenge, and consequently a good supervisor is also someone who can distinguish between them and know that, as Heifetz (Heifetz and Linsky, 2002) goes on to suggest, applying technical forms of solution to adaptive challenges can only lead to failure.

## Key phases of the supervision landscape

Lee and Green (2009), in their article 'Supervision as metaphor', enumerate the many ways in which the supervision process has been characterised. One of the most-used metaphors is that of a journey or a learning journey (Wisker et al., 2007: 305; Jackson et al., 2009: 89; Heinze and Heinze, 2009: 295) characterised by a number of 'stages' or 'phases', where different 'thresholds' are encountered and need to be crossed:

> [Y]ou will go through different phases of feeling confident ... I do see that I've been climbing you know, a mountain and I've got past base camp and I have got to some of the other earlier camps up the hill ... and I do actually feel so different than I did at the start I do see, understand and believe in that sense of working at different thresholds ... trying to get to that peak! (Student 'Julie' quoted in Wisker and Savin-Baden, 2009: 244)

Other pieces of research (see Tables 9.1–9.4) suggest that projects have a 'lifecycle' where the stages or phases are marked by changes of activity or changes in focus. These phases may be determined by administrative or award requirements, by the nature of the project and its research methods, by the nature of the discipline, by the requirements of the institution, by the mode of participation (e.g., part-time, full-time or distance learning) or even by the temperament of individual supervisors. If we were to consider process phases in a project then there is broad agreement that in undertaking most academic projects there are 'starting-off/exploring' processes, 'understanding/agreeing/getting started' processes, 'carrying-on/maintaining' processes and 'finishing-off' processes.

There is no real agreement on names for the phases so, in keeping with the generic processes identified above, they will be referred to here as 'contracting' (an orientation phase), 'establishing', 'sustaining' and 'concluding' as set out in Figure 9.1.

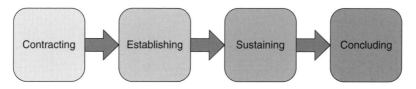

**Figure 9.1**    Meeting the challenges of complex supervision – the supervisor as navigator

Navigating the complex landscape of supervision requires supervisors to have an effective mental map, a set of flexible intelligences – cognitive, emotional and behavioural – and an open mind so that they can 'have' frames of mind but not be 'had' (dominated) by them (Kegan and Lahey, 2002). They need to have the ability not only to maintain student-centredness but also to develop different kinds of conversation across the lifecycle and know when particular kinds of conversation are required, depending on the phase of the project. For example, stretching and challenging the supervisee with motivating goals can only take place if the supervisee has already developed basic capability in the 'establishing' phase.

Table 9.5 overleaf sets out just some of the aspects of this navigation task by combining examples from the research and the good supervision 'frames' developed in earlier sections.

## Conclusion

Academic supervision is a complex process offering considerable challenge to those involved in the supervisory relationship and new forms of supervision are evolving to meet the demands of that complexity. The ability to create empathic, dialogue-focused relationships while simultaneously supporting students in balancing technical and adaptive challenges across the project lifecycle represents just one, but the most crucial, of the new elements that need to be integrated into the supervisor's repertoire.

Those elements are, of course, not new to anyone who may be familiar with the form of supervision that is enjoyed and employed by professionals in counselling, social work, nursing and other forms of health and social care, in what might be called 'professional practice' supervision. Those models and frameworks need some adaptation and adjustment for a higher education (HE) context since supervision in those fields is designed for quite a different purpose. Nevertheless, there are a number of process principles that inform this field of 'professional practice' supervision that are clearly applicable to the new academic supervision landscape.

**Table 9.5** Challenges and possible actions in the different phases of the supervision process

| Phase | Challenges (for example) | Possible actions/supervisory conversations |
|---|---|---|
| **Contracting** | *Technical challenges*<br>• Registration /understanding Requirements<br>• Timescales/deadlines<br>• Resources (e.g., funding)<br><br>*Adaptive challenges*<br>• Sharing experience (supervisor and supervisee)<br>• Cognitive development of supervisee<br>• Support/conflict between current supervisee physical/social environment and project | • Agreeing responsibilities<br>• Setting boundaries (especially supervisor availability)<br>• Connecting/integrating supervisee/project/environment<br>• Project guidelines (institution)<br>• Building relationship – active listening<br>• Discussing expectations of each other – how you will work together<br>• How will disagreements/conflicts be handled<br>• Summarising<br>• Agreeing direction of project (initial – scoping) |
| **Establishing** | *Technical challenges*<br>• Design/format of project<br>• Firming scope of project<br>• Indicative content and research skill acquisition<br>• First deadlines/indicators of progress<br><br>*Adaptive challenges*<br>• Starting to research/write (when, how, what)<br>• 'Progressing'<br>• Sensemaking – research/researcher/ researching | • Agreeing direction of project (exploring scope/establishing)<br>• Goal-setting<br>• Modelling (supervisor being a model for, and helping supervisee create own mental models of, research/researcher/researching)<br>• Reflecting for learning<br>• Giving feedback/being critical friend – being none-directive<br>• Supporting<br>• 'Scaffolding'<br>• Enabling networks for supervisee (introduction to peers/academic colleagues/external networks) |

| Phase | Challenges (for example) | Possible actions/supervisory conversations |
| --- | --- | --- |
| **Sustaining** | *Technical challenges* | • Motivating plus goal-setting and feedback |
| | • Transferring MPhil to PhD (where appropriate) | • Challenging plus goal-setting and feedback |
| | • Building drafts into structure/keeping writing | • Formative assessment and evaluation – with feedback |
| | • Organising teaching for supervisee | • Tension regulating/balancing for supervisee |
| | • Research skill widening/deepening | • Connecting with peer-based project/personal development resources, e.g., peer-supervision groups or Action Learning sets |
| | *Adaptive challenges* | • Being more directive |
| | • Staying focused | • External networking/conferences/forums for supervisee |
| | • Staying motivated | • Being an advocate for the project |
| | • Balancing tensions | |
| **Concluding** | *Technical challenges* | • Who should examine? |
| | • Recruiting external/internal examiners (where appropriate) | • When/how/why of finishing writing |
| | • Preparing final version of project | • Preparing for assessment |
| | • Arranging Viva (where appropriate) | • Dissemination of research |
| | • Assessing work | • Next moves, job-hunting/career development |
| | *Adaptive challenges* | |
| | • Finishing writing (concluding) | |
| | • Preparing for Viva (where appropriate) | |
| | • Letting go | |
| | • Moving on and out | |

Academic supervision is clearly at a point where it needs to acknowledge the many changes taking place in HE and the complexity of the process as it has been outlined in earlier parts of this chapter. It is, in fact, beginning to experience its own set of adaptive challenges and there is some evidence that new and appropriate responses are beginning to emerge. Based on the growing recognition that supervision needs to become more process-orientated and less product- or problem-orientated, these new approaches view reflection and 'generative reactiveness' (Johnson, 2007: 259) rather than 'direction' as the core dynamic of the process. There is the coaching approach (or 'attitude') to supervision – which is process-orientated and has, at its core, both empathic concern and mutuality (Manek, 2004; Robinson, 2011). Similarly, in an attempt to introduce peer voices into the supervision process and include elements of social learning, academic supervision is beginning to embrace action learning (AL). AL is essentially facilitated (or self-facilitated) group-based learning based on participants' self-nominated projects. It has a long pedigree as a developmental tool in business and in education.

The nature of academic institutions and ways in which knowledge may be represented is also changing and other new elements with which some supervisors may now be confronted include learning to work with students in locations remote from the supervisor – which could also be complicated by needing to communicate across different time-zones – or learning to work with projects in different modalities other than text – web- or video-based, for example.

Finally, however, while it is clear that academic supervision demands a far more diverse set of abilities than required in previous years, an additional and, perhaps, ultimate ability is (as Boud and Costley, 2007: 129 suggest) for supervisors to acquire the capacity not only to identify when the supervision process is not being effective but also the flexibility to act on that observation.

## Questions for reflective practice and professional development

1  What are the most challenging things that you face as a supervisor? How would you match them against the 'technical' or 'adaptive' category descriptions in the chapter?

2  If you had to draw a 'map' of the supervision process from your own perspective, would you add anything and would you remove anything from the elements in Table 9.5?

3 After reading this chapter, how would you describe the purpose(s) of academic supervision to a student that you will shortly be supervising?

4 If, after reading the chapter or from your reflections on Question 1 above, you were now to assess your strengths as a supervisor, what would you say they were? What would you say you need to develop? Would you be prepared to receive feedback from a colleague or a student on your supervision and if so, how would you go about doing that?

## Further reading

Carnell, E., MacDonald, J. and Askew S. (2006) *Coaching and Mentoring in Higher Education: A learning-centred approach*. London: The Institute of Education, University of London.

This is an excellent resource on the coaching approach to supervision.

Brockbank, A. and McGill, I. (2013) *Coaching with Empathy*. Buckingham: Open University Press.

On a similar theme, of developing a learning relationship through dialogue. While it is not HE centred, both authors have extensive experience of working with HE audiences – both staff and student.

### Action learning (AL)

There are a number of good references on the use of AL in HE settings, but these are particularly useful:

Bourner, T. and Frost, P. (1996) 'In their own words: The experience of action learning in higher education', *Education & Training*, 38: 22–31.

Coghlan, D. and Pedler, M. (2006) 'Action learning dissertations: Structure, supervision and examination', *Action Learning: Research and Practice*, 3: 127–39.

Brockbank, A. and McGill I., (2003) *The Action Learning Handbook: Powerful techniques for education, professional development and training*. London: Routledge.

More information about the relationship between such psychological growth and academic learning can be found in:

Baxter Magolda, M. B. and King, P. (2004) *Learning Partnerships: Theory and models of practice to educate for self-authorship*. Sterling, VA: Stylus.

Chickering, A. W. and Reisser, L. (1993) *Education and Identity* (2nd edn). San Francisco, CA: Jossey-Bass.

Kegan, R. (1983) *The Evolving Self: Problem and process in human development.* New York: Harvard University Press.

# References

Abiddin, N. Z. (2007) 'The role of an effective supervisor: Case studies at the University of Manchester, United Kingdom', *European Journal of Scientific Research*, 16: 380–94.

Acker, S., Hill, T. and Black, E. (1994) 'Thesis supervision in the social sciences: Managed or negotiated?', *Higher Education*, 28 (4): 483–98.

Anderson, C., Day, K. and McLaughlin, P. (2006) 'Mastering the dissertation: Lecturers' representations of the purposes and processes of Master's level dissertation supervision', *Studies in Higher Education*, 31: 149–68.

Armitage, A. (2006) 'Consultant or academic?: Frameworks of supervisory practice to support student learning and postgraduate research', paper presented at the Higher Education Academy Annual Conference, Royal Holloway College, London.

Armstrong, S. J. (2004) 'The impact of supervisors' cognitive styles on the quality of research supervision in management education', *The British Journal of Educational Psychology*, 74: 599–616.

Boud, D. and Costley, C. (2007) 'From project supervision to advising: New conceptions of the practice', *Innovations in Education and Teaching International*, 44: 119–30.

Brabazon, T. (2013) '10 truths a PhD supervisor will never tell you', *Times Higher Education*, 13 July. Available at http://tinyurl.com/ptwzod3 (accessed 3.10.14).

British Association for Counselling and Psychotherapy (BACP) (2013) *Ethical Framework for Good Practice in Counselling & Psychotherapy.* London: BACP. Available at http://tinyurl.com/mz3bzyh (accessed 3.10.14).

Brown, M., Brown, G. A. and Atkins G. (1988) *Effective Teaching in Higher Education.* Abingdon: Routledge.

Crossouard, B. (2008) 'Developing alternative models of doctoral supervision with online formative assessment', *Studies in Continuing Education*, 30: 51–67.

Cullen, S., Dowling, S. and Webb, T. (2009) *Dissertation Supervision: Enhancing the experience of tourism and hospitality students.* York: Network for Hospitality, Leisure, Sport and Tourism, Higher Education Academy. Available at: www.studynet2.herts.ac.uk/intranet/lti.nsf/Teaching+Documents/D3F14D79 895A51C280257A9300364648/$FILE/2009%20HEA%20resource%20dissertation_ supervision.pdf

de Beer, M. and Mason, R. B. (2009) 'Using a blended approach to facilitate postgraduate supervision', *Innovations in Education and Teaching International*, 46 (2): 213–26.

Delamont, S., Atkinson, P. and Parry, O. (2004) *Supervising the Doctorate: A guide to success* (2nd edn). Maidenhead: Open University Press.

Deuchar, R. (2008) 'Facilitator, director or critical friend?: Contradiction and congruence in doctoral supervision styles', *Teaching in Higher Education*, 13, 489–500.

Dysthe, O., Samara, A. and Westrheim, K. (2006) 'Multivoiced supervision of Master's students: A case study of alternative supervision practices in higher education', *Studies in Higher Education*, 31: 299–318.

Emilsson, U. M. and Johnsson, E. (2007) 'Supervision of supervisors: On developing supervision in postgraduate education', *Higher Education Research & Development*, 26: 163–79.

Gatfield, T. (2005) 'An investigation into PhD supervisory management styles: Development of a dynamic conceptual model and its managerial implications', *Journal of Higher Education Policy and Management*, 27: 311–25.

Goleman, D. (2007) *Social Intelligence: The new science of human relationships*. London: Arrow.

Gore, C., Bond, C. and Steven, V. (2000) 'Organisational self-assessment: Measuring educational quality in two paradigms', *Quality Assurance in Education*, 8 (7): 76–84.

Grant, B. (2003) 'Mapping the pleasures and risks of supervision', *Discourse: Studies in the Cultural Politics of Education*, 24: 175–90.

Grant, B. M. (2005) 'The pedagogy of graduate supervision: Figuring the relations between supervisor and student', PhD thesis, University of Auckland.

Green, B. and Lee, A. (1995) 'Theorising postgraduate pedagogy', *Australian Universities' Review*, 40–45.

Gurr, G. (2001) 'Negotiating the rackety bridge: A dynamic model for aligning supervisory style with research student development', *Higher Education Research & Development*, 20 (1): 81–92.

Halse, C. (2011) '"Becoming a supervisor": The impact of doctoral supervision on supervisors' learning', *Studies in Higher Education*, 36: 557–70.

Hampes, W. P. (2001) 'Relation between humor and empathic concern', *Psychological Reports*, 88 (1): 241–4.

Hasrati, M. (2005) 'Legitimate peripheral participation and supervising PhD students', *Studies in Higher Education*, 30 (5): 557–70.

Healey, M., Lannin, L., Stibbe, A. and Derounian, J. (2013) *Developing and Enhancing Undergraduate Final Year Projects and Dissertations*. York: Higher Education Academy. Available at www.heacademy.ac.uk/node/8079 (accessed 23.7.15).

Heifetz, R. A. and Linsky, M., (2002) *Leadership on the Line: Staying alive through the dangers of leading*. New York: Harvard.

Heinze, A. and Heinze, B. (2009) 'Blended e-learning skeleton of conversation: Improving formative assessment in undergraduate dissertation supervision', *British Journal of Educational Technology*, 40: 294–305.

Jackson, D., Darbyshire, P., Luck, L. and Peters, K. (2009) 'Intergenerational reflections on doctoral supervision in nursing', *Contemporary Nurse*, 32 (1–2): 83–91.

Johnson, W. B. (2007) 'Transformational supervision: When supervisors mentor', *Professional Psychology: Research and Practice*, 38: 259–67.

Kamler, B. and Thomson, P. (2006) *Helping Doctoral Students Write: Pedagogies for supervision* (Kindle edn). Abingdon: Taylor & Francis eLibrary.

Kegan, R. and Lahey, L. (2002) *How the Way We Talk Can Change the Way We Work: Seven languages for transformation*. San Francisco, CA: Jossey-Bass.

Kiley, M. (2009) 'Identifying threshold concepts and proposing strategies to support doctoral candidates', *Innovations in Education and Teaching International*, 46 (3): 293–304.

Kilminster, S., Cottrell, D., Grant, J. and Jolly, B. (2007) 'AMEE Guide No. 27: Effective educational and clinical supervision', *Medical Teacher*, 29: 2–19.

Lee, A. (2007) 'Developing effective supervisors: Concepts of research supervision', *South African Journal of Higher Education*, 21: 680–93.

Lee, A. and Green, B. (2009) 'Supervision as metaphor', *Studies in Higher Education*, 34: 615–30.

Leonard, D., Becker, R. and Coate, K. (2005) 'To prove myself at the highest level: The benefits of doctoral study', *Higher Education Research & Development*, 24: 135–49.

Light, G. and Cox, R. (2001) *Learning and Teaching in Higher Education: The reflective professional*. London: Sage.

Malfroy, J. and Webb, C. (2000) 'Congruent and incongruent views of postgraduate supervision', in M. Kiley and G. Mullins (eds), *Quality in Postgraduate Research: Making ends meet*. Adelaide: Advisory Centre for University Education, University of Adelaide, pp.165–77.

Manathunga, C. (2005) 'The development of research supervision: "Turning the light on a private space"', *International Journal for Academic Development*, 10 (1): 17–30.

Manek, N. (2004) 'Developing coaching skills: A practical approach for education supervision', *The Clinical Teacher*, 1 (2): 74–6.

Murphy, N., Bain, J. D. and Conrad, L. (2007) 'Orientations to research higher degree supervision', *Higher Education*, 53: 209–34.

Noble, H. (2011) 'Exploring the experience of supervising pre-registration nursing students through their literature review dissertation', *Learning at City Journal*, 1 (1): 25–32.

Park, C. (2007) *Redefining the Doctorate*. York: Higher Education Academy. Available at: https://www.heacademy.ac.uk/sites/default/files/redefining_the_doctorate.pdf

Parks, S. D. (2005) *Leadership Can Be Taught: A bold approach for a complex world*. New York: Harvard.

Phillips, E. and Pugh, D. S. (2000) *How to Get a PhD: A handbook for students and their supervisors* (3rd edn). Buckingham: Open University Press.

Polonsky, M. J. and Waller, D. S. (2011) *Designing and Managing a Research Project: A business student's guide* (2nd edn). New York: Sage, ch. 3.

Robinson, L. A. (2011) 'Supervision: A meeting of minds and hearts; a coach and facilitator of adult learning reflect on the experience of engaging in supervision as a professional doctoral student in practical theology', *Work Based Learning*, 2.

Salmon, P. (1992) *Achieving a PhD: Ten students' experiences*. Stoke-on-Trent: Trentham Books.

Schön, D. A. (1991) *The Reflective Practitioner: How professionals think in action*. Aldershot: Ashgate.

Todd, M., Bannister, P. and Clegg, S. (2004) Independent inquiry and the under-graduate dissertation: Perceptions and experiences of final-year social science students', *Assessment & Evaluation in Higher Education*, 29 (3): 335–55.

Ulriksen, L. (2009) 'The implied student', *Studies in Higher Education*, 34 (5): 517–32.

Vilkinas, T. (2008) 'An exploratory study of the supervision of PhD/research students' theses', *Innovative Higher Education*, 32: 297–311.

Watts, J. H. (2009) 'From professional to PhD student: Challenges of status transition', *Teaching in Higher Education*, 14 (6), 687–91.

Wisker, G. and Savin-Baden, M. (2009) 'Priceless conceptual thresholds: Beyond the "stuck place" in writing', *London Review of Education*, 7 (3): 235–47.

Wisker, G., Robinson, G. and Shacham, M. (2007) 'Postgraduate research success: Communities of practice involving cohorts, guardian supervisors and online communities', *Innovations in Education and Teaching International*, 44: 301–20.

Wisker, G., Robinson, G., Trafford, V. and Warnes, M. (2003a) 'From supervisory dialogues to successful PhDs: Strategies supporting and enabling the learning conversations of staff and students at postgraduate level', *Teaching in Higher Education*, 8: 383–97.

Wisker, G., Waller, S., Richter, U., Robinson, G., Trafford, V., Wicks, K. and Warnes, M. (2003b) 'On nurturing hedgehogs: Developments online for distance and offshore supervision', in *Learning for an Unknown Future*, Proceedings of the 26th HERDSA Annual Conference, Christchurch, New Zealand, 6–9 July. Available at http://tinyurl.com/p7gqcgk (accessed 3.10.14).

Woolhouse, M. (2002) 'Supervising dissertation projects: Expectations of supervisors and students', *Innovations in Education and Teaching International*, 39: 137–45.

# 10

# Work-related and Professional Learning

## Sibyl Coldham and Pauline Armsby

### Chapter overview

This chapter explores:

- influences in the development of work-related learning (WRL)
- differences in roles, responsibilities and relationships in work-related, professional and disciplinary learning
- learning design strategies for WRL and their uses in generic and discipline-specific learning
- teaching, learning and assessment approaches for WRL

## Introduction

This chapter outlines a range of approaches to developing work-relevant skills, attributes and practices, looking at the openings they offer in terms of developing students' confidence in, and experience of, work processes during their university study. We also explore key learning design and assessment strategies used in the various approaches, drawing on literature from workplace learning and practice, as well as higher education (HE) and employability. To illustrate different approaches we draw in examples from a range of disciplines, our own experience and offer links to substantial case study repositories as further reading.

## Context

In the UK from the late 1990s, a series of government and industry reports set out and developed the inter-related agendas of mass HE, the introduction of tuition fees for 'home' students, and expectations that university courses take some responsibility for preparing graduates for the world of work (cf CBI, 2011; Leitch, 2006; Scott, 1995). For an analysis of these policy developments, see Hayward and James, 2004). The development of a highly skilled workforce able to adapt to change and innovation was proposed by policymakers, as essential for an economy no longer grounded in manufacturing. The list of skills and attributes varies slightly with each report, but generally includes: self-management, communication, team working, business and customer awareness, literacy, numeracy and IT skills. More recently (CBI, 2011) the language has shifted to a focus on attributes such as a 'can do' approach and creativity, which the report writers believe all students should have the opportunity to develop, and will potentially demand. In response to these demands employability forms the focus of significant strands of work for the UK's JISC network (www.jisc. ac.uk/ accessed 29.9.15) focused on using digital technology to enhance employability, the outputs of which can be found in the resources list at the end of this chapter.

A recent Higher Education Academy (HEA) report (Pegg et al., 2012), which showcases a range of approaches to developing employability, suggests that no single approach is emerging as 'best practice'. What is clear from their case studies is that development of skills and attributes for employability seems to be more successful when students take responsibility for decisions around evaluating and progressing their own development through self-determined planning and reflection. Alongside this is an emerging body of work whose authors propose practice-orientated curriculum frameworks that draw on understandings of learning that have emerged from research into how learning (individual and collective) comes about in workplaces and professions (Reich et al., 2015; Billett et al., 2014; Hager et al., 2012; Green, 2009; Higgs et al., 2012). The influence of this work is summarised in Table 10.1.

## The terminology of work-related learning

'Work-related learning' (WRL) is an umbrella term in the UK for curriculum design to support both professional, discipline-specific learning and the general development informed by the employability agenda described above. In Australia, 'work-integrated learning' (WIL) (Cooper et al., 2010; Billett, 2009) or 'practice-based learning' (Billett et al., 2014; Higgs et al., 2012;

Green, 2009; Kemmis, 2005) are more generally used, while in the USA these activities are called 'cooperative learning' or 'coop'. Figure 10.1 sets out the key terms used for activities that come under the WRL umbrella.

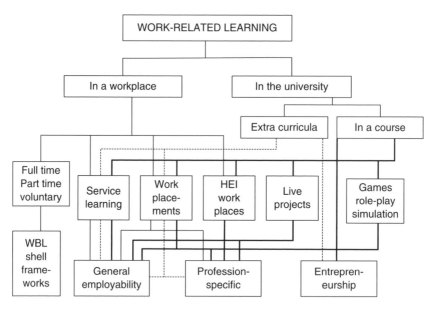

**Figure 10.1**   Typology of work-related learning

Different disciplines or professions also prefer different terms. For example, medical and architecture professionals often explain themselves as 'developing practice' rather than work, where 'practice' implies disciplinary or theoretical knowledge personally embedded with capabilities and attributes that together form know-how or competence in the field. 'Practice-based learning' is used to imply this sort of professional formation, but can also be used to imply development of a way of being and the attributes of the responsible citizen (Higgs et al., 2012; Kemmis, 2005). Practice-orientation moves the focus away from the skills themselves and towards the 'whole person', and is often described as 'a process of becoming' (Dall'Alba and Sandberg, 2014; Hodkinson et al., 2008).

One primary division in WRL relates to the site where the main activities take place: in the university or in a workplace. The primary division of WRL activity inside a university tends to be around the type of activity and the focus of the learning. Some approaches concentrate specifically on job-seeking and career development skills. These approaches tend to draw on central careers departments. Other approaches focus on the attributes of work and professional practice, and it is these approaches that we focus on in this chapter, although we offer references to sources for career development at the end of the chapter. Activity in a workplace with the roles and relationships of work tends to be called 'work-based learning' (WBL) if the programme is designed for workplace learners, or 'placement learning' if it is designed as part of or additional to a course of study, and we use this distinction here.

Before looking at these various approaches to WRL in more detail, we will look at insights emerging from research into workplace learning, and explore some learning and teaching approaches that seem to be key.

# Teaching and learning approaches for WRL

HE has traditionally developed knowledge as a demonstrable product disassociated from the person being assessed. Knowledge is demonstrated through writing essays and exams and analysing case studies designed to test application of theory. Courses in the creative industries and other practice-orientated fields may focus on creativity, personal intention and judgement, but in most courses the aim is for students to learn the theory and to selectively apply it to the topic under consideration. This is very different from a workplace where problems do not arrive fully formed, and where knowledge and know-how is distributed across individuals, teams and professional communities, who construct or frame the problem and the resolution. In that world, knowledge is not separate from the way it is practised. The intention of much of WRL is to bring this different understanding of learning to the fore. In the main, this is done either by starting from work or starting with a loosely defined problem. Before discussing these approaches in detail, we will briefly outline aspects of learning design that underpin them.

## Experiential and practice-orientated learning

There are two aspects to experiential learning. First, experiential learning involves an active process of reflection, review and critical analysis of things that the learner is involved with in the present or in reviewing their past experience (Boud et al., 2006; Boud and Miller, 1996; Schön, 1987). Work-based and placement learning take this starting point. Learning is seen as bound up with personal growth, and built up through sensemaking (Hodkinson et al., 2008; Chappell et al., 2003; Kolb, 1984). Experiential learning can also be used as a constructivist learning-design approach to incorporate critical reflection with structured activities to facilitate problem-framing and review. This might be as independent or team-working, and might be online, in the classroom or as additional activities. The activities for experiential learning need to be specific, including key characteristics of the setting and other participants, and with a clear task or goals for individuals and teams. Problem-based learning (PBL) is one such approach (Hmelo-Silver, 2004; Savin-Baden, 2000; further case studies in the ACEN repository, listed at the end of the chapter,). PBL takes complex problems as the drivers for delivery of the curriculum. It can also involve further release of information which unfolds in relation to how students work through the layers of the problem. The problem should exemplify a real-world situation, often without a preferred solution. (See vignette 2 for an example and also Chapter 2: Course and Learning Design and Evaluation.)

Experiential learning challenges the notion that theory can be internalised without personal experience to make sense of it (Hodkinson et al., 2008; Chappell et al., 2003). More recently, insights from research into how professional people learn in workplaces has shown the significant influence of the context, in which the learner and learning are situated, on what is learned and has led to a focus on practices and attributes of learning and professional work (Reich et al., 2015; Billett et al., 2014; Higgs et al., 2012; Hager et al., 2012; Green, 2009). At its simplest, attention to practices or experience shifts the educational focus away from the knowledge content or theory focus and towards developing the attributes of the particular practice, and to preparing students to make judgements in novel situations. A focus on practice foregrounds considerations of how the learner internalises attributes and judgement through interaction with the setting, its features, processes and participants. For example, becoming a graphic designer will involve more than knowing what others in the field have done and mastering techniques. It also involves developing a personal style (intention) that may challenge and disrupt whilst also referencing the community of practice.

## Reflection and reflective facilitation

Second, learning from experience requires the learner (or team) to unpick how they construct and internalise personal knowledge and practices. Structured critical reflection can assist with this (Boud et al., 2006; Coldham, 2004; Moon, 2004; Schön, 1987). A critically reflective approach aims to explore people's assumptions, reactions and other connections with a view to framing or reframing a problem, developing greater understanding, and planning future actions and learning. In WBL it is used to articulate personal understanding as a starting point for exploring relevant theories, and building critically informed practice. In team-working and work that involves interpersonal working, reflection also offers an ethical framework in which to give feedback and to explore others' actions reactions, and assumptions, by taking a starting position that each person's experience is equally valid, and working with an exploratory rather than a judgemental mind-set.

Reflective questioning is a key strategy for tutor facilitation of experiential learning to develop students' self-awareness and criticality (Heron, 1999). In a one-to-one setting this might be described as mentoring or coaching (Brockbank and McGill, 2012). It involves techniques of reflecting ideas back to probe for consequences, and other possibilities and their consequences. This is important when facilitating group discussion or team presentations, in order to keep the thinking in the group rather than focused on the teacher as the source of a 'correct' answer. Some useful strategies here are:

- setting a ground-rule expecting people to talk only from their own experience, and using examples from their own experience;
- keeping the discussion non-judgemental (including avoidance of words such as 'good', 'right', 'wrong', which tend to close down further thought) to encourage unusual ideas and to build confidence;
- cycling questions back to the group to explore answers;
- asking for different perspectives from the ones expressed up to that point;
- asking 'What if ...?' and 'What else ...?' questions.

This form of facilitation supports students in taking responsibility for their work while guiding them to necessary research and considerations in framing their practice, and developing their professional approach (Coldham, 2004).

## Roles, responsibilities and relationships

The influence of roles, responsibilities and relationships as contextual influences on what can, and may not, be learned in workplaces is well studied (cf. Reich et al., 2015; Hager et al., 2012; Billett, 2009; Boud and Garrick, 1999). This was borne out in several evaluation interviews for projects funded by the University of Westminster Centre for Excellence in Professional Learning from the Workplace (Coldham, 2011). Students seemed to accept supervisor advice more readily or even interference when they were working for a client. They also readily took responsibility for working to professional standards when working on a real-world project or simulation (see vignettes below). Table 10.1 sets out key contextual factors that impact on workplace learning, as identified in the research, and compares how these tend to play out in workplaces and in educational settings.

**Table 10.1**  Key contextual factors in work, with relevance to activity and place

| Factor | Workplaces | Education places |
|---|---|---|
| **Reasons for learning** | To get the job done; career advancement; to advance the organisation (process focused) | To acquire a knowledge base; pass exams; gain qualifications (content-focused). |
| **Responsibilities of learners** | The worker/learner has responsibility to the organisation for outcomes of their work, and not just to themselves. A worker follows a negotiated plan, guidelines, including professional and ethical guidelines, rules, regulations etc. | The learner is responsible to her/himself. Students are entitled to a set of opportunities, but how they use them is largely up to the individual. Rules and guidelines are limited to societal obligations and the regulations governing the award of qualifications. |
| **Responsibilities of supervisors** | The person supervising the work is primarily responsible for productivity. The learner/worker is not the central focus of the work enterprise. Learning is a means to those ends rather than solely for the benefit of the learner. | The learner is at the centre of the learning enterprise. The tutor's primary responsibility is to promote and facilitate effective learning. Students' learning is an end in itself. |
| **Role/impact of the 'client' for the work** | Depending on the type of organisation, the activity and any associated learning is usually, directly or indirectly, for an external client (third party), or for another section in the organisation (i.e. proto-external). Work supervisor and worker are jointly engaged in delivering the best output/outcome. | In traditional education there is no external client. Activity is geared towards learning the subject content, which is set by the tutor. The learner is the recipient (client) of the tutor's work and the tutor has set the brief (ie taken the client role) for the student's assessment or work output. In this sense they are not in a shared enterprise. |
| **Relationships with peers** | Peer relationships are inter-dependent, set through roles and responsibilities and not primarily through choice. Cooperation is likely to lead to gains for the organisation and reward (promotion, enhanced CV etc.) for the individual. | Peer relationships are optional. No specific work relationships are required for a standard academic course, unless there is a group work assessment. Cooperation can be seen as having a negative impact on personal success. |
| **How learning is demonstrated** | Learning is demonstrated through contextualised performance; showing/mentoring others; the focus is on outcomes and outputs and learning is likely to be implicit in team-working and outputs rather than demonstrated separately. | Learning needs to be explicitly demonstrated in relation to explicit criteria around knowledge and aspects of practice. Criteria are set in advance of the learning, and the assessment output is taken to equate with learning. |

It is well established that learning is more likely to carry forward from one context (such as an educational setting) to another (such as a workplace) if the two contexts are similar (Tennant, 1999). This suggests that formal learning is more likely to be applicable in a work place if at least some of the context can replicate the work setting. One strategy is to introduce a 'client' for the work as in live projects, in-house companies and productions (Reich et al., 2015; Coldham, 2011). Another is to replicate the roles and responsibilities of real-world settings as a simulation in the learning environment, or through work placements. All these examples draw on experiential learning and reflection as their underlying teaching and learning strategies. A range of approaches and case studies are outlined in Armsby (2011).

# WRL in the university

One of the differences between WRL and disciplinary learning relates to the focus. Disciplinary learning tends to focus on the acquisition of specific knowledge, whereas WRL, at its best, focuses on workplace practices, where sourcing and evaluation of knowledge is key. The advantages of bringing work into the formal course context are that all students take part and the work can be structured at a pace suitable for the learners, and supported by teaching input and facilitation. WRL projects can bring in the kinds of roles, relationships and responsibilities for decision making that might not be available to a student on a placement.

## Live projects and consultancy

Live projects and consultancy have many similarities in terms of how they are set up and managed. Both involve working for a client and to the client's brief, with the aim of developing something of use to that client or market. This might be a website, a marketing plan, a field or data-set analysis, professional services (clinical, legal, architectural), a media programme or a community history or 'story-telling' project (the ACEN repository, listed at the end of the chapter, has several examples). Students may pitch to be assigned to a specific project or role or have these allocated to them, and depending on their prior learning, there may be taught or online sessions aligned with the knowledge and skills the project draws on. It is important that the client engages with the process at least once during the work, even if remotely. Working to the client's specification is a key feature of live projects and consultancy. The client's involvement is essential to bringing workplace relevance into the course environment. Students or teams may work on different aspects of a larger project, or in competition with each other, which can achieve greater value from a small number of projects.

Supervision of these projects should be planned at the time of developing the activity to align with key stages in the brief and the timeline, such as presentation of a draft plan, and other scheduled points for review and feedback to support the developing project plan need to be included. The learning outcomes and criteria need to reflect the whole task and so should include decision making, response to feedback, aspects of roles and so on as well as response to the brief. In cases that include competition, however, acknowledgement of a winner would normally be made outside of the assessment criteria.

## Vignette 1: Live project – working with a local urban regeneration initiative

Using links with their local authority, a postgraduate programme in urban regeneration worked with the project manager for a neighbourhood regeneration project in a run-down area of London that includes a street market selling fruit and vegetables and antiques. The project included student teams researching the history of market and its buildings and analysing current use of the market and other similar developments in order to propose solutions to various aspects of regeneration such as traffic flow, community spaces and public realm, and pedestrian access to nearby leisure spaces. A firm of architects, whose offices were situated at the top of the market, offered access to their archives and mentoring support to the student teams. This, in turn, supported the small course team and built links with the local authority project manager. The student teams consulted with local stakeholder groups, researched potential solutions, and drew up and defended proposals for regeneration (their module assessment) that were exhibited in the area, which in turn enabled local stakeholders to influence the final shape of the regeneration.

The sourcing of suitable projects and writing briefs requires some resourcefulness and good relationships with local networks including the university's careers advice and guidance staff. A key question to ask is, 'Who in the local area would want the kinds of products and services that this course relates to, and how can we access them?' The rationale for live projects and consultancy is to shift the context of the students' learning activities closer to the work environment so that they experience working in different roles and inter-related responsibilities (see Table 10.1).

Enterprise and entrepreneurship education is usually structured and facilitated in a similar way to live projects, but instead of working to a brief, students develop their own enterprises and usually work with successful entrepreneurs as mentors. Fuller discussion of enterprise education is beyond the scope of this chapter. However, the Enterprise Educators listed at the end of the chapter is a useful starting point for further information and guidance.

## Games, role play and simulations

Games and simulations can be anything from a simple set of steps through to complex scenarios with well-defined roles, and with alternative avenues replicating world events. Some role play simulations use bespoke equipment, particularly in high-risk fields, such as medicine where there is a need to develop a level of competence before working in real-world settings. More recently computer-based scenario games have been shown to increase self-directed learning, problem framing and solving, and motivation to learn (Gee, 2007).

Virtual learning environments (VLE) and online resources enable the development of virtual companies and conferences where different players with different roles can build up their 'position', working in teams or individually. Games and simulations enable students to experience multifactorial situations and can help them develop higher order skills of strategic and critical thinking, and negotiation in scenarios that they would be unlikely to have access to through a work placement. For example, online companies can be set up to focus on specific aspects of business, and can bring in an element of competition, or international or interdisciplinary dimensions if done in collaboration with other institutions/ disciplines. Through this medium students can take roles with levels of responsibility that would not be possible in a work placement. Even if the student was an observer at the 'top table', without experience of what was involved they would be unlikely to notice nuanced positions, interpersonal dynamics and risk calculations. The online environment makes it possible for teams to research the background to their context and develop their position and strategies in private. It also makes it possible for the simulation tutor to progressively release information at strategic times so that the participants experience the issues, challenges and ethical dilemmas of live situations. In this way, they can practise relevant strategic thinking and respond to the consequences of theirs and others actions.

In addition, many fields use scenario modelling in the workplace and so in some senses the simulation itself can build familiarity and efficacy with a workplace practice.

## Vignette 2: Simulations and games in politics and international relations

The teaching team of an undergraduate course in politics and international relations developed a web tool to manage team preparation for simulated international diplomatic summits. World events are used as the context; however, this can lead to the need to adapt the storyline if political circumstances change. Teams, with individually assigned roles and responsibilities, prepare by researching their country's background, the history behind the crisis, their own and their opponent's political strengths, weaknesses and resources. Each side (and there may be several) develops their position and negotiation tactics. Position statements are exchanged, but not each side's tactics for formal and behind-the-scenes working, and alternative positions depending on how the negotiations developed. The online environment enables the release of simulated 'world news' and additional information to be controlled by the course team. It also enables private group areas, the potential for sub-group and cross-group communication so that negotiations can take place at a number of levels. The actual summit is a live event where each team negotiates on the basis of the information they have gleaned and their strategy in the evolving context.

The course team also developed board and online games to build experience of strategy and negotiation. They are currently extending the work-related potential by working with computer science and graphic design students to develop the games in electronic formats, thereby extending the WRL collaboratively with other subject areas.

Students in classroom settings can be resistant to role play, which can leave them feeling exposed, especially if there is too much 'acting' involved. In-class role plays need to have very clear instructions for each of the roles. For example, if role-playing a job interview to develop awareness of how to talk about generic skills, then the interviewer's instructions could include the actual questions to be asked, and both roles need the background of the particular job. It also helps to encourage participants to think about how and where they should sit (behind a desk, casually or formally) to help them get into role. As the purpose is to emulate the real world it is important to structure how the students will capture and build on their experience. Two key ways of doing this are through individual reflection and facilitated plenary sessions as discussed above.

All these techniques offer different approaches to simulating the work context, setting or situation, and are often used as part of the preparation for experience in workplace settings.

## WRL in the workplace

This section begins with outlining the development of workplaces within universities, before moving to external initiatives: placements, and WBL programmes where people in employment bring their work in as their field of study.

### Workplaces within universities

Universities are large and complex organisations and many draw on their internal departments as a source of work placements, as well as offering services to their communities. Some universities have facilities that are modeled on commercial workplaces (e.g., newsrooms, television studios, performance theatres, interpreting suites). However, although universities may have professional equipment they may simply use it to develop technical proficiency and not to develop the contextual factors of work set out in Table 10.1. Some universities do offer commercial or community services to the general public through bespoke units, with students working under supervision (e.g., treatment or law clinics, commercial design studios, IT services, architecture and urban design, and music and theatre performances). The extent to which these replicate workplaces can be gauged through the expectations on students in terms of their taking responsibility for the consequences of their judgements, team working and the supervisory relationship. The closer these expectations replicate the work context, as shown in Table 10.1, the more likely the learning will transfer usefully into a work setting.

### Placements and internships

The Quality Assurance Agency (2012) sets out a code of practice for managing student placements in work environments. ASET (listed at the end of the chapter) also offers comprehensive advice and resources for setting up and managing work placements and internships, and so we will not go into detail here. Some professions, particularly health-related professions and teacher education, set specific expectations for the work experience and for the training of workplace supervisors, but generally the learning is more opportunistic and guidance to students tends to focus on strategies for self-appraisal of learning, problem-framing and self-determined planning that draw on experiential learning and reflection. Volunteering is effectively a form of placement, although the student may be more likely to find the placement themselves, and 'service learning' is the term often used for learning through voluntary work where there is a focus on values and citizenship (Annette, 2005).

A placement may range from two or three weeks' casual work on a commercial project in a subject-related field, which is quite common in media, arts and communication industries, to a year's employment in a field related to the student's discipline. It is generally accepted that learning from placements is enhanced by preparation and follow-up that is integrated throughout the course (Jackson, 2015; Cooper and Ord, 2014; Billett, 2010, 2009). The form this preparation takes can draw on simulations as described above, and on developing responsibility for learning through self-appraisal, problem-framing and goal-setting, with experiential learning and reflection as part of the assessment strategy of the course. Where the placement is not integrated into subject learning and might not be credit rated, students will still need to have developed these practices and be given guidance on how to identify learning opportunities and internalise their learning in ways that will help them develop employability skills, promote themselves in the job market, develop their capabilities in self-managed learning, and develop their awareness of cultural and community or global issues (Pegg et al., 2012; Billett, 2010; Cooper et al., 2010; Cranmer, 2006).

## Work-based learning

In WBL the curriculum is centred around the participants' employment. The validated programme typically takes the form of a 'shell course' that allows students to negotiate their own learning outcomes, tailored to their professional role and adapted to their specific contexts, needs and experience. Learning outcomes are often articulated in terms of both generic and academic processes and skills. The learner can negotiate the focus and forms of assessment that draw on their roles, responsibilities and personally identified developmental needs. This means that WBL can be assessed as a field rather than a mode of study (Costley and Armsby, 2007). The course structure may include some core modules such as research methods and work-based projects, and usually allows for the recognition of prior learning (RPL) (see Chapter 4: Assessment for Learning). The learner negotiates a learning programme around their work activity, experience and responsibilities using a learning agreement, and time in work usually forms a significant portion of the learning hours.

Typically, WBL agreements involve each of the key stakeholders (the student, the university and the employer) agreeing on the programme of study. This can involve a university programme approval panel that considers and agrees the content and coherence of the programme. In cases where the individually negotiated study is only within a single module, rather than a programme, the approval of the learning agreement may be incorporated within the module. A key issue is the balance between the various needs and requirements of these stakeholders (Gibbs, 2009). For example, for a negotiated work-based project, the balance might be between progressing a development that the organisation wants implemented, providing an opportunity for high-level critical and ethical understanding of relevant knowledge and practices for the university, and enabling a feasible project for the individual.

## Vignette 3: BA WBL (Primary school special needs learning and teaching)

Sanjay had been working as a teaching assistant in a Primary School for three years when he decided to undertake a work-based learning (WBL) degree that would qualify him to apply for the Graduate Teacher Programme and become a primary school teacher. He first completed an RPL claim that made it possible for the learning from his:

- in-service training in learning and teaching;
- experience of facilitating learning with children with a range of different special needs;
- modules undertaken on a relevant subject (psychology) at another university to be accredited and used as the foundational knowledge for his degree.

Following this, Sanjay undertook a 'planning work-based projects' module in which he planned two projects. In the module he:

- learned about various approaches to undertaking work-based research, such as action research;
- detailed the project activity and intended learning from each project;

*(Continued)*

> *(Continued)*
>
> - outlined how the credit and knowledge he had received for his RPL claim, and this module qualified him to undertake his projects;
> - negotiated his work-based study title.
>
> One of the projects aimed to improve regular home and school liaison of learning objectives for special needs students and evaluate effects on learning. The school had been struggling with this problem and were pleased that Sanjay decided to focus his project on this. Mentors with relevant experience in the school were provided for Sanjay. The university provided him with a project adviser who helped him apply the standard work-based assessment criteria to his planned project.

The essential feature of a WBL programme is that the starting point for the learner is experiential, with theory developed and critiqued from that base (Garnett et al., 2009; Boud and Solomon, 2001). The learning of pre-identified theory is not a goal in itself. Learning at, through and in work, underpinned by theories of experiential learning and reflective practice as described above, drives the entire programme of study. The learner's existing knowledge is articulated as an individualised foundation and brought in through RPL in the form of general credit and to underpin further study (Armsby et al., 2006).

The individually negotiated elements of WBL can make it costly for universities. Negotiation with an employer can provide economies of scale through devising programmes suitable for organisational cohorts. These groups may all undertake specified organisational training and experience, and undertake well-defined, sometimes collaborative, group projects. These approaches are argued to be most authentic to employer and employee needs but have been criticised for putting organisational priorities before individual learners' needs (Gibbs, 2009).

## Assessment of WRL

In the educational setting and for traditional courses, the demand for reliability and validity of assessments has favoured assessment tasks that are externalised from the characteristics of the learner. However, many of the strategies for WRL described above aim to develop the person and their practice and not just their understanding and application of subject content. In WBL and live projects there is often a product or output around which assessment criteria that bring in academic processes at the relevant year level can be negotiated (Gibbs, 2009). However, WRL integrated into courses also needs to assess aims and learning outcomes that include a focus on learning processes, reflection and workplace competence (Cooper and Ord, 2014; Yorke, 2011; Boud and Falchikov, 2007). Assessment criteria need to address processes, such as how students have worked through the tasks and roles, framed problems, researched and come to solutions. Typically, this might include fairly generic work-based competencies such as 'working with others' and 'consideration of resource issues'. One approach to assessment is to set out requirements for a portfolio of evidence that demonstrates process-orientated learning outcomes. Another is for students to use reflective learning logs, journals or blogs to capture and reflect on their experience, to identify their learning needs and develop their ability to learn through critical review, encouraging them to take responsibility for their learning (Pegg et al., 2012). Boud and Falchikov (2007) argue for assessment tasks and criteria that reflect what the learners themselves value. In other words they propose that criteria should be worked out in collaboration with the learners. All these approaches support assessment linked to learners evidencing their change, through reflective self-appraisal in relation to identified (and agreed) process- and practice-related criteria. In this framework assessor judgements can be made as to the extent to which learning and capability can be inferred from their reflections and other evidence mapped to criteria (Reich et al., 2015; Cooper and Ord, 2014).

## Conclusion

The further development of WRL will be influenced by the expectations of students and employers, but more significantly, perhaps, it will be influenced by academics and others who support learning; how they engage with the possibilities offered by online learning environments, by the emerging thinking around practice and learning; and the growing interest in international interdisciplinary and collective learning.

## Questions for reflective practice and professional development

1 Consider your own learning; how do you go about learning in and from your own work and what might this tell you about how your students learn?
2 What would a practice-led curriculum look like in your field?
3 How does the idea of prioritising the learning of practices, rather than the learning of theory, challenge your approach to teaching and learning design?
4 How might we develop students' abilities to work with uncertainty, and to assess the legitimacy of emergent (for them or for the field) knowledge?

# Useful websites, further reading

### ASET

www.asetonline.org/
ASET is a membership network that sees itself as the professional body for placement and employability staff. It offers resources and events for staff development, debate and best practice dissemination in relation to developing learning through placements.

### Australian Collaborative Education Network

http://acen.edu.au/wil-vignettes/
ACEN is a recognised national professional body for strategic leadership in work-integrated learning research, scholarship and practice in Australia. Its resources repository holds a large and diverse range of case studies, with many related to live projects.

### Centre for Recording Achievement

www.recordingachievement.org/higher-education.html
CRA is concerned with developments in Personal Development Planning, e-portfolios and the HE Achievement Record.

### Enterprise Educators UK

www.enterprise.ac.uk/
EEUK is a UK HE network that supports its members to increase the scale, scope and effectiveness of enterprise and entrepreneurship teaching within

their institutions. They offer awards, networks and resources for enterprise education, and European conference on enterprise education.

### Higher Education Academy

www.heacademy.ac.uk/resources
HEA offers an extensive repository of case studies and other resources related to employability and placement learning.

### Joint Information Services Committee

www.jisc.ac.uk/rd/projects/developing-student-employability
JISC includes a series of case studies showcasing innovative uses of technology to support the development of skills and attributes for employability.

Helyer, R. (ed.) (2015) *Facilitating Work-based Learning: A handbook for tutors.* London: Palgrave.
A detailed account of how work-based learning programmes work, including examples to support tutors working with a range of approaches such as the accreditation of prior learning, learning agreements and work-based projects.

## References

Annette, J. (2005) 'Character, civic renewal and service learning for democratic citizenship in higher education', *British Journal of Education Studies*, 52 (3): 326–40.

Armsby, P. (ed.) (2011) 'The impact of CETLs on the development of work-related learning', Special Edition, *Higher Education, Skills and Work Based Learning*, 1 (3).

Armsby, P., Costley, C. and Garnett, J. (2006) 'The legitimisation of knowledge: A work-based learning perspective of APEL', *International Journal of Lifelong Education*, 25 (4): 369–83.

Billett, S. (2009) 'Realising the educational worth of integrating work experiences in higher education', *Studies in Higher Education*, 34 (7): 827–34.

Billett, S. (2010) *Learning Through Practice: Models, traditions, orientations and approaches.* Dortrecht: Springer.

Billett S., Hartels, C. and Gruber, H. (2014) *International Handbook in Professional and Practiced-based Learning.* Dortrecht: Springer.

Boud, D. and Falchikov, N. (2007) *Rethinking Assessment in Higher Education: Learning for the longer term.* London: Routledge.

Boud, D. and Garrick, D. (1999) *Understanding Learning at Work.* London: Routledge.

Boud, D. and Miller, N. (1996) *Working with Experience: Animating learning.* London: Routledge.

Boud, D. and Solomon, N. (2001) *Work-based Learning: A new higher education.* Buckingham: SRHE/Open University Press.

Boud, D., Cressey, P. and Docherty, P. (2006) *Productive Reflection at Work.* London: Routledge.

Brockbank, A. and McGill, I. (2012) *Facilitating Reflective Learning: Coaching, mentoring and supervision.* London: Kogan Page.

CBI (2011) *Working towards your future: Making the most of your time in higher education.* London: CBI. Available at www.cbi.org.uk/media-centre/news-articles/2011/03/working-towards-your-future/ (accessed 17.7.15).

Chappell, C., Rhodes, C., Solomon, N., Tennant, M. and Yeates, L. (2003) *Reconstructing the Lifelong Learner.* Abingdon: RoutledgeFalmer.

Coldham, S. (2004) 'Using reflective practice in an interprofessional complementary therapies programme', in S. Tate and M. Sills (eds), *The Development of Critical Reflection in the Health Professions.* York: Higher Education Academy.

Coldham, S. (2011) 'CETL for professional learning from the workplace: Using activity theory to facilitate curriculum development', *Higher Education, Skills and Work Based Learning,* 1 (3): 262–72.

Cooper, S. and Ord, J. (2014) 'Developing "know how": A participatory approach to assessment of placement learning', *Journal of Vocational Education and Training,* 66 (4): 518–36.

Cooper, L., Orrell, J. and Bowden, M. (2010) *Work-Integrated Learning: A guide to effective practice.* London: Routledge.

Costley, C. and Armsby, P. (2007) 'Work-based learning assessed as a field or a mode of study', *Assessment and Evaluation in Higher* Education, 32 (1): 21–33.

Cranmer, S. (2006) 'Enhancing graduate employability: Best intentions and mixed outcomes', *Studies in Higher* Education, 31 (2): 169–84.

Dall'Alba, G. and Sandberg, J. (2014) 'A phenomenological perspective on researching work and learning', in S. Billett, C. Hartels and H. Gruber (eds), *International Handbook in Professional and Practice-based Learning.* Dortrecht: Springer.

Garnett, J., Costey, C. and Workman, B. (2009) *Work-based Learning: Journeys to the core of higher education.* London: Middlesex University Press.

Gee, J. P. (2007) *What Video Games have to Teach us about Learning and Literacy.* New York: Palgrave Macmillan.

Gibbs, P. (2009) 'Learning agreements and work-based higher education', *Research in Post-Compulsory Education,* 14 (1): 31–41.

Green, B. (2009) *Understanding and Researching Professional Practice.* Rotterdam: Sense.

Hager, P., Lee, A. and Reich, A. (2012) *Practice, Learning and Change: Practice-theory perspectives on professional learning.* Dordrecht: Springer.

Hayward, G. and James, S. (2004) *Balancing the Skills Equation: Key issues and challenges for policy and practice.* Bristol: Policy Press.

Heron, J. (1999) *The Complete Facilitator's Handbook.* London: Kogan Page.

Higgs J., Barnett R., Billett S., Hutchings M. and Trede F. (2012) *Practice-based Education: Perspectives and strategies.* Rotterdam: Sense.

Hmelo-Silver, C. (2004) 'Problem-based learning: What and how do students learn?', *Educational Psychology Review,* 16 (3): 235–66.

Hodkinson, P., Biesta, G. and Thorpe, M. (2008) 'Understanding learning culturally: Overcoming the dualism between social and individual views of learning', *Vocations and Learning*, 1: 27–47.

Jackson, D. (2015) 'Employability skill development in work-integrated learning: Barriers and best practice', *Studies in Higher Education*, 40 (2): 350–67

Kemmis, S. (2005) 'Knowing practice: Searching for saliences', *Pedagogy, Culture and Society*, 13 (3): 391–426.

Kolb, D. A. (1984) *Experiential Learning: Experience as the Source of Learning and Development*. Englewood Cliffs, NJ: Prentice-Hall.

Leitch, S. (2006) *The Leitch Review of Skills. Prosperity for All in the Global Economy: World class skills*. London: HMSO.

Moon, J. (2004) *A Handbook of Reflective and Experiential Learning: Theory and practice*. London: RoutledgeFalmer.

Pegg, A., Waldock, J., Hendy-Isaac, S. and Lawton, R. (2012) *Pedagogy for Employability*. York: Higher Education Academy.

Quality Assurance Agency for Higher Education (2012) UK *Quality Code for Higher Education: Chapter B10: Managing higher education provision with others*. London: QAA. Available at www.qaa.ac.uk/en/Publications/Documents/quality-code-B10.pdf (accessed 17.7.15).

Reich, A., Rooney, D. and Boud, D. (2015) 'Dilemmas in continuing professional learning: Learning inscribed in frameworks or elicited from practice', *Studies in Continuing Education*, 37 (2): 131–41.

Savin-Baden, M. (2000) *Problem-based Learning in Higher Education*. Buckingham: SRHE/Open University Press.

Schön, D. (1987) *Educating the Reflective Practitioner*. San Francisco, CA: Jossey-Bass.

Scott, P. (1995) *The Meanings of Mass Higher Education*. Buckingham: SRHE/Open University Press.

Tennant, M. (1999) 'Is learning transferable?', in D. Boud and D. Garrick (eds), *Understanding Learning at Work*. London: Routledge.

Yorke, M. (2011) 'Work-engaged learning: Towards a paradigm shift in assessment', *Quality in Higher Education*, 17 (1): 117–30.

# 11

# Professional Development

Jennifer Bright, Rebecca Eliahoo and
Helen Pokorny

## Chapter overview

This chapter explores:

- mentoring practice
- approaches to peer review of teaching
- the Scholarship of Teaching and Learning (SoTL)
- the role of mindfulness in professional development

## Introduction

'Professional development' refers to the development of a person in their professional role. Professional growth and development occurs through increased experience of teaching and ongoing evaluation and examination of your practice in this role (Glattenhorn, 1987). The decisions made in relation to the development of practice are underpinned by an individual's professional values and ethics. Values such as equality of opportunity, access to higher education (HE), an understanding of how students learn, a concern for student development, a commitment to scholarship and reflective practice drive both professional development and the development of practice in learning and teaching in HE. These values underpin the

*UK Professional Standards Framework for Teaching and Supporting Learning in Higher Education* (UKPSF, 2011) and other similar professional development frameworks. Professional development is therefore wider than workshops and courses, although these might form part of the process of developing one's professional practice as an educator. It is concerned with examining the cycle of teaching and assessing from different standpoints both individually and collaboratively. In this chapter we consider a range of approaches to professional development.

## Mentoring

Many educators will have had some mentoring at the start of their career; however, there is a growing move towards developing schemes through which experienced colleagues mentor others through their career development sharing experiences and expertise. Traditionally, the more senior mentor passes on knowledge and guidance as the mentee finds their feet in a new role; however, mentoring is increasingly seen not as a passive relationship but one which values mentees actively engaging in their own learning and development (Zachary and Fischler, 2014). Mentoring as a long-term professional relationship differs from coaching, which is more instrumental in character and designed to identify and solve particular problems. Mentoring requires a more gradual and reflective approach. Increasingly mentor–mentee relationships are regarded as valuable within education and industry as an effective part of supporting people's professional development (Clutterbuck and Lane, 2004; Cullingford, 2006; Buchanan et al., 2008).

Mentoring others also facilitates deep reflection about the quality and effectiveness of one's own professional work. It could involve enhancing the teaching and learning of colleagues, researching and modelling good practice for staff and supporting them to improve and experiment with new strategies and techniques, whether in curriculum development, teaching, assessment or feedback. This allows mentors to demonstrate their pedagogic and subject-specific knowledge and skills. Mentors may have a specialist area of expertise perhaps in modelling innovative ways of using technology and may demonstrate different ways to evaluate the effectiveness and impact of teaching and learning strategies, not just for quality assurance purposes but also to improve and share good academic and professional practice in education.

These sorts of activities are linked to mentoring values, such as the willingness to create an inclusive learning environment and the desire for social justice through widening participation. Such mentoring activities and values could therefore provide a thorough understanding of effective approaches to teaching and learning, as well as effective support and guidance for colleagues leading to better outcomes for learners.

## What makes a good mentoring relationship?

There are no firm requirements on what makes a good mentor, but there are some ground rules which mentors should follow, such as the need to maintain appropriate confidentiality about aspects of their mentees' practice. Mentors should be able to negotiate and agree the boundaries of their professional relationship with their mentees, for example, the time and number of meetings. They should have the experience and skill to observe the mentees' teaching if this is to form part of the relationship and to give appropriate feedback which is both constructive and challenging. Mentors need to develop good listening and interpersonal skills as well as being able to use questioning, challenging and re-framing techniques.

### Characteristics of good mentors

- Proven effectiveness as an educator.
- Good learning design and classroom management skills.
- The ability to form and maintain effective professional relationships.
- High-level communication skills.
- An ability to counsel.
- Strong subject knowledge.

Zachary and Fischler (2014) suggest the following elements make for a successful mentoring relationship:

- *Reciprocity* – defined as equal engagement and shared responsibility in the relationship. Both have much to gain. Mentors often report both satisfaction from sharing their experience and also new perspectives that arise from this sharing. It may help them to reconnect to areas of the organisation they have not used for some time and ideas they have left behind.
- *Learning* – the quality of the relationship is important but the product is learning. This requires a deliberate focus and active engagement through critical reflection on behalf of both parties.

- *Relationship* – working at the quality of the relationship takes time and effort on behalf of both parties. Trust is the key element and necessary to avoid blaming and demotivation. A commitment to honesty and following through on ideas and actions builds trust.
- *Partnership* – rather than a process driven by the mentor, the relationship works best when both parties are involved, make agreements about mutually defined goals and actions, get to know each other well and value the individuality each brings to the relationship.
- *Development* – mentoring is future focused and benefits from planning and goal-setting for development rather than dwelling in the present.

Research shows that mentoring has advantages not just for mentees and mentors, but for their own students and their organisations and the mentors themselves (Clutterbuck and Lane, 2004; Eliahoo, 2011; Gravells and Wallace, 2012).

## Does mentoring always work well?

Since there is a relationship between learning and risk, mentoring relationships do not necessarily always work well, for various reasons: mentor and mentee may be badly matched in terms of age, gender, culture, language or personality; some mentors or mentees may exhibit 'toxic' behaviour, subverting the relationship in subtle and not so subtle ways (Feldman, 1999). In addition, there may be a lack of time on either side for meetings or communication.

For mentees, change can involve loss and the unknown. Leaving a familiar context where you are a practitioner or subject expert to embark on a university career can pose difficulties for new lecturers. Often the mentor's role is about managing this transition (Bridges, 2009) and introducing mentees to a new community of practice where they slowly become second-order practitioners – both practitioner and teacher (Murray and Male, 2005). Mentees may feel that they are not being sufficiently challenged or not being given enough responsibility or freedom to innovate in their teaching practice (Hobson et al., 2009).

Gravells and Wallace (2007) describe this journey as 'walking the tightrope', a way of expressing the many conflicting impulses that mentors may experience when trying to help someone develop. A greater awareness of these potential conflicts is a first step towards managing them successfully. The next steps comprise simple but effective practices which mentors can use to support colleagues, discussed below.

An important way of enabling this is for management to start to build a good mentoring 'architecture' in their own institution. For example, institutions could recognise and reward mentors. Mentors should be selected rather than 'landed with' the role. Institutions could draw up appropriate selection criteria and make it clear that status and kudos will accrue to mentors. Mentoring has the potential to assuage the effects of a challenging environment on new lecturers, as the psychosocial functions of mentoring improve mentees' sense of competence and professional effectiveness (Noe, 1988).

Another way of interpreting the mentoring role is to develop good listening skills so that mentees could talk through any anxieties about their context, or practice, as well as identifying the successes of their teaching week. Mentors can advise on how to manage workloads and how to avoid undue stress in the workplace.

This potential adoption of affective objectives is significant as it reflects the demands on lecturers which place greater emphasis on motivating learners, dealing with vulnerable and diverse learners and developing their broader academic and study skills. These aspects of teaching lie in what Schön (1983) would call 'the swampy lowlands' of professional knowledge where mentors are asked to handle myriad mentee problems from managing a class to coping with deadlines. Last, the induction of mentees into disciplinary and institutional communities of practice (Lave and Wenger, 1991) is important as it helps to support their subject pedagogy. Increasingly the mentoring role is seen as a way to extend and develop this community of practice, perhaps through additional activities such as peer observation.

## Peer observation and review

The observation of teaching by colleagues aims to help stimulate reflection on practice and the enhancement of teaching and learning. It is seen by many as a cornerstone of professional development in teaching, particularly in the compulsory education sector. It is widely used in the USA, UK, Australian and other HE systems. The purposes of peer observation vary from accountability (such as individual performance review) to professional development and sharing of practice. Gosling (2002) identified three main models:

- *Evaluation (management) model* – involving senior staff observing.
- *Developmental model* – involving educational developers and/or expert teachers often observing as part of a formal programme of study.
- *Peer review model* – where academics observe colleagues to share practice.

There is a growing shift from peer observation, usually focused on the classroom, to peer review of a range of learning and teaching activities, such as assessment design, feedback practices, virtual learning environments, learning resources, course/module design and evaluation. Various benefits of teaching observation and peer review have been identified, as listed in the box below.

## Benefits of peer review of teaching: Opportunity for dialogue about teaching

- Insight into what helps learners to learn.
- Feedback on teaching skills and style.
- Exchange/dissemination of good practice.
- Spread of innovation, encouragement for experimentation.
- Enhanced motivation and enthusiasm.
- Increased confidence.
- Fostering reflection on teaching and learning.
- Reassurance for new lecturers.
- Sharing solutions to known problems.
- Learning about one's hidden strengths.
- Improved teaching performance/practice.
- Benefits of observing such as gaining new ideas, viewing a variety of teaching methods, reflecting on one's own approach.
- Transformation of educational perspectives.
- Better communication within teams and departments; development of collegiality.
- Evidence for teaching awards and promotions.

(Drawn from Lomas and Nicholls, 2005)

## What are the issues and challenges in implementing peer observation and review?

Observation is not always valued by those being observed, for a number of reasons, and observations may not always be viewed as being developmental in nature. A range of studies (Shortland, 2004; Hatzipanagos and Lygo-Baker, 2006) have suggested that the process of observing lecturers can be ineffective and even detrimental, which can result in mistrust and resistance. It can be seen as an intrusion into an individual's professional domain, and there may be concerns about the representativeness of what is reviewed and the objectivity of those who review.

It may be that negative views of observation arise because lecturers have either not been supported in the way that feedback was given to them or that the feedback given was negative or badly expressed. Some of the considerations include the importance of treating the process as supportive and developmental, not as a management tool, maintaining confidentiality while enabling relevant issues to be aired for the benefit of others. Gosling (2005) has also stressed the fatigue that develops through repeated classroom observations and the need to think more widely about useful peer review activities to avoid colleagues 'going through the motions'. He also points out the limitations of observation schemes confined to the classroom which ignore parts of the teaching that are important but not directly observable (Gosling, 2002).

Although the most effective use of observation is developmental in nature, it has to involve judgement. It is therefore essential for observers to develop skills and knowledge in peer observation methods and strategies, so that they are able to collect evidence and to give feedback appropriately. Allen (2002) argues for a focus on the 'exploration of what works' rather than on 'individual performance'. Consequently, one of the key characteristics of a peer review scheme should be that the design ensures mutuality, trust and respect; for this, it is essential that participants are genuinely regarded as peers. Such schemes also make demands on time and have logistical implications which need to be addressed. Lomas and Nicholls (2005: 145) stress the importance of establishing a 'formative and developmental process that involves collegial conversations and collaborations about teaching and not just peer judgements'. The evidence reviewed here is that this process stands or falls by the relationship between reviewer and reviewed, observer and observed.

## The use of peer observation for new lecturers

The first years of teaching are often described as a stressful period, as novice lecturers begin to join a new community of practice (Lave and Wenger, 1991) by extending their role from that of subject specialist to include that of lecturer, thus gaining a dual identity. Furlong and Maynard (1995) identify five stages of new teacher development: early idealism, personal survival, seeing the difficulties, hitting a plateau and moving on. Observers may need to take these stages into consideration when choosing their feedback strategies. Lecturers may find the idea of being observed very stressful, which only adds to their levels of anxiety. Observers should take the time to explain the positive benefits of the process.

New lecturers may feel pressured by the workload associated with preparation for teaching. They may also feel bewildered when they encounter unmotivated or bored students and these barriers to learning may make lecturers feel out of their depth in trying to cope with behaviour management issues. At this early stage, an observer's key focus may be on helping the new lecturer to develop the skills of planning sessions, managing classroom dynamics and re-engaging reluctant learners (see also Chapter 3: Teaching by Leading and Managing Learning Environments and Chapter 6: Student Engagement).

## The use of observation for experienced lecturers

Peer observation is acknowledged to be an effective professional development tool for experienced lecturers, where the process is based on collaboration and mutual respect between colleagues (Taylor, 2009; Hatzipanagos and Lygo-Baker, 2006). The role of the observer is to be a critical friend and colleague in order to help lecturers develop their own practice. Observers do this by honing their skills so that they can

- act as a sounding board;
- shine a light on practice;
- hold up a mirror to a colleague's practice.

## Suggestions for good practice in classroom observation

It is essential for observer and observee to meet prior to the observation or, if this is not practicable, to communicate by email or telephone. The purpose of this is to agree the format and focus of the observation, including, for example, the time and place, the length of the observation and any specific aspects of the observee's practice that they would like the observer to focus on. It would also be useful for the observee to describe the student cohort and to identify any aspects of the lesson or the context that the observee sees as professionally challenging.

If you are observing a teaching session remind the lecturer to explain to the students who you are. Choose a seat in the room which allows you as good a view of the events that take place as possible.

*(Continued)*

*(Continued)*

The lecturer should give you a copy of the session plan and any other relevant documentation (e.g., hand-outs, task briefings, worksheets).

Arguably the most important question concerns what you should record and how you should do this. Some observers find that they are asked to complete an observation form that is so complex and detailed that they find it difficult to use during the observation and prefer to make their own notes and fill in the form as soon as possible afterwards. Most experienced observers like to make a note of what took place at each stage of the lesson, jotting down comments on the lecturer's behaviour, the timing, the response of the class to specific activities, whether there was any concept checking or formative assessment and so on. Some use a blank page, while others prefer to use a few simple headings.

Teaching is a complex activity. Detailed notes and diagrams written down during the observation help observers to offer factual evidence for what happened during a session. This is particularly important, as it is easy for lecturers to forget, or fail to notice, some of the detail when many things are happening in a classroom.

## Giving feedback

One of the most important skills of an observer is the ability to give effective and non-judgemental feedback to facilitate the development of professional skills and knowledge. Harvey (2006) describes the process as 'informed professional dialogue'. What is needed is a balance of support and challenge, appropriate to the lecturer's development needs. For example:

- use real examples from the session ('two students were texting on their mobile');
- seek out good practice and note it ('your use of questioning elicited more analytical answers');
- offer suggestions on how to improve as food for thought ('you did x really well perhaps now you might try …'; try to avoid saying: 'you didn't do this and you haven't …').
- ask the observee to self-evaluate before you give feedback by jotting down strengths and areas for development so that this becomes a collegial conversation.

Both mentoring and peer review of teaching are used extensively to form part of a number of activities for professional development and enhancement of teaching and learning. They provide a way of bringing professionals together to discuss teaching issues and innovations. This feature of peer dissemination and discussion is an important cornerstone of the Scholarship of Teaching and Learning.

## Scholarship and professional development

Trigwell describes the Scholarship of Teaching and Learning (SoTL) as: 'first about improving student learning (mostly enacted through teaching and second about scholarship (a systematic, peer-supported, research-like scholarly process). Together they lead to higher quality teaching' (2013: 254). This definition has its roots in the writing of Boyer, who called for a broadening out of the traditional definition of disciplinary scholarship and research to encompass: 'the scholarship of teaching and learning that is the systematic study of teaching and learning processes. It differs from scholarly teaching in that it requires a format that will allow public sharing and the opportunity for application and evaluation by others' (1997: 67).

Thus the focus of SoTL is on improving students' learning outcomes and disseminating learning and teaching practice within and across institutions. SoTL aims to understand how student learning has been developed and to share that knowledge with other practitioners. Curriculum evaluation, designed accordingly, can be a basis for SoTL (see Chapter 2: Course and Learning Design and Evaluation).

## Six stages of SoTL development

Trigwell (2013: 255) describes a six-stage process through which SoTL might develop, beginning with an idea of how student learning might be developed:

1 Using a theory, model, framework or possibly even a substantial teaching tip to ground the initiative and provide the justification for action.
2 Identifying an intervention designed to enhance learning, or current practice thought to be affecting learning, or a collection of

*(Continued)*

*(Continued)*

    information that might lead to enhanced learning (the approaches identified are usually derived from the model or theory).

3 Formulating an investigative question related to teaching and/or student learning in the chosen context.

4 Conducting an investigation (empirical, theoretical or literature-based) designed to address the question.

5 Producing a result and some form of public artefact.

6 Inviting peer review on the clarity of each of the theory, practice, question, method and result steps of the procedure.

Blair suggests that there are emancipatory ideas to SoTL whereby 'the removal of the false divide between teaching and researching propagates a practice in which one enhances the other – leading to "new" revelations in research and a movement from unexamined practice to self-augmenting praxis' (2013: 330). However, the divide between teaching and research is deeply entrenched in the university system and SoTL has been valued for its contribution to student learning and professional development in teaching rather than as a pathway to a research career. Brew and Ginns (2008) provided evidence of a significant relationship between the scholarship of teaching and learning and students' course experiences. Additionally, Kreber (2006) notes that while SoTL is often linked to the notion of professionalism its value comes from not just gaining a better understanding of best practice and what works in particularly instructional contexts, but also from asking questions about the goals and purposes of HE and relating student learning to these purposes through wider curriculum and co-curriculum change. Thus SoTL also involves consideration of the political, social, cultural, environmental and economic challenges of our times. Kreber positions SoTL as a way of promoting different levels of reflection, moving from subjective or instrumental understanding and consensus within a given context or community to a 'critical analysis of the processes and conditions by which certain norms we have come to take for granted have evolved and how "consensus" was reached' (2006: 91). She notes the relationship to Mezirow's (1991) three levels of reflection on content, process and premise. Content refers to the use of our present knowledge and understanding of a situation to state and solve problems, while process focusses on reviewing the effectiveness of the approach within the community, and premise calls into question underlying assumptions and the presuppositions on which present knowledge is based, which may lead to different questions as well as alternative responses.

Within institutions committed to improving student learning through professional development a number of initiatives and structures are often in place to support SoTL. These include small grants to support teaching interventions and their evaluation, time to conduct larger studies, awards for scholarly teaching, conferences and symposia dedicated to sharing and disseminating SoTL, networks, journals, websites and forums of different types internal and external to institutions where practitioners can come together to share their insights and findings.

SoTL has as its purpose the improvement of student learning outcomes. A key benefit of SoTL is that it is context-specific and data may come from many practice-based sources. The local context is influential in what can be achieved in many areas of student learning, and generating SoTL communities of practice within an institution can be a powerful way of enhancing student learning and promoting change. Healey (2000) has also argued for the development of disciplinary-based communities around SoTL (see Cleaver et al., 2014 in the further reading section at the end of this chapter). Nancy Chick provides a list of evidence that might be collected and used in SoTL to help us see what students know, do and learn including:

> samples of students' work, classroom assessment techniques, process captures, scores, counts, first hand reports, and institutional research data. There are essays, presentations, online or recorded discussions, minute papers, muddiest points, clicker data, annotations of a text, thinkalouds, process logs, concept maps, a single exam question, a whole exam, quizzes, online postings, office visits, numbers of pages read or written, hours studied, survey results, interviews, focus groups, retention rates, and course GPAs. They can document everything from the specific experiences of individual students in a single course to larger patterns across institutions—and beyond. (2014: 7)

Creanor (2014) also demonstrates how SoTL and models of distributed leadership can work together to promote change and development in that practitioners sharing their scholarship can become informal leaders of change and influence the practice of others. This type of influence and impact can provide the basis for recognition within professional recognition frameworks such as the *UK Professional Standards Framework for Teaching and Supporting Learning* (UKPSF, 2011).

SoTL's role in improving student learning empowers academics to make positive evidence-based changes to their practice. Not only does this alleviate some of the stresses that accompany challenging teaching experiences, but it also brings together networks of colleagues to provide support and guidance, through the peer process. There is no single best solution when designing learning and teaching, and new interventions often come with unintended consequences which can be stressful. Managing the pressures and stresses of teaching is increasingly challenging, and it is to this issue of developing resilience and caring for the self that we now turn and examine the role of mindfulness in professional development.

## Mindfulness and professional development

Mindfulness as a term and a practice is ubiquitous. It seems that scarcely a week passes without some mention of it being made in the media. It is increasingly being used in business, education and health settings to assist in stress-reduction, to support well-being, reduce anxiety (Schoeberlein, 2009; Krusche et al., 2013) and to enhance learning (Langer, 1998; Poulin et al., 2008; Bright and Pokorny, 2012).

Mindfulness is also generating interest as an aspect of academic professional development in that it enables one to be more centred and self-aware, allows one to better manage stress and develop resilience, and to be more present to both students and colleagues and responsive to the learning environment. In other words, it creates a sense of both spaciousness and groundedness that can allow us to choose to respond rather than react, to develop creative projects, to initiate curriculum development, writing or research, or to design learning so that it inspires creativity and curiosity. Bolton (2010) notes that mindfulness can also be an aid to reflexivity, allowing insight into one's own motivations, agency and assumptions. It is closely related to emotional intelligence without which Alan Mortiboys argues 'the value of both your knowledge of your subject and your learning and teaching methods can be seriously diminished' (2005: 2).

Watt describes mindfulness as 'a simple idea ... that means being in the present moment – right here, right now, without wanting it to be somehow different' (2014: 8). She describes simple, quick and immediate techniques such as being aware of the movement of the breath in and out of the body or pausing and noticing the body, the environment or sounds; practices that can be done in a few minutes before going into the classroom. Other less immediate and longer practices might be yoga or running or walking. Watt points out that the quick and immediate practices are not substitutes for those that are longer and more disciplined, but that they act as a complement in strengthening the 'mindfulness muscle' (2014: 23).

## Mindfulness practice: Pausing and noticing

Take a few seconds break from your reading to notice whatever is here, in yourself and your environment. How does your body feel? Are you tired or energised, tense or relaxed, buzzy or lethargic? Are there any thoughts whirling about, or emotions? Notice the space around you, the sights, sounds or smells. See if you can open up your aware-ness to whatever is present without judging or analysing what you find.

Now take a few mindful breaths, being aware of the movement of the breath in and out of the body. You don't have to change your breath. Let it be as it is. Notice the breath wherever you feel it, per-haps in the nostrils, throat, chest or belly.

Then carry on. Without making a big deal of it, continue with your day. Each time you find yourself stuck in fast-forward mode, press the pause button and take a few moments out. If you do this often, it will start to puncture holes in your busyness and create a greater sense of spaciousness in your daily life.

(Watt, 2014: 21)

The return to a more contemplative approach – interestingly, a tradition which, as Barnett (2011) acknowledges, gave rise to modern universities – creates fertile ground for nourishing, inspiring and energising interactions through which, as Weimer (2002) encourages, 'we aim not to cover the content but to uncover some of it'. Fostering curiosity through inquiry-based approaches has the potential to open up new ways of knowing and learning.

Hunt (2009), in exploring spirituality as a dimension of lifelong learning, echoes Parker Palmer (2004) when she speaks of the fragmentation that many feel and of the desire for a sense of integration between the personal and professional. Mindfulness can heal this divide in providing the space to develop an awareness of the ways in which we can bring more of our-selves into the classroom and to allow our students to do the same. Mindfulness practices can also encourage a connection to our students and to accord them what psychologist Carl Rogers (1956) termed 'unconditional positive regard'. According to Weimer, 'a bevy of research establishes that student-faculty relationships are important on a number of fronts. For example, they predict persistence and completion in college. They impact the amount of effort students make in courses. They affect the development of students' academic self-concepts' (2013: 41). The teacher's role in creating the learning–teaching relationship is central and clearly has an impact on student learning and performance (see Chapter 6: Student Engagement and Chapter 7: Embracing Student Diversity).

## Case study

### Mindfulness and presence in teaching and learning

David Kahane (2011) describes how he began teaching feeling full of anxieties, using his ability to be highly organised to handle student questions and 'paper over a sense of inadequacy'. He focused on the material rather than on the meanings and insights dialogue could generate.

On moving to a new university, circumstances led to his being responsible for redesigning a large course that was being delivered by a loose sequence of 10 lecturers to 250 passive and often disengaged students and which, not surprisingly, was performing poorly. He moved to an inquiry-based curriculum accompanied by inquiry into teaching practice by the team. 'We had from the beginning encouraged active learning methods ... but it was the authenticity of learning about our own teaching that built a culture of inquiry able to animate active learning ...'. One of the effects of the team culture of enquiry, through the honest sharing of each person's areas of strengths and weaknesses in relation to teaching, was the ability of staff members to become more themselves when in the classroom; the need to defend and protect diminished and teaching became both more enjoyable and successful resulting in the course winning both national and university awards four years after its redesign.

At the same time Kahane 'stumbled across' mindfulness practices that connected to his desire to be more present to the nuances of the classroom in each moment, to feel a sense of fundamental adequacy rather than lack and found a rigorous practice for cultivating presence. In time, he began each class with eight minutes of mindfulness meditation. He found this had a number of effects: 'bringing everyone into the room together, we would calm down ... compassionately noticing when our minds got caught up in thoughts and allowing focus on the conversations to follow.' This helped to increase both his own and his students' capacity for presence and awareness of the sometimes challenging emotions (anxiety; not understanding; not knowing) that are attendant when teaching and learning, and also the ability to observe them without judgement, and to return to the breath. It showed how each person in the room had a 'plenitude of experience and knowledge relevant to the course' and that 'none of us was operating from a place of lack'. He concluded that 'increasing our ease with not knowing provides a foundation for our most authentic and joyful learning.'

Kahane (2011: 17–22)

## Case study

### Learning to stop, stopping to learn

Similarly, Richard Brady (2007) describes a different example of a mindful practice that he has taken into the maths classroom as a way of providing focus and attention to the present and supporting concentration and engagement.

'Our students have very full schedules. They do their Maths quickly, at best mastering the material and using it to solve problems successfully but rarely aware of their relationship to the work. Could students become more mindful of their thinking? I thought they could if I gave them time specifically dedicated to doing so. Thus, for the past three years my students have done five minutes of free writing. My instructions are, "Spend the next five minutes writing down whatever comes into your awareness. Do not stop writing. Should you find nothing in your mind, write 'my mind is blank' over and over until something shows up." I never read this writing. It is only for the students. Many take to it from the start. Others report being initially put off by the randomness of their minds but over time find their thinking becoming more coherent. The exercise of writing takes on real value.'

Brady (2007: 372)

It is true that engaging in such explorations takes time, which is often a concern expressed by lecturers. However, we need to ask ourselves what we see our role as lecturers to be: whether we see ourselves as deliverers of content that has to be covered, or if we see ourselves as facilitators of a deep engagement with part of the content (designing learning that will inspire our students to explore the remaining 'content' independently) and as a partner in the development of the whole person, that of both ourselves and our students.

In summary, effective teaching for learning rests on adopting a scholarly and reflexive approach through which our own practice is reviewed and refreshed in the light of new ideas and findings from educational literature, peer exchange, feedback and engagement in continuing professional development. Such an approach is intrinsic both to the ethics of good teaching and to the current global trend (particularly in the UK, USA, Australia and New Zealand) towards the professionalisation of university teaching (Abbas and McLean, 2003; Canning, 2007). The ideas in this chapter offer ways forward in this journey of discovery that can improve both student learning outcomes and our own love of teaching.

## Questions for reflective practice and professional development

1 What aspect of your practice would it be beneficial to look at within the context of peer review of teaching? What would enable you to do this?
2 Are there opportunities for you to undertake a reciprocal mentoring relationship with a colleague? What would be the purpose of this for your both?
3 Where could you share the outcomes of a SoTL investigation of an aspect of your practice within your own institution/outside the institution?
4 What moments have you felt most connected or disconnected to a learning situation? How has this affected your teaching and your students?

## Useful websites, further reading

### The Centre for Contemplative Mind in Society

The centre has a wide range of resources for daily individual practice as well as practices in the workplace. There are downloadable audio files for guided practice, as well as links to reports on the effects of contemplative practices, such as mindfulness.

www.contemplativemind.org/

## Staff and Education Development Association

SEDA's objective is the advancement of education for the benefit of the public, particularly through improvement of educational and professional development in HE. To this end, SEDA offers its members and the wider education community, including university- and college-based HE, relevant and valued activities, professional recognition opportunities, and publications.

www.seda.ac.uk/

Wallace, J. and Gravells, D. (2012) *Dial M for Mentor: Critical reflections on mentoring for coaches, educators and trainers (coaching and mentoring)*. St Albans: Critical Publishing.

This book uses humour and insight to explore stories of learning relationships taken from film, TV and literature as a tool for reflecting on, understanding and evolving current mentoring and coaching practice.

O'Leary, M. (2013) *Classroom Observation: A guide to effective observation of teaching and learning*. Abingdon: Routledge.

This book explores the role of lesson observation in the training, assessment and development of new and experienced teachers and lecturers. Offering practical guidance and insights into an aspect of training that is a source of anxiety for many teachers, Matt O'Leary critically analyses the place, role and nature of lesson observation in the lives of education professionals.

Cleaver, E., Lintern, M. and McLinden, M. (2014) *Teaching and Learning in Higher Education: Disciplinary approaches to educational enquiry*. London. Sage.

This text explores broad best-practice approaches to undertaking scholarship and enquiry into learning and teaching in HE. This is complemented by chapters exploring what educational enquiry means in the context of different academic disciplines, including physical sciences, mathematics, engineering, the life sciences, the arts, the humanities, the health professions, and law.

Murray, R. (ed.) (2008) *The Scholarship of Teaching and Learning in Higher Education*. Maidenhead: Open University Press.

This book provides practical guidance for lecturers undertaking their own scholarship through developing, investigating and evidencing innovations in learning, teaching and assessment.

Watt, T. (2012) *Introducing Mindfulness: A practical guide*. London: Icon Books. Written in a simple and straightforward style, this book introduces the reader to a number of practical mindfulness exercises and gives sufficient background information to make sense of the practices. Unlike many other books on the same subject, it acknowledges that there are sometimes obstacles to practice and it nicely addresses these. The author has many years of practical experience, which shows in the clarity of the writing.

# References

Abbas, A. and McLean, M. (2003) 'Communicative competence and the improvement of university teaching: Insights from the field', in *British Journal of Sociology of Education*, 24 (1): 69–81.

Allen, L. (2002) 'Consenting adults in private – union and management perspectives on peer observation of teaching', paper for Learning and Teaching Support Network (LTSN) Generic Centre.

Barnett, R. (2011) 'The idea of the university in the twenty-first century: Where's the imagination?', keynote speech at the *International Higher Education Congress: New trends and issues*, Istanbul, 27–29 May.

Blair, E. (2013) 'Academic development through the contextualization of the scholarship of teaching and learning: Reflections drawn from the recent history of Trinidad and Tobago', *International Journal for Academic Development*, 19 (4): 330–40.

Bolton, G. E. J. (2010) *Reflective Practice: Writing and professional development*. London: Sage.

Boyer, E. L. (1997) *Scholarship Reconsidered: Priorities of the professoriate*. San Francisco, CA: Jossey-Bass.

Brady, R. (2007) 'Learning to stop, stopping to learn: Discovering the contemplative dimension in education', *Journal of Transformative Education*, 5 (4): 372–94.

Brew, A. and Ginns, P. (2008) 'The relationship between engagement in the scholarship of teaching and learning and students' course experiences', *Assessment & Evaluation in Higher Education*, 33 (5): 535–45.

Bridges, M. (2009) *Managing Transitions: Making the Most of Change*. London: Nicholas Brealey.

Bright, J. and Pokorny, H. (2012) 'Contemplative practices in higher education: Breathing heart and mindfulness into the staff and student experience', *Educational Developments*, 13 (4): 22–5.

Buchanan, J., Gordon, S. and Schuck, S. (2008) 'From mentoring to monitoring: The impact of changing work environments on academics in Australian universities,' *Journal of Further and Higher Education*, 32 (3): 241–50.

Canning, J. (2007) 'Pedagogy as a discipline: Emergence, sustainability and professionalisation', *Teaching in Higher Education*, 12 (3): 393–403.

Chick, N. (2014) 'Methodologically sound "under the big tent": An ongoing conversation', *International Journal for the Scholarship of Learning and Teaching*, 8 (2): 1–12.

Clutterbuck, D. and Lane, G. (2004) *The Situational Mentor: An international review of competences and capabilities in mentoring*. Aldershot: Gower.

Creanor, L. (2014) 'Raising the profile: An institutional case study of embedding scholarship and innovation through distributive leadership', *Innovations in Education and Teaching International*, 51 (6): 573–83.

Cullingford, C. (2006) *Mentoring in Education: An international perspective*. Farnham: Ashgate.

Eliahoo, R. (2011) 'Dilemmas in measuring the impact of subject-specific mentoring on mentees' learners in the lifelong learning sector', *Practitioner Research in Higher Education*, 5 (1): 39–47.

Feldman, D. C. (1999) 'Toxic mentors or toxic protégés? A critical re-examination of dysfunctional mentoring', *Human Resource Management Review*, 9 (3): 247–78.

Furlong, J. and Maynard, T. (1995) *Mentoring Student Teachers: The growth of professional knowledge*. London: Routledge.

Glattenhorn, A. (1987) 'Cooperative professional development: Peer-centered options for teacher growth', *Educational Leadership*, 45 (3): 31–5.

Gosling, D. (2002) 'Models of peer observation of teaching', keynote address at the *Learning and Teaching Support Network Generic Centre, Peer Observation of Teaching Conference*, Birmingham, 29 May.

Gosling, D. (2005) 'Peer observation of teaching', SEDA Paper 118. London: SEDA.

Gravells, J. and Wallace, S. (2007) *Mentoring in the Lifelong Learning Sector*. Exeter: Learning Matters.

Gravells, J. and Wallace, S. (2012) *Dial M for Mentor: Critical reflections on mentoring for coaches, educators and trainers*. St Albans: Critical Publishing.

Harvey, P. (2006) *Improving Teaching Observation Practice in the Learning and Skills Sector: A literature review*. Norwich: The Research Centre, Norwich City College.

Hatzipanagos, S. and Lygo-Baker, S. (2006) 'Teaching observations: Promoting development through critical reflection', *Journal of Further and Higher Education*, 30 (4): 421–31.

Healey, M. (2000) 'Developing the scholarship of teaching through the disciplines', *Higher Education Research and Development*, 19 (2): 169–89.

Hobson, A. J., Ashby, P., Malderez, A. and Tomlinson, P. D. (2009) 'Mentoring beginning teachers: What we know and what we don't', *Teaching and Teacher Education*, 25 (1): 207–16.

Hunt, C. (2009) 'Seeking integration: Spirituality in the context of lifelong learning and professional reflective practice', in R. L. Lawrence (ed.), *Honoring our Past, Embracing our Future – Proceedings of the 50th American Adult Education Research Conference*. Chicago, IL: National-Louis University/AERC, pp.155–60.

Kahane, D. (2011) 'Mindfulness and presence in teaching and learning', in I. Hay (ed.), *Inspiring Academics: Learning with the world's great university teachers*. Maidenhead: Open University Press, pp.17–22.

Kreber, C. (2006) 'Developing the scholarship of teaching through transformative learning', *Journal of Scholarship of Teaching and Learning*, 6 (1): 88–109.

Krusche, A., Cyhlarova, E. and Williams, M. G. (2013) 'Mindfulness online: An evaluation of the feasibility of a web-based mindfulness course for stress, anxiety and depression', *British Medical Journal Open*, 3 (11). Available at http://bmjopen.bmj.com (accessed 1.5.15).

Langer, E. (1998) *The Power of Mindful Learning*. Boston, MA: De Capo Press.

Lave, J. and Wenger, E. (1991) *Situated Learning: Legitimate peripheral participation*. Cambridge: Cambridge University Press.

Lomas, L. and Nicholls, G. (2005) 'Enhancing teaching quality through peer review of teaching', *Quality in Higher Education*, 11 (2): 137–49.

Mezirow, J. (1991) *Transformative Dimensions of Adult Learning*. San Francisco, CA: Jossey-Bass.

Mortiboys, A. (2005) *Teaching with emotional intelligence: A step-by-step guide for further and higher education professionals*. London: Routledge.

Murray, J. and Male, T. (2005) 'Becoming a teacher educator: Evidence from the field', *Teaching and Teacher Education*, 21: 125–42.

Noe, R. A. (1988) 'An investigation of the determinants of successful assigned mentoring relationship', *Personnel Psychology*, 41 (1): 457–79.

Palmer, P. (2004) *A Hidden Wholeness: The journey toward an undivided life*. San Francisco, CA: Jossey-Bass.

Poulin, P. A., Mackenzie, C. S., Soloway, G. and Karayolas, E. (2008) 'Mindfulness training as an evidenced-based approach to reducing stress and promoting well-being among human services professionals', *International Journal of Health Promotion and Education*, 46: 35–43.

Rogers, C. (1956) *Client-centred Therapy*. Boston, MA: Houghton-Mifflin.

Schoeberlein, D. R. (2009) *Mindful Teaching and Teaching Mindfulness*. Somerville, MA: Wisdom.

Schön, D. (1983) *The Reflective Practitioner: How professionals think in action*. London: Temple Smith.

Shortland, S. (2004) 'Peer observation: A tool for staff development or compliance?', *Journal of Further & Higher Education*, 28 (2): 219–28.

Taylor, L. (2009) *Promoting The Development Of Teaching And Learning Through A Participatory Observation Model*. London: Westminster Partnership CETT.

Trigwell, K. (2013) 'Scholarship of teaching and learning', in L. Hunt and D. Chalmers (eds), *University Teaching in Focus: A learning-centred approach*. London: Routledge.

UKPSF (2011) *UK Professional Standards Framework for Teaching and Supporting Learning in Higher Education*. York: The Higher Education Academy. Available at www.heacademy.ac.uk/sites/default/files/downloads/UKPSF_2011_English.pdf (accessed 9/9/15).

Watt, T. (2014) *Mindful London: How to find calm and contentment in the chaos of the city*. London: Virgin.

Weimer, M. (2002) *Learner-centered Teaching: Five key changes to practice*. San Francisco, CA: Jossey-Bass.

Weimer, M. (2013) 'Are student–professor relationships more important in hard courses?', *Faculty Focus*, 12 September. Available at www.facultyfocus.com/articles/teaching-and-learning/are-student-professor-relationships-more-important-in-hard-courses/ (accessed 1.5.15).

Zachary, L. J. and Fischler, L. A. (2014) *Starting Strong: A mentoring fable*. San Francisco, CA: Josey-Bass.

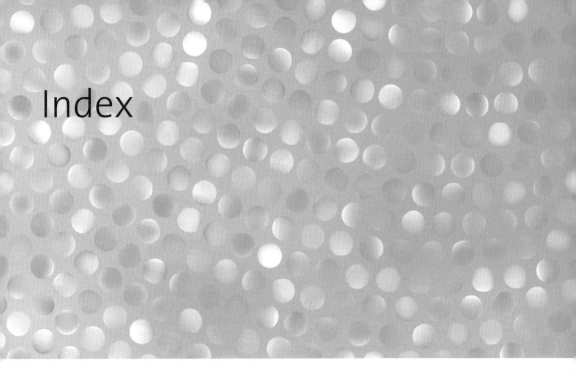

# Index